Foreign Migrants
in
Contemporary Japan

JAPANESE SOCIETY SERIES

General Editor: Yoshio Sugimoto

Foreign Migrants in Contemporary Japan

Hiroshi Komai

Translated by
Jens Wilkinson

Trans Pacific Press

Melbourne

First published in Japanese in 1999 by Akashi Shoten (Tokyo) as *Nihon no gaikokujin imin*.
This English edition first published in 2001 by
Trans Pacific Press, PO Box 120, Rosanna, Melbourne, Victoria 3084, Australia
Telephone: +61 3 9459 3021 Fax: +61 3 9457 5923
E-mail: enquiries@transpacificpress.com
Website: http://www.transpacificpress.com

Set in CJR Times New Roman by digital environs Melbourne
enquiries@digitalenvirons.com

Printed in Melbourne by Brown Prior Anderson

Distributors

Australia
Bushbooks
PO Box 1958, Gosford, NSW 2250
Telephone: (02) 4323-3274
Fax: (02) 9212-2468
Email: bushbook@ozemail.com.au

Japan
Kyoto University Press
Kyodai Kaikan
15-9 Yoshida Kawara-cho
Sakyo-ku, Kyoto 606-8305
Telephone: (075) 761-6182
Fax: (075) 761-6190
Email: sales@kyoto-up.gr.jp
Web: http://www.kyoto-up.gr.jp

USA and Canada
International Specialized Book
Services (ISBS)
5824 N. E. Hassalo Street
Portland, Oregon 97213-3644
USA
Telephone: (800) 944-6190
Fax: (503) 280-8832
Email: orders@isbs.com
Web: http://www.isbs.com

ISSN   1443–9670 (Japanese Society Series)
ISBN   1–8768–4306–3

National Library of Australia Cataloging in Publication Data

Komai, Hiroshi.
[Nihon no gaikokujin imin. English]
Foreign migrants in comtemporary Japan.

Includes index.
ISBN 1 876843 06 3.
1. Aliens - Japan - Social conditions - 20th century. 2.

Immigrants - Japan - Social conditions - 20th century. 3.
Japan - Emigration and immigration - History - 20th century.
I. Wilkinson, Jens. II. Title.

305.906910952

Contents

Tables

Japan

The Kanto region

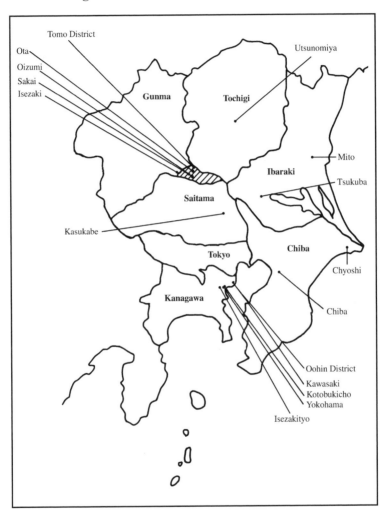

Tokyo's central wards

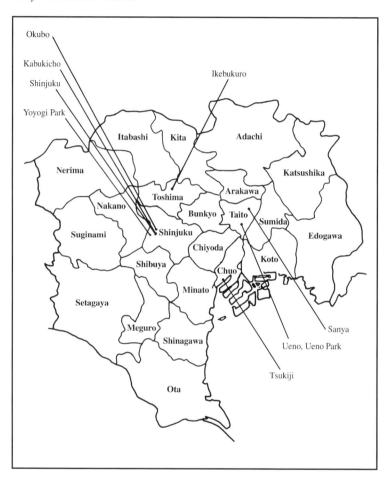

Preface to the English Edition

It was in 1995 that my first comprehensive English-language work on foreign workers in Japan, entitled *Migrant Workers in Japan*, was published by Kegan Paul International. It has been eight years since the original work was published in Japanese, in 1993. During that period, there have been major changes in the migration of foreigners into Japan. The economic recession, which has gone on for a decade since the bursting of the economic bubble, has had a serious effect on foreign migrants. Moreover, a significant number of migrants have begun to walk down the path toward settlement in Japan. In order to grasp this situation, I published the original Japanese version of this work in December 1999. This is the English version of that book. *Migrant Workers in Japan* was very well received internationally, and I hope very much that this work will also receive acclaim from an international readership.

As I also stated in the preface to *Migrant Workers in Japan*, publishing a book in English entails many sacrifices for Japanese authors. Since writing a book in readable English is impossible for many of us, we must rely on translators. However, there are practically no sources of either public or private funding for such endeavors, and in the end the author is often forced to bear the burden. I decided, in spite of this hardship, to go forward with this publication because of the conviction that, as a member of the global community, I have a responsibility to inform others of the situation faced by migrants in Japan. On top of this, I believe it is highly probable that this book will help contribute to forming a network with other parts of the global community, and through this will contribute to enhancing the status of foreign migrants in Japan. I would like also to express my sincere hope that a stable support system for publishing the achievements of Japanese academia in English can be established as soon as possible.

It is partially thanks to Jens Wilkinson, who translated with such prowess, that *Migrant Workers in Japan* was so well received.

After graduating from the State University of New York, he has come to love and settle in Japan, and from his base in Tokyo has been active in movements to protect and improve the rights of foreigners here. Not only is his Japanese excellent, but his English prose is clear and beautiful. It was a great fortune for me to have been able to get his cooperation for the publication of this book.

I would like to thank the following people who gave me enormous assistance in realizing this project. First, I would like to thank Yamaka Junko, from Lingua Guild, Inc. where Mr. Wilkinson works, for her invaluable work checking the translation. I am also grateful to Yamazaki Tazuko, who works in my office, for her help with the charts and figures as well as the index to the book. Ishii Akio, the president of Akashi Shoten, the publisher of the Japanese edition, was kind enough to give his consent to the English version. And finally, I would like to thank Professor Yoshio Sugimoto of La Trobe University, Australia, who not only understood the significance of this book and agreed to publish it, but who also provided me with lavish support on many occasions.

Komai Hiroshi
January 23, 2001

Preface

Two years after Japan was defeated in the Second World War, I was brought back to Japan from the beautiful city of Dalian, with its acacia trees, and returned to the Japanese countryside, where I entered primary school. There was among my classmates a cute girl named Mieko, who lived in my neighborhood. As was the custom in Dalian, I invited her to walk to school together. However, this became a trigger for bullies at the school, who started to call me names. I had to undergo this humiliation on a daily basis, and still cannot forget it. I believe this experience is the source of the deep sense of incompatibility that I feel toward Japanese society. In retrospect, I think it is fair to say it was an interaction of different cultures, between a person brought up in the open culture of the *gaichi* (Japan's overseas colonies) and those raised within Japan's closed culture. Hence, like other people from the *gaichi*, I was able to fit into Japanese culture superficially, but was resistant to attacks, and found myself shouldered with the fate of challenging the limitations of this culture. My aim in writing this work can be seen very much as an extension of this fate that I share with other people from the *gaichi*.

In other words, the basis for this book is my perception that foreigners coming into Japan are similar to those of us from the *gaichi*, and I see them not simply as strange neighbors who need protection, but rather as reformers with the potential to open up new horizons in our society. I believe that the discoveries I outlined in Chapter 7 of this book will have some significance for the future of Japanese society.

This book is based on papers published since my 1994 book, *Imin shakai Nihon no koso* (Vision for Japan as a country of immigrants), published by Kokusai Shoin, and covers the period from 1993 to 1999. However, it was completely rewritten from the originals, and much of the material is new. In particular, Sections 2 to 4 in Chapter 7 were written specifically for this book.

Around the late 1980s and early 1990s, when I was writing my 1995 book, *Migrant Workers in Japan*, which was published by Kegan Paul International, most of the available literature focused on the experiences of other countries, and very few studies had been done on the situation in Japan. As a result, I had no choice but to collect and analyze data on my own. Now, roughly a decade later, the number of researchers has grown, and I am amazed to see the body of literature that has steadily accumulated.

I would like to first thank all the people who supported me and gave me the strength to live during the past seven years. Also, I am very grateful to Iwasaki Jun of Akashi Shoten, who gave me his full support on the original Japanese edition of this book like so many of my others. I received great assistance from Yamazaki Tazuko, from my office, who did a tremendous range of valuable work including helping with the collection and sorting out of data, and creating the index to the book. And finally, I would like to express my sincere thanks to Ishii Akio, the president of Akashi Shoten, who by coincidence came into this world in the same year as me, for graciously accepting to publish the original Japanese edition.

It is my great desire, as an author, that this book will make some contribution to transforming Japan into a society of multicultural coexistence.

September 30, 1999
Komai Hiroshi

Introduction:
Hateful Peoples, Liberated Peoples

Peoples: The revenge of the nation and ethnic groups

With the reunification of Germany and the collapse of the Soviet Union, Europe entered an age of dramatic transformation. At the very core of this change lay problems of nations. The breakaway of the Baltic states, followed by the Ukraine and Belarus, were all, needless to say, movements toward ethnic independence. In the countries of Eastern Europe, as well, where ethnic relations had traditionally been unstable, the existing states broke up, inter-ethnic tensions intensified, and in the case of the former Yugoslavia, we witnessed war, genocide, and the emergence of large numbers of refugees. Western European countries are also facing issues of ethnicity on top of their traditional problems involving local minorities, though the scale of these problems varies from country to country. The ethnic groups in these countries traditionally included groups who came from former colonies, who were imported as foreign workers, and who were accepted as political refugees, but now they have been joined by new influxes caused by the destabilization of the old Eastern bloc. In the midst of this situation, ultraconservative groups such as the neo-Nazis in Germany and the National Front in France have emerged, calling for the expulsion of foreigners, and they have received a measure of popular support. As exemplified by the Islamic residents of France, the integration of these ethnic groups has proven to be very difficult.

In the United States, too, ethnic problems are shaking the very foundation of that country's founding philosophy. As seen by the Rodney King riots of 1992, in Los Angeles and other places, tensions between whites and other groups, including not only

African Americans but also Hispanics (Spanish-speaking people) and Asian Americans, have become complex.

Alain Minc has coined a term for this situation, 'the vengeance of nations.'[1] What this indicates is that 'nations,' which once appeared to have been overcome by internationalism and socialism, have reared their head again as a fundamental factor in world history.

In Japan, as well, foreign workers, who started flowing into the country in large numbers in the late 1980s, have begun to form major ethnic groups, along with the Ainu, an indigenous people, and minority groups such as the resident Koreans. This points to the possibility that Japan may soon confront the same types of social problems which now face the United States and Europe.

In the background of this eruption of nations and ethnic groups on a global scale lies a simple fact. Ethnicity is connected to the ideas of liberation from oppressors and respect for the rights of minority groups, and hence accords to some extent with universal human ideals. However, the principle of tribalism or ethnicity has a darker aspect: the danger of a descent into intolerant exclusionism, which involves putting absolute value on oneself, often accompanied by an ill-boding state of seclusiveness, exclusion of the other, hatred, and ultimately massacre. We should remember that the mass slaughter carried out by Nazi Germany against the Jews (the tragedy of Auschwitz) was done under the name of the nation, and led to tragedy on a truly historical scale. In this context, I would like to consider the following question: under what conditions can the principles of tribalism or ethnicity approach the human ideal of liberation for all of humanity?

Here, I would like to provide a definition of ethnic groups or ethnicity in contrast to tribes, races, peoples, and nations. The concept of 'ethnic groups' or 'ethnicity' refers to a group whose social boundaries are set when individuals identify themselves as members, or are identified by others as component members, within a process of mutual interaction with others in a more comprehensive society, based on common attributes which individuals cannot choose, such as origin, culture, religion, physical features, and language.[2] In other words, ethnic groups are one component of a more comprehensive society, which in most cases, though not all, is a nation-state. Ethnic groups are formed as members and non-members set social boundaries through their mutual interactions, and do not exist in the absence of such mutual interactions. In addition, they are fluid, because the boundaries are created subjectively or through the subjective stereotypes of others, and the objective features which cannot be chosen by individuals are merely materials used for the identification of subjective boundaries. Moreover, ethnicity can be interpreted as a principle based on ethnic groups, and an ethnic society refers to a society composed of multiple ethnic groups.

The term 'ethnic groups' has only recently come into use. It began to be utilized in the 1950s in the United States, at the height of the Civil Rights Movement, which sought the liberation of African Americans. It derives from ancient Greek, and came into use when a necessity arose to find a term to refer to the minority groups who were confronting the ruling groups within the comprehensive society of the United States. In Europe, it came into use in the 1970s, when foreign workers began to settle into those societies. It can be pointed out that in the background of this term is a change in attitudes toward ethnic groups, basically from assimilation toward multiculturalism. Within multiculturalism, one must give consideration to the relationships that arise from the position of an ethnic group within society, or to its mutual interactions with other ethnic groups. As an example of ethnic groups, one can cite the Ainu people, Korean residents, and foreign workers who confront the dominant Japanese in Japan. In addition, however, though the Japanese make up the mainstream of society in Japan, in Brazil they constitute an ethnic group.

Theoretically, ethnicity can be generally divided into 'ethnicity as intrinsic nature,' where importance is placed on emotional ties created by common features which are felt as shared, and 'ethnicity as an instrument,' where the focus is on the motivation of gaining real economic or political benefits.[3] Good examples of the former can be found among African Americans, Jews, and Catholics, as well as Puerto Ricans, Italians, and Irish groups in the United States. These groups have formed communities bound together by newspapers or places of worship, and are tied by cultural identities rather than politics.[4] When ethnicity is used as an instrument, ethnic groups are formed politically. They are constituted in order to gain benefits for their members, and historical, racial, or cultural conditions emerge from this process. Within this second stream, there are theorists of ethnic collective movements who focus in particular on ethnic actions against discrimination, and those who focus on the division of the labor market.

The term 'tribe,' which is often used in anthropology, is gradually giving way to 'ethnic groups,' as a reflection of the danger inherent in the use of 'tribes,' of placing too much emphasis on isolation and on fixed attributes. The concept of race, for its part, is different from ethnicity in that it is defined based on physical attributes such as skin color. On the other hand, the idea of people (folk) generally signifies a group which shares a common language, culture, and history, but generally is a concept that was formed historically as the basis for the creation of nation-states. Thus, unlike the situation of ethnic groups, it does not include the idea of a more comprehensive society, and is not based on the premise of mutual interactions with others. Furthermore, there is a strong tendency for it to be defined on objective grounds, and for it to have a more substantial nature than ethnicity. Finally, the concept of the nation refers to the totality of the individuals who make up a nation-state. This concept was born in Europe following the invention of letter printing technology. As publishing activities centered around national languages became profitable, the concept of the nation emerged through those publishing activities, and the nation-state was born. In this way, the nation is no more than an 'imagined community.'[5]

The necessity of multiculturalism and the establishment of the public sphere

When minority and majority groups co-exist within a society, the rights of the minorities are often violated, to a smaller or greater extent, by the majority groups. Members of minority groups sometimes find this pressure unbearable, and either try to hide their origins, or choose to escape from the particular country. Generally speaking, however, they tend to gradually strengthen their cohesiveness, and to come to make group demands toward the majority group. If these demands are not met, tensions arise in that society, leading to social divisions.

Past debates on the demands of minority groups have tended to focus on the desire for socioeconomic rights,[6] but have often neglected the underlying desire for the recognition of group identity, and in particular demands for cultural rights.[7]

In many societies, majority groups have adopted assimilationist policies toward minority groups, which can generally be divided into two forms: one which attempts to assimilate others into one's own culture, and a second, republicanism, which attempts to assimilate them into the republican system.[8] As an example of the former one can cite Japan, which attempted to 'Japanize' Korean residents under the ideology of a 'homogeneous nation,' and as examples of the latter one can mention France and the United States. Although difficult in practice, it is possible for the state to desire to grant equality with regard to socioeconomic demands even while maintaining assimilationism. However, it is impossible to respond to cultural demands under assimilationism. In this way, ethnic conflicts erupt even under republicanism. Multiculturalism, thus, is the only mechanism that can prevent social tension and division.

The aim of multiculturalism is to create a society that is culturally unified even while the cultures of minority groups are respected. In recent years, societies which embrace multiculturalism have sometimes been described using the metaphor of a 'salad bowl.' In a salad bowl, the tomatoes and lettuce, while maintaining their own special tastes, contribute to the beautiful flavor of the dish as a whole. In the same manner, within a multicultural society, different ethnic groups contribute to society as a whole while maintaining their own unique attributes.

Recently, however, there has been increasing criticism that multiculturalism can lead to both exclusiveness and seclusiveness. The argument runs as follows. In the process of the liberation of colonies, the idea of national spirit created by national racialism, was succeeded by cultural relativism, which absolutizes cultural differences and cultural identity in opposition to European ethnocentrism. This idea then developed into multiculturalism, but according to Finkielkraut, it represents exclusivism as opposed to the universal liberation created by the Western Enlightenment, as well as the enslavement of the individual, who ought to be free.[9] This type of argument can be seen as a critique of multiculturalism under republicanism, but fails to grasp the Western Enlightenment itself as relative. I would argue, in opposition to such critiques that the merits of multiculturalism go beyond simply the passive acknowledgement of cultural rights. What is far more important is the positive merit it holds of opening to all the possibility of rectifying the defects in their own cultures and creating new cultures.

In order to acknowledge the sociopolitical and cultural rights of minority groups, it is indispensable to establish the public sphere, as emphasized by Habermas. Here, the public sphere refers to an interest among the members of the society in forming a social consensus, through critical discourse, in opposition to public authority.[10] The public sphere, in this sense, can only be established with the participation of the members of the society. It is an absolute precondition for the recognition of various rights and tolerance for other cultures.

From this point of view, we can shed new light on the charge of reverse discrimination, which is often used as a critique of multiculturalism. This claim, which is often made in the United States, charges that affirmative action policies (preferential quotas for certain ethnic groups) represent discrimination in reverse as they take away opportunities from members of the majority group. One can recognize, indeed, that when the decisions on these preferential quotas are made by public authorities, there is no guarantee of real fairness. Only a public sphere established through the participation of all parties with an interest in the issue can guarantee decision-making which contains real fairness.

From this perspective, the responses toward resident Koreans in Japan can be seen in a positive light. The refusal of local governments to uphold the 'Nationality Clause'[11] carries not only the passive significance of guaranteeing rights, but also opens the door for the participation of members of minority groups as residents in local governments, which are organized as providers of service to residents. It thus has the positive significance of contributing to the establishment of the social public sphere. In the same way, for example, allowing citizen foreigners to participate in decision-making meetings will, from the position of a public sphere divorced from bureaucratic discretion, contribute to the establishment of broad socioeconomic as well as cultural rights for citizen foreigners.

Part One

The History and Current Situation of Migration

1 The History and Overall Situation of Migration

The age of migration

Since the dawn of humanity, history has been made by people repeatedly moving to and settling into unknown lands. The movement of populations since the 15th century, when the capitalist economic system emerged in Europe and began its phenomenal growth on a worldwide scale, can generally be divided into four categories.

The first is the movement of populations as the labor power which fuelled this global economic system. At the core of the system was a constant demand, albeit with fluctuations caused by economic upturns and downturns, for labor. On the other hand, in peripheral areas where the concept of the exchanging wages for labor was not yet established, there was a decisive shortage of labor power, which needed to be created, sometimes through forced movements. There are other regions, such as the Middle East in the 1970s, which absorbed labor power due to a concentration of economic surplus.

Secondly, there are movements of populations as refugees, by people for whom a 'fear of persecution' exists. They include, in addition to the traditional concept of refugees, people who are forcibly moved during wars or internal conflicts or as the result of disputes (war refugees) and movements caused by poverty or natural disasters (economic refugees).

Third, there are movements of people in search of self-actualization. People sometimes leave the land where they were born and raised to test their own potential in new worlds. Studying abroad falls within this.

Fourth, there are movements of people for marriage or to join their families. However, these four patterns are merely ideal types. In addition, movements from regions that were once colonies into the former imperial centers, which fall outside of these four categories, are very important.

In the following section, I would like to provide an outline of world population movements since the 15th century. I will divide it into two periods: before World War II, and after it.

First, the classical events of the first period, in terms of movements into the peripheries of the world economic system, were the forced move of African slaves into the Caribbean region and Latin America, and, in the period between the latter half of the 19th century and the Great Depression, the movement of Chinese into Southeast Asia. On the other hand, in terms of population movements into the core, one can cite the movements from Ireland and Eastern Europe into England beginning in the second half of the 19th century. For the United States, there was, first, the import of African slaves, which reached its peak in the middle of the 19th century, and second, the mass migrations primarily between the early 19th century and the Great Depression, beginning with Western Europeans, and later involving Eastern and Southern Europeans. A total of 60 million Europeans migrated to various places throughout the world during that period.

Turning to the postwar period, in terms of movements of labor power into the core of the world economic system, England and Switzerland began to vigorously import foreign workers immediately after World War II.[1] Germany and other European countries later followed suit. In the beginning, this labor power was primarily drawn from Eastern and Southern Europe, but later on began to be supplied from Third World regions such as the Middle East and Asia. In the United States, there were large flows of irregular workers[2] (I use this term instead of 'illegal,' which I believe is too strong), mostly from Mexico and the Caribbean region. In Japan, the full-fledged influx of foreign workers began in the 1980s. In addition, there was an important influx of migrant workers from Asia into the Middle East during the period following the oil boom, which triggered later movements of labor power within Asia. Among Asian countries, Pakistan and the Philippines acted as important providers of labor. Furthermore, in the Asian NIEs and in ASEAN, economic development was accompanied by a phenomenon of 'billiard ball migration,' where these countries simultaneously sent workers to Japan, but also imported migrant workers from peripheral areas.

One major feature of population movements in the period following the Second World War was that many involved people from former colonies flowing into the former imperial centers after the process of decolonization. This took place in a limited form, sometimes as movements of labor power and at other times in the form of refugees, and in a sense can be seen as a 'payback' for colonization. England received people from the Indian subcontinent, the Caribbean and Africa; for France the flow from Algeria was particularly large. Moreover, the former British colonies formed their own channels of movement. Specifically, these international labor paths began with the Third World countries, and ended in Australia and Canada. For the United States there was a continuing flow from the Philippines, a former colony, but also a major movement from the American territory of Puerto Rico in the Caribbean.

Many of the large refugee flows that emerged following the conclusion of World War II were results of the Cold War. People who had fought on the United States' side in Eastern Europe, Cuba, and Indochina, and particularly Vietnam, became refugees and moved into the U.S. Later, the collapse of the socialist regimes added pressure to the movements of refugees, as people from Eastern Europe and Russia moved into Western Europe. In other areas, many refugees from Afghanistan continue to live in Pakistan and Iran. The problem of refugees is also particularly serious in Africa, and there are especially large numbers in Rwanda and Somalia. The problem of 'conflict refugees' is also serious in the former Yugoslavia. According to the UNHCR, as of January 2000, there were a total of 22.30 million refugees around the globe.

As a result of the Oil Shock of 1973, the core countries of Western Europe all fell into recessions, and an era of labor surpluses began. Because of this, they began to restrict the entrance of foreign workers and enacted measures to promote their repatriation. However, these workers, once they had entered those countries, did not leave, and gradually settled into the societies. Not only this, but they added to the weight of population movements by bringing in their families from home or by getting married and bringing their spouses. It is well known, of course, that this led to social tension as citizens of the host countries who held racist ideologies called for the exclusion of foreigners. This was followed by growing incidents of violence and destruction. As of 1990, there were a total of 15 million foreigners living in the nine major countries of Western Europe. In addition, there has been increasing migratory pressure from a mass movement of refugees, many of whom are considered economic refugees, as a result of the breakdown of the socialist bloc and the destabilization of these societies, and the countries of Western Europe all face the dilemma of how to prevent this influx. In this way, in Europe in the 1990s, the tendency to 'close the countries' to new migration from outside the European Union has been strengthening.[3]

In the case of the United States as well, which since its founding has been a 'nation of immigrants,' a negative stance toward immigration has emerged. The 1986 Immigration and Naturalization Act abolished, for the first time, the principle of immigration, specifically as a countermeasure to the increase in the immigration of Asian and Hispanic people. In the 1980s, more than 7 million people immigrated into the U.S. legally, while there were several millions of irregular immigrants. The new Immigration and Naturalization Act of 1997 was characterized in particular by strengthened measures against irregular immigrants and residents. In addition, bilingual education and affirmative action measures for minority groups were rolled back in the state of California, where there are many Hispanics, and are now under fire in other states as well.

Looking at Southeast Asia, we find that during the era of economic prosperity, nations such as Malaysia, Singapore and Thailand actively recruited foreign workers from other regions, and in particular from their neighbors. The inflow of irregular workers also increased. When the economic recession hit, Malaysia and Thailand in particular carried out large-scale crackdowns; in Singapore the measures were much less noticeable.

Summing up world migration since World War II, we find that it was largely regulated by two conditions: economic trends and international tensions. As a result of the large-scale migration and settlement of populations, all of the core countries of the world economic system were transformed into states composed of multiple ethnic groups. This has shaken the very concept of the nation-state. It is fair to say that today the doors are being closed to new immigrants. This is not simply due to labor surpluses, but also to the recognition that the social problems brought about by immigrants may be intractable.

From multinational statism to homogeneous nationalism

Japan first confronted the problems of ethnicity and peoples in a full-fledged way in 1895, when it colonized Taiwan following the Sino-Japanese War. The problem emerged of how to treat the Taiwanese, a distinct people from the Japanese, but whose land had become a Japanese territory. At about the same time, it became necessary to allow foreigners to live among the Japanese (foreigners were only allowed to live in specified enclaves) in order to achieve the revision of the unequal treaties with the Western powers. There was great conflict between proponents and opponents on this point. The proponents pointed out that many people had come into Japan from the Korean Peninsula in ancient times, and that the Japanese were in fact a people of mixed blood. Partly thanks to this argument, the Mixed Residence Order was promulgated in 1899. Then, the annexation of Korea in 1910 presented Japan with the serious issue of how to treat people from the Peninsula. In the end, Taiwanese and Koreans were nominally given the status of Japanese, but under the policy of 'Kominka' (transformation into subjects of the Emperor) were denied suffrage when they lived in Taiwan and Korea. In this way, up until its defeat in World War II, Japan showed the desire to become a multiethnic state.

Here, I must make some mention of the Chinese workers who came to Japan in the period between the promulgation of the Mixed Residence Order of 1899 and the 1920s. Many worked in three professions which required the use of knives or razors, i.e., as barbers, cooks, and tailors, and also kimono fabric merchants, coolies, longshoremen, and laborers. Most returned to China after the Manchuria Incident of 1931.[4]

A great number of Koreans came to Japan in the years between the Annexation and the end of World War II. Between 1910 and the 1930s, there was an influx of peasants who had been deprived of their basis for livelihood by the colonization. The majority worked as construction workers, miners, and gravel diggers, while others were employed as factory workers in small- and tiny-sized companies. They were discriminated against in terms of wages, receiving only half or so of those given to Japanese workers. In addition, to make up for the extreme labor power shortage caused by wartime conscription, Koreans were forcibly brought to Japan to work as miners, as well as construction, steel, and agricultural workers. It is believed that in 1945, the total population of Koreans in Japan was 2.3 million. Shortly after Japan was defeated, more than 1.5 million returned to their homeland. However, some 500,000 others decided to stay on in Japan. They were mainly those who had been longer and had built up a livelihood. They were pushed to stay partly because of the political instability and hyperinflation on the Peninsula, as well as the stringent restrictions on the repatriation of assets.[5]

I will use the term 'old-comer foreigners' to refer to the Chinese and Koreans who came to Japan during the period up until the end of World War II and became long-term resident foreigners, as well as their descendents. [6]

In spite of the existence of these old-comers, the concept of a 'homogeneous nation' emerged after the end of the War, and replaced the trend toward a multiethnic society as Japan's ruling ideology. The symbolic emperor system (*shocho tennosei*) was used as a basis to support the idea of homogeneity, with the sharing of the royal blood becoming an important marker of membership in this homogenous nation. In addition, the existence of discrimination against blacks in the United States was cited as an argument against multiethnic societies.[7] The result of this idea of homogeneity is that although Japan's policies toward immigration as well as toward long-term foreign residents have been gradually relaxed, they are still fundamentally colored by the fact that they are seen as policies for the maintenance of public order. This stance of seeing foreigners above all subjects of rule and control emerged primarily through a series of laws which were enacted during the period leading up to the coming into force of the San Francisco Peace Treaty and Japan's independence in 1952.

In that year, a directive issued by the head of the Interior Ministry's Civil Affairs Bureau stated that 'All Koreans and Taiwanese, including those residing in Japan, are divested of Japanese nationality.' With this, they were firmly placed under the immigration system. The main legal instruments which accomplished this were (1) the Nationality Law (revised in

1950), which was based on the transmission of nationality through the paternal line, (2) the 1951 Immigration Control Regulation, and (3) the 1952 Foreign Registration Law, which was revised based on the Foreign Registration Regulation.

Given this goal of control, the 1952 Foreign Registration Law set up the system under which foreigners were required to carry registration cards and present them to authorities upon demand, and under which they were fingerprinted. Penalties, including imprisonment, were set for offenders. Under the law, all foreigners were required to register within 90 days of arriving in Japan, and if children were born, to report the birth within 60 days of the birth. They were even required to provide their occupations as well as names and addresses of the companies where they were employed. Those who were at least 16 years of age and had permission to stay for one year or more were forcibly fingerprinted at the time of registration, and had to go through this procedure once every five years. Violations of these provisions were punishable by up to one year's imprisonment or a fine of up to ¥200,000.

Moreover, resident Koreans were deprived of their right to leave and re-enter Japan by the re-entry permit system. Under this system, the Ministry of Justice has the discretionary right to decide whether to grant a re-entry permit, and being denied such a permit is tantamount to being forbidden to leave. The denial of re-entry permits was sometimes used as a sanction against people who refused to be fingerprinted.

Hence, the defining feature of the 1952 immigration legislation was that it ignored or placed little importance on human rights, while imposing a system of strict surveillance. Furthermore, it anticipated assimilation, with deportation seen as the penalty of last resort for people who resisted this assimilation. Thus, a structure of extreme discrimination emerged against foreigners in general, but was used particularly harshly against resident Koreans.

Given the 1952 legal system, there was no large-scale influx of foreigners, including workers, into Japan until the late 1970s. The exceptions to this rule were an estimated 150,000 people who were smuggled into the country from the Korean Peninsula, as well as a significant number of foreign workers who entered the country beginning in the late 1960s under the pretext of training. This was because in 1965, after the Tokyo Olympics, the Japanese economy entered into a boom, and began experiencing labor shortages. However, these shortages came to an end with the recession caused by the Oil Shock.

The shaking of the ideal of the homogenous nation, and the focus on a society of multicultural coexistence

It was the arrival of newcomer foreigners beginning in the late 1970s, as well as Japan's accession in 1982 to the Convention Relating to the Status of Refugees, that provided the first shock to the foundations of the ideology of Japan as a homogeneous nation.

During the period between the end of the 1970s and the early 1980s, in spite of the fact that the Japanese economy had not yet recovered from the Oil Shock recession, there were four new patterns of influx of foreigners into Japan. These can be seen as the 'initial period' of the entry of newcomer foreigners.

The first pattern consisted of foreign women who came in beginning at the end of the 1970s to work in the sex industry. At first, the majority were Filipinas, and later they were joined by women from Korea, Taiwan, and Thailand. The Filipinas were often brought into Japan using the status of 'entertainer,' which included the provision that they could engage in activities including 'theatrical performances, musical performances, sports, or any other show businesses.'

The second pattern involved Indochinese refugees, from Vietnam, Cambodia, and Laos, who eventually became the trigger for Japan's accession to the U.N. Treaty on Refugees. Starting in the 1970s, international demands emerged for Japan to begin accepting refugees, and it was in the 1980s that Japan was most active in this area. However, the total number of refugees accepted by Japan has failed to go beyond 10,000 or so, and in practical terms ended in 1989 with the beginning of screening procedures. Incidentally, a negligible number – just a few more than 200 – of political refugees have been accepted from outside of Indochina.

The third pattern was the second and third generation descendants of Japanese who had been left in China at the end of World War II. There was a significant number of Japanese who either moved to or were born in northeastern China, a colony of Japan at the time, and were left behind. As I will discuss further in Chapter 3, some 5,000 of these individuals have returned to Japan, in many cases along with their spouses, children, and grandchildren. In other cases, they brought their families over later. These people are called the second and third generation returnees from China. Of them, between 50,000 and 60,000 have Chinese nationality.

Finally, a fourth pattern involved business people from Europe and North America.

Another important event in this period was Japan's ascension to the International Convention Relating to the Status of Refugees. Japan had been reluctant to join either the original treaty of 1951, or the Protocols formulated in 1967. However, in 1979, a Summit on Indochinese Refugees was held, and this, along with the ensuing international pressure, compelled Japan to sign the Convention in 1982.

The Convention prescribed that Japan provide equal treatment to nationals and non-nationals; as a result, there was some alleviation of the discrimination against foreigners which existed in areas related to social security. Specifically, in 1982 foreigners became eligible for the National Pension, Childcare Allowance, and Dependent Childcare Allowance systems. And in 1986, foreigners who did not work at workplaces which had health insurance were granted the right to join National Health Insurance plans managed by the local governments where they lived. (There were no restrictions based on nationality for workplace-based health insurance plans, the Employees' Pension Insurance, Employment Insurance, and Workers Compensation Insurance.) These measures ended up helping not just refugees, but also ordinary foreigners and resident Koreans.

In the later half of the 1980s, the influx of newcomer foreigners increased dramatically. This period, which continued until the bursting of the economic bubble in the early 1990s, can be termed an 'expansion period.' The specific character of this time was an influx of low-wage labor power in various forms in response to the shortages accompanying the economic boom, as well as the entry of people seeking self-actualization.

The first pattern of entrance of low-wage labor power involved irregular foreign workers, meaning people working outside of the scope permitted by their residency status and overstayers. Many of the people working outside of the scope of their visas used the status of technical trainees or students at Japanese language schools. At the same time, there was a tremendous increase in the number of overstayers; when the economic bubble burst in the early 1990s, there were nearly 300,000. Most were men, and they came not only from neighboring countries such as South Korea, China, and the Philippines, but from other Asian countries, and in fact from all over the world. The second pattern involved Latin Americans of Japanese descent (Nikkeijin), who began to arrive in Japan in the late 1980s.

During this period, in addition to the influx of low-wage labor power, Japan witnessed the entry of people who could be said to be in search of 'self-actualization.' They were people who wanted to take on the challenge of testing themselves in Japan as a foreign country, or who wanted to broaden their horizons or points of view. Many of them entered as foreign students (*ryugakusei*) or as '*shukagusei*,' or 'pre-college students,' meaning students at language and technical schools. This influx began in 1983 with the 'Plan to Accept 100,000 Foreign Students.' The number of pre-college students began to increase tremendously in the late 1980s.

To deal with this enormous influx, the government presented a bill for a revised Immigration Control Act to the National Diet at the end of 1989. The intent was to preserve the spirit of the existing law, but to shut out irregular foreign workers. The bill was enacted into law, and went into force on June 1, 1990. The first major feature of the new law was that it imposed a system of penalties for employers. Specifically, it established the crime of abetting illegal labor, which could be applied both to employers who knowingly hired irregular workers and to brokers who mediated the employment of such workers; it imposed penalties of up to three years imprisonment or ¥2 million in fines. The second characteristic was that it gave Nikkeijin, meaning foreign people of Japanese descent, as well as their non-Nikkeijin spouses, permission to live and work in Japan freely. This triggered an enormous influx of people from Latin America, mainly from Brazil, who came with the aim of working in Japan. In connection to this, incidentally, in 1991 the requirement for fingerprinting was eliminated for old-comers. It was finally abolished for all foreign residents in 1999.

However, in the second half of 1991, just one year after the new Immigration Control Act was put into force, the economic bubble burst and Japan was plunged into a prolonged recession from which it has yet to recover. As a result, the existing labor shortage became a surplus. Consequently, I would like to call the period after the second half of 1991 the 'stagnation period' for the entry of newcomer foreigners. During this time, partly as a result of the revised Immigration Control Act, the number of irregular workers hit a peak, and began to decrease slightly, though there was no precipitous fall. By contrast, the number of Nikkeijin from Latin America continued to grow dramatically even after the collapse of the bubble, and to increase at a smaller pace in later years. In addition, during the period of stagnation, there were notable increases in the number of international marriages as well as the hiring of foreign nationals by Japanese companies moving into foreign markets. The overseas operations of Japanese firms became clearly visible in the second half of the 1980s. This trend has accelerated, along with the hollowing of industry, since the bursting of the economic bubble. As a result, it has become necessary to bring in foreign language teachers and other specialists in international business to provide support in this area.

Seen in this light, economic factors may be very important in explaining the arrival of newcomer foreigners, but there is a limit to their explanatory power. In the expansion period during the bubble economy years in which foreign labor alleviated the labor shortage, push-pull theory or Todaro or Lewis models can be applied to some extent,[8] and during the period of stagnation it is certain that there were some movements in response to the globalization of production, as pointed out by Sassen. However, in the initial period and the period of stagnation, non-economic factors also played vital roles.

Not only this, but the arrival of newcomer foreigners was directly related to Japanese immigration control policies themselves. For example, the policy of accepting Nikkeijin was realized with the background of the labor shortage in the Japanese economy. Moreover, the influx of workers from Bangladesh, Pakistan, Iran and Malaysia was influenced by the signing, and subsequent suspension, of agreements on mutual visa exemptions. In other words, although the effects of economic cycles cannot be ignored, there were other patterns of influx which are also important.

The current state of migration

Basic information on the population of foreign migrants in Japan can be obtained from the Statistics on Registered Foreigners, and Number of Overstayers, both of which are released by the Ministry of Justice (http://www.moj.go.jp). I touched upon the issue of registered foreigners in the second section of this Chapter. However, it should be noted that unregistered foreigners are not eligible for administrative services, and consequently the possession or non-possession of registration has decisive significance for the living and work of foreigners in Japan.[9] Considering this, the statistics on the number of registered foreigners are of much greater importance than those in other areas. The number of overstayers is calculated from the numbers of embarkation and disembarkation cards that are presented by foreigners arriving and departing from Japan. However, the Ministry of Justice has noted that there are several factors which cause errors, such as a lack of matching processing, so that these numbers cannot be called definitive, and must be considered approximate figures (estimates). Data on the number of overstayers are issued every six months.[10]

Table 1.1 is an aggregation of data on foreigners in Japan, for the end of 1992, the date when data for overstayers first became available, for the end of 1995, and for the end of 1998 or beginning of 1999. The chart is arranged so that the figures for old-comer foreigners are shown on the far left side. The subtotals for newcomer foreigners are shown in the second column from the right, and the far-right column shows totals for these groups combined. This chart does not, however, show all foreigners living in Japan. It does not include American military personnel and their families, or diplomats, who are not required to register under the Foreign Registration Law. In addition, needless to say, it does not include people who were smuggled into the country or entered through other unlawful channels.

Another complicating factor is that the task of alien registration is entrusted by the national government to local governments, and some progressive municipalities have begun to provide registration even to foreigners with irregular residency status, such as overstayers. Therefore, the alien registration figures also include some people with irregular status, who are shown in Table 1.1 as

Table 1.1.1 *Number of Foreigners by Nationality (or Region of Origin) and by Residence Status (as of the end of December 1992, or November 1, 1992)*

	Old-comer foreigners — No. of registered persons — Special permanent Resident	Newcomer foreigners — Number of registered persons (1) Prof/Business	Specialist	Cultural	Entertainer	Trainee	Student	Dependent	Temporary Visitor	Spouse	Permanent Resident	Special residency	Visa-less (3)	Sub-total	No. of irregulars (2) Over-stayers	Sub-total (1)+(2) −(3)*	Total
South/North Korea	585,170	1,988	2,892	373	646	711	19,890	10,118	3,159	35,630	19,462	3,186	4,919	102,974	37,491	135,546	720,716
China/Taiwan	4,796	6,781	9,669	1,729	673	10,185	65,872	14,631	5,380	52,885	21,592	149	992	190,538	36,374	225,920	230,716
Brazil	-	100	117	37	187	252	324	308	1,945	143,575	290	6	662	147,803	**	147,141	147,141
Philippines	1	806	433	1,057	20,090	1,907	1,646	512	2,418	30,968	1,625	121	634	62,217	34,296	95,879	95,880
Thailand	-	160	441	106	215	1,976	1,732	222	659	4,509	241	14	185	10,460	53,219	63,494	63,494
Peru	-	20	21	10	-	62	53	45	5,311	25,300	56	-	173	31,051	6,241	37,119	37,119
United States	37	9,933	8,149	529	243	48	1,416	7,194	810	11,001	2,883	71	168	42,445	**	42,277	42,314
Malaysia	2	298	336	21	103	806	2,633	446	279	655	157	2	6	5,742	34,529	40,265	40,267
Indonesia	1	99	123	71	14	1,534	1,317	673	116	1,071	152	12	18	5,200	**	5,182	5,183
Iran	2	78	53	21	2	20	136	374	3,372	312	87	6	53	4,514	32,994	37,455	37,457
Bangladesh	-	69	107	23	3	164	1,117	342	652	366	29	7	26	2,905	8,161	11,040	11,040
Pakistan	-	104	100	11	4	43	139	230	2,629	635	83	19	127	4,124	8,056	12,053	12,053
Myanmar	-	62	54	19	1	78	1,181	79	1,460	153	18	17	10	3,132	5,425	8,547	8,547
Others	184	9,919	9,855	3,868	569	1,451	5,497	9,597	5,143	25,023	6,418	398	608	78,346	36,005	113,743	113,927
Total	590,193	30,417	32,350	7,875	22,750	19,237	102,953	44,771	33,333	332,083	53,093	4,008	8,581	691,451	292,791	975,661	1,565,854

* (3) = Visa-less persons granted foreign registration

***There may be a small number, but they are included in Others.

Prof/Business = Investor/Business Manager, Legal/Accounting Services, Medical Services, Researcher, Instructor, Engineer, Professor, Artist, Religious activities, Journalist

Specialist = Specialist in Humanities/International Services, Intra-company Transferee, Skilled labor

Cultural = Cultural activities, Designated Activities

Student = College Student, Pre-college Student

Spouse = Spouse or child of Japanese national, Long term Resident

Permanent Resident = Permanent Resident, Spouse or Child of Permanent Resident

Special residency = Special residency status (for refugees), others

Visa-less = Visa-less persons who have been granted foreign registration

21

Table 1.1.2 Number of Foreigners by Nationality (or Region of Origin) and by Residence Status (as of the end of December 1995, or November1, 1995)

	Old-comer foreigners	Newcomer foreigners — Number of registered persons (1)													No. of irregulars (2)	Sub-total	Total
	Special permanent Resident (No. of registered persons)	Prof /Business	Specialist	Cultural	Entertainer	Trainee	Student	Dependent	Temporary Visitor	Spouse	Permanent Resident	Special residency	Visa-less (3)	Sub-total	Over-stayers	(1)+(2) −(3)*	
South/North Korea	557,921	2,038	3,773	490	564	600	19,157	11,324	3,168	33,853	27,460	3,168	2,860	108,455	49,530	155,125	713,046
China/Taiwan	4,685	9,047	13,587	3,643	683	9,610	58,475	23,930	4,469	67,963	24,419	256	2,224	218,306	46,674	262,756	267,441
Brazil	3	95	127	40	249	252	391	357	3,010	169,749	503	99	1,565	176,437	**	174,872	174,875
Philippines	9	743	536	1,288	12,380	1,718	1,293	662	4,260	44,649	4,363	1,163	1,233	74,288	41,122	114,177	114,186
Thailand	1	112	533	134	68	1,376	1,649	236	2,796	7,564	475	582	509	16,034	43,014	58,539	58,540
Peru	-	32	25	18	20	61	69	52	8,392	26,766	192	50	592	36,269	14,693	50,370	50,370
United States	108	9,980	7,309	462	249	33	1,286	6,864	814	12,107	3,716	87	183	43,090	**	42,907	43,015
Malaysia	2	214	261	18	80	332	2,467	412	459	870	221	-	9	5,343	13,460	18,794	18,796
Indonesia	1	104	100	846	154	1,888	1,217	725	252	1,411	201	16	41	6,955	**	6,914	6,915
Iran	3	74	42	12	1	6	146	337	6,982	473	142	110	317	8,642	14,638	22,963	22,966
Bangladesh	-	108	228	43	2	119	1,310	698	1,829	425	48	73	52	4,935	6,836	11,719	11,719
Pakistan	4	120	147	16	13	35	152	305	2,655	869	147	152	138	4,749	5,865	10,476	10,480
Myanmar	-	91	94	17	5	40	1,083	147	1,868	213	29	23	33	3,643	6,022	9,632	9,632
Others	313	10,943	11,566	3,100	1,499	1,643	6,431	10,643	7,722	28,612	8,418	719	879	92,175	42,890	134,186	134,499
Total	563,050	33,701	38,328	10,127	15,967	17,713	95,126	56,692	48,676	395,524	70,334	6,498	10,635	799,321	284,744	1,073,430	1,636,480

* (3) = Visa-less persons granted foreign registration

**There may be a small number, but they are included in Others.

Prof/Business = Investor/Business Manager, Legal/Accounting Services, Medical Services, Researcher, Instructor, Engineer, Professor:Artist, Religious activities, Journalist

Specialist = Specialist in Humanities/International Services, Intra-company Transferee, Skilled labor

Cultural = Cultural activities, Designated Activities

Student = College Student, Pre-college Student

Spouse = Spouse or child of Japanese national, Long term Resident

Permanent Resident = Permanent Resident, Spouse or Child of Permanent Resident

Special residency = Special residency status (for refugees), others

Visa-less = Visa-less persons who have been granted foreign registration

Table 1.1.3 *Number of Foreigners by Nationality (or Region of Origin) and by Residence Status (as of the end of December 1998, or January 1, 1999)*

	Old-comer foreigners	Newcomer foreigners													No. of irregulars (2)	Sub-total	Total
	No. of registered persons	Number of registered persons (1)															
	Special permanent Resident	Prof /Business	Specialist	Cultural	Entertainer	Trainee	Student	Dependent	Temporary Visitor	Spouse	Permanent Resident	Special residency	Visa-less (3)	Sub-total	Over-stayers	(1)+(2) −(3)*	
South/North Korea	528,450	3,156	4,313	441	695	240	18,604	11,435	6,499	31,494	30,615	971	1,915	110,378	62,577	171,040	699,490
China/Taiwan	4,349	14,153	17,467	10,543	931	15,646	52,420	30,408	6,974	84,840	32,646	398	1,455	267,881	44,237	310,663	315,012
Brazil	14	109	141	42	199	217	406	297	1,895	214,359	2,691	193	1,654	222,203	**	220,549	220,563
Philippines	21	825	638	1,687	24,278	2,122	1,129	724	4,972	54,004	10,907	2,479	1,522	105,287	40,420	144,185	144,206
Thailand	1	130	637	170	103	1,865	1,622	252	4,584	10,762	948	1,860	628	23,561	30,065	52,998	52,999
Peru	2	29	30	10	5	52	74	55	6,651	30,475	3,285	122	527	41,315	10,320	51,108	51,110
United States	181	9,694	7,257	483	223	15	1,285	6,557	746	11,483	4,677	55	118	42,593	**	42,475	42,656
Malaysia	4	269	275	18	46	314	2,254	413	1,609	1,017	349	20	11	6,595	9,989	16,573	16,577
Indonesia	3	169	131	4,968	285	3,709	1,395	1,039	748	2,117	297	70	31	14,959	**	14,928	14,931
Iran	5	99	53	18	3	11	156	318	4,802	1,103	227	349	73	7,212	7,304	14,443	14,448
Bangladesh	1	204	307	59	2	88	1,296	1,035	2,452	581	101	237	59	6,421	4,936	11,298	11,299
Pakistan	6	128	235	26	19	42	164	389	2,700	1,347	282	554	113	5,999	4,307	10,193	10,199
Myanmar	1	114	266	34	5	67	951	230	2,356	358	58	59	57	4,555	5,487	9,985	9,986
Others	358	13,114	16,182	4,891	2,077	2,720	8,583	12,523	12,827	32,179	12,500	1,031	1,134	119,761	51,406	170,033	170,391
Total	533,396	42,193	47,932	23,390	28,871	27,108	90,339	65,675	59,815	476,119	99,583	8,398	9,297	978,720	271,048	1,240,471	1,773,867

* (3) = Visa-less persons granted foreign registration

**There may be a small number, but they are included in Others.

Prof/Business = Investor/Business Manager, Legal/Accounting Services, Medical Services,
Researcher, Instructor, Engineer, Professor,Artist, Religious activities, Journalist
Specialist = Specialist in Humanities/International Services, Intra-company Transferee, Skilled labor
Cultural = Cultural activities, Designated Activities

Student = College Student, Pre-college Student
Spouse = Spouse or child of Japanese national, Long term Resident
Permanent Resident = Permanent Resident, Spouse or Child of Permanent Resident
Special residency = Special residency status (for refugees), others
Visa-less = Visa-less persons who have been granted foreign registration

Source: For numbers of registered old-comer and newcomer foreigners, Ministry of Justice, Immigration Bureau, *Zairuu gaikokujin tokei* (Statistics on resident foreigners November 1,1992);Japan Immigration Association, 1993, 1995, 1999.
For the number of irregulars, Ministry of Justice, Immigration Brureau. 'Honpo ni okeru fuho zairyusha su' (The number of illegal foreigners in the country)(as of November 1 ,1995, and January 1,1999).

'Visa-less persons granted foreign registration.' This double counting has been corrected through a subtraction carried out in the 'Subtotal' columns.

Estimating the number of people who have entered Japan illegally is a difficult task. However, in 1998, a total of 8,191 persons receiving deportation orders were either irregular entrants (people who had entered Japan's territory without a proper visa) or irregular landers (people who had landed in Japan without receiving a landing permit), a figure equivalent to 20.6% of the number of overstayers receiving deportation orders in the same year, 39,835. Generalizing from this, we can estimate that in addition to the 271,048 overstayers as of January 1, 1999, there were 55,727 persons who had entered the country in irregular ways.

Summarizing the table (taking the beginning of 1999 to be equivalent to the end of 1998), we find that the total migrant population in Japan, excluding people who were smuggled into the country, increased from 1,570,000 in 1992 to 1,640,000 in 1995 and 1,770,000 in 1998, an increase of 210,000 people in six years. Foreigners now make up 1.4% of Japan's total population.

Looking first at the number of newcomer foreigners by country of origin, we find that Chinese (including Taiwan) held the uncontested first place, with 310,663 persons as of the end of 1998; this position has not changed since 1992. Other groups that made up more than 100,000 individuals were Brazilians (220,549), Koreans (171,040), and Filipinos (144,185), with their relative positions also unchanged. The remaining major countries of origin were Thailand (52,998), Peru (51,108), the United States (42,475), Malaysia (16,573), Indonesia (14,928), Iran (14,443), Bangladesh (11,298), Pakistan (10,193), and Myanmar (9,985). Although the number of Indonesians remains small, the increase is remarkable.

Looking at the statuses of residence of all foreign residents, we see that 533,396 were 'Special permanent residents,' a clear decrease compared to the 590,193 in 1992. The vast majority of these individuals are people from Japan's former colonies and their descendants (concretely, 528,450 from Korea and a much smaller number, 4,349, from China). They constitute the old-comers. The Chinese are, in terms of numbers, on the verge of extinction. The newcomers now represent the main body of foreigners in Japan, with 1,240,471 persons.

In terms of residence status, the largest group of newcomer foreigners has the status of 'Spouse or Child of Japanese National' or 'Long Term Resident' (476,119), and their numbers have been increasing consistently over the noted three-year periods. The status of 'Spouse or Child of Japanese National' is granted to foreigners who are married to Japanese or whose parents are Japanese, whereas that of 'Long Term Resident' is typically granted either to refugees or to grandchildren of Japanese, or to the families of children or grandchildren of Japanese. Since there are only 10,000 or so officially recognized refugees in Japan, we can conclude that the main body of long-term resident foreigners in Japan is composed of foreign spouses of Japanese, as well as Nikkeijin.

The next largest body of newcomer foreigners is overstayers (271,048 individuals), whose number hit a peak of 298,646 in May 1993, showing a slight decreasing tendency in subsequent years. Though there has been some turnover, the absolute number has not fallen significantly, indicating that the aim of the revised Immigration Control Law, which was to exclude them, has been a failure. The number of Iranians, Bangladeshis, and Pakistanis, which at one time was large, has now decreased to between 7,000 and 4,000 each. These individuals constitute the core of foreign workers in Japan who are employed in manual or service labor.

The third largest grouping is the 99,583 'Permanent residents' and their spouses or children, a number that has been growing rapidly. The fourth largest is 'College students' or 'Pre-college students,' with 90,339 persons, though this number has been decreasing after hitting a peak in 1992. The number of college students, however, has remained fairly consistent. Following are Dependents (65,675), Temporary visitors (59,815), Business specialists and skilled laborers (typically chefs in restaurants serving non-Japanese food) (47,932), and professionals or managers in areas such as 'Investor/business manager, Legal/ accounting services, Medical services, Researcher, Instructor, Engineer, Professor, Artist, Religious activities, or Journalist' (42,193). In addition, there are Entertainers, of which many are actually workers in disguise (28,871), and Trainees (27,108), who demonstrate the same tendency. These last two groups both decreased in 1995, but began to grow again in 1998.

Incidentally, those with professional or managerial ability, or skilled labor, are people with high abilities or mature skills; the aim of the revised Immigration Control Law was precisely to open the door to them. However, their number had not risen beyond the level of 100,000 or so, showing that the goals of the revisions were not met. One of the main reasons for this failure, ironically, is that many professionals find jobs in Japan after graduating as foreign students, but the number of students has fallen due to restrictions against them working part-time to raise tuition, a policy which was taken to prevent illegal labor.

Finally, with regard to the occupations of registered foreigners in 1998, excluding those who were either unemployed or for whom an occupation could not be determined, out of 536,688, 213,053 were working as technicians or in production facilities, 94,354 were office workers, 51,354 were working in service industries, and 41,820 were sales people; thus the majority were technicians or productive workers.[11] This reflects the reality of legal foreign workers in Japan, with Nikkeijin at their center.

The specific features of ethnic groups, genders, and occupations

Examining the figures in Table 1.1 for 1998 by ethnic group, we find first that among the largest group of newcomer foreigners, Chinese (including Taiwanese), the largest category is the spouses, children, or grandchildren of Japanese (with about 85,000 individuals); most of them came to Japan along with Japanese spouses or parents who remained in China during the period following World War II, or are the descendents of such families. This category has grown rapidly since 1992. The next largest group is college and pre-college students, with roughly 50,000 individuals, but this number has been consistently decreasing since 1992. The next is the approximately 45,000 overstayers, most of whom are former pre-college students who were unable to enter universities. Their number peaked in 1995, and in 1998 began to fall. In addition, there were slightly over 30,000 long term residents, spouses or children of Japanese nationals, or people working in non-manual occupations, 30,000 staying with their families, and 15,000 trainees. The number working in non-manual occupations has climbed significantly since 1992. In many of these cases students, upon graduation from university, went on to find jobs at Japanese companies. Thus, this represents a group of people whose social status has risen. In summary, the Chinese ethnic group is very diverse.

With regard to Brazilians, the second largest group of newcomers, nearly all are Nikkeijin with the status of spouse or child of Japanese national or long term resident. In comparison to the Chinese, they are a very homogenous group. Nikkei Brazilians and their families are allowed to work legally, and their occupations are overwhelmingly biased toward manual labor.

Among the third largest group, Koreans, the predominant category is overstayers, of which there are just over 60,000. This category has been growing consistently since 1992. The second largest category is the slightly more than 30,000 spouses and children of Japanese nationals, or long term residents; quite a few of them are spouses of Japanese, reflecting the increasing number of international marriages. There are also roughly 30,000 permanent residents, or spouses or children of permanent residents. Following this are nearly 20,000 college and pre-college students, and slightly more than 10,000 people staying with families. The categories of spouses, long-term residents, and students are all showing slight downward trends.

With regard to the fourth largest group, Filipinos, the major categories are 'Spouse or child of Japanese national' and 'Long term resident,' with slightly over 50,000. In substance this number represents marriages between Japanese men and Filipina women. This category has grown substantially since 1992. This group is followed by overstayers, with slightly over 40,000 individuals, though this number dropped slightly in 1998. The large number of 'Entertainers,' slightly over 20,000, is also a characteristic of the Filipino group. The majority of these women entered the country as dancers or singers, and are employed in the sex/entertainment industry.[12] This category decreased in 1995, but grew again in 1998.

Among the fifth largest group, from Thailand, the largest category is overstayers, with more than 30,000 persons. There are more women than men among them, and they work principally in the sex and entertainment industry. The number of overstayers, however, has been decreasing consistently since 1992. Of the sixth largest group, Peruvians, more than 30,000 are spouses or children of Japanese nationals, or long term residents, in a pattern similar to that for the Brazilians. However, unlike the Brazilians, there are also more than 10,000 overstayers. The number of people in this category grew in 1995, but decreased in 1998.

The number of men and women in each ethnic group is shown in Table 1.2. It is important to note, however, that a total of 9,297 individuals, who are overstayers with foreign registration, are counted twice in this table. Moreover, there are no statistics that differentiate between old-comers and newcomers, and therefore the table includes old-comers. The table shows that there are slightly more men than women among overstayers, but that in total there are 881,484 men versus a slightly larger number, 901,680, of women.

Looking separately at different ethnic groups, it is interesting to note that there is a clear distinction between those where men predominate and those where women are in the majority, with the exception of Chinese, where the number of women and men are almost the same. Women predominate among Koreans, Filipinos, and Thais. Many of the women from these three nationalities have come to Japan to work in the sex and entertainment industry. In addition, there has been a phenomenal increase in the number of Filipinas married to Japanese men.

By contrast, the number of men predominates among Iranians, Bangladeshis and Pakistanis, all from Islamic areas. However, among Malaysians and Indonesians, which are also predominantly Islamic countries, there are a considerable number of women. Men also predominate among Brazilians, Americans, and Myanmarese.

Looking from Immigration Bureau statistics on registered foreigners at the age composition of ethnic groups, we note that with the exception of Koreans, where the presence of old-comers gives greater weight to older groups, there is a division between groups which are overwhelmingly people in their 20s, and others where the largest group is people in their 30s. The first group includes Brazilians, Peruvians, Malaysians, and Indonesians. With the exception of Malaysians, these groups share the feature that they came to Japan predominantly as labor power. In the case of Indonesians there are a large number of trainees, but this residency status is often used as a cover for labor, so in reality many of these people can be seen as laborers. Among Malaysians, there are many students.

Table 1.2   Status of residence of Foreigners by Nationality (or Region of Origin) and Sex (As of the end of December 1998, or January 1,1999)

	Men			Women			Total		
	Registered persons	Over-stayers	Subtotal	Registered persons	Over-stayers	Subtotal	Registered persons	Over-stayers	Subtotal
South/North Korea	308,189	24,434	332,623	330,639	38,143	368,782	638,828	62,577	701,405
China/Taiwan	125,176	25,142	150,318	147,104	19,095	166,199	272,280	44,237	316,517
Brazil	122,753	**	122,753	99,464	**	99,464	222,217	0	222,217
Philippines	15,663	14,722	30,385	89,645	25,698	115,343	105,308	40,420	145,728
Thailand	6,841	13,552	20,393	16,721	16,513	33,234	23,562	30,065	53,627
Peru	23,489	6,885	30,374	17,828	3,435	21,263	41,317	10,320	51,637
United States	26,604	**	26,604	16,170	**	16,170	42,774	0	42,774
Malaysia	3,901	5,195	9,096	2,698	4,794	7,492	6,599	9,989	16,588
Indonesia	11,463	**	11,463	3,499	**	3,499	14,962	0	14,962
Iran	6,683	7,024	13,707	534	280	814	7,217	7,304	14,521
Bangladesh	5,323	4,685	10,008	1,099	251	1,350	6,422	4,936	11,358
Pakistan	5,541	4,156	9,697	464	151	615	6,005	4,307	10,312
Myanmar	2,713	3,870	6,583	1,729	1,617	3,346	4,442	5,487	9,929
Others	71,920	35,560	107,480	48,263	15,846	64,109	120,183	51,406	171,589
Total	736,259	145,225	881,484	775,857	125,823	901,680	1,512,116	271,048	*1,783,164

*The chart includes 9,297 persons who are overstyers but registered, so the actual total is 1,773,867.

**There may be a small number, but they are included in Others.

Sources: Ministry of Justice, Immigration Bureau, *Zairyu gaikokujinn tokei* (Statistics on resident foreigners), Japan Immigration Association, 1999, Ministry of Justice, Immigration Bureau, 'Honpo ni okeru fuho zairyusha su' (The number of illegal foreigners in the country) (January 1,1999).

The 30-somethings predominate among Chinese, Thais, Americans, Iranians, Bangladeshis, Pakistanis, and Myanmarese, but the background behind this composition of population differs from group to group. For Chinese it indicates a tendency toward employment in upper stratum jobs as well as the presence of second- and third-generation returnees; for Thais it represents the number of spouses of Japanese men; for Americans it shows a tendency to be employed in upscale jobs; and for Iranians and the others it reflects a tendency to have been in Japan for long periods of time. Filipinos are an exception, in that the number of people in their 20s and 30s are roughly equivalent.

Looking at occupational composition by ethnic groups from the same Immigration Bureau statistics, we can state the following facts. It is notable that a great number of Koreans, many of whom are old-comers, work in professional, managerial, or office jobs, as well as in sales, as technicians and in production processes. Chinese hold a variety of occupations; some find work in professional, managerial, or office jobs after coming to Japan as foreign students, and others work as technicians, in production processes, or in the service industry. Filipinos demonstrate a similar pattern, with women working predominantly in services, followed, for the population as a whole, by professional, managerial, and technician or production process jobs, in that order.

The majority of the Brazilian and Peruvian populations are Nikkeijin working as technicians or in production processes, but there are also a significant number who have moved up into office jobs. Among Thais, Iranians, Bangladeshis, and Indonesians, the majority work as technicians or in production processes. The pattern is similar for Pakistanis, though there are also a significant number in office jobs, with quite a few of these people working in trade.

The overwhelming majority of Americans are classified as working in professional or managerial jobs, but in fact most are English language instructors. For Malaysians as well, the majority are professionals or managers, with office work holding second place.[13]

Future prospects

When examining the future prospects of migration into Japan, the first important issue to consider is that economic conditions will have a major impact. Currently, in spite of the economic recession, the number of foreign workers has remained at a fairly stable level. Considering this, it seems likely that when recovery arrives, a number of policies will be established to allow the entry of foreign workers, and there will be a new large-scale influx. However, there is also a need to give consideration to factors which will act as brakes on any future expansion of labor demand. First of all, under the ongoing industrial hollowing, Japanese manufacturers are relocating their production bases to China, Southeast Asia, and the rest of the world. It is thus unlikely that we will witness any considerable increase in labor demand in that sector for the foreseeable future. However, also in the long term, Japan's society is aging at a very rapid pace. As the population of elderly people swells to previously unheard of levels, it seems likely that there will be a strong demand for the labor power of young people, and this will be pushed even further by the need for nursing care for the elderly. Under these circumstances, I believe there will be increasing calls for a reliance on foreign workers in the long-term.

When this occurs, a problem will arise regarding how to find this labor force. There are only 1.3 million or so Nikkei Brazilians, and it is unrealistic to expect a much larger influx into Japan. Turning to China, there are only 1,000 or so Japanese who were left behind during the War and who would like to return. And there are not a great number of Asian Nikkeijin.

'Asian Nikkeijin' usually refers in broad terms to the descendants of Japanese people living in other parts of Asia, but here I will limit its meaning to the descendents of Japanese who went to various regions of Asia before and during World War II. The majority of such individuals living in Japan are second- and third-generation people, who came to Japan from China along with Japanese nationals who had been left behind at the end of the War. I will address the question of this group in Chapter 3. In the following section, I would like to provide an overview of Asian Nikkeijin from other parts of the region.

There are Nikkeijin spread throughout the Philippines, although there is a large concentration in Davao, Mindanao. They are the descendents of Japanese who went there as settlers to cultivate Manila hemp. In 1938, the number of Japanese living in Davao had reached 16,745. Partly because of the problem of land ownership, many Japanese men married indigenous women, especially from the Bagobo tribe. After the end of World War II, the surviving Japanese were repatriated to Japan by the U.S. military, but the general policy for second generation people of mixed blood was to repatriate them if they were at least 16 years of age, and to leave them behind if they were 15 or under. Many of the members of this second generation, who were unable to return to their fathers' homeland, reached school age at a time of strong anti-Japanese sentiment, and were unable even to attend school. Many were left with no choice but to take jobs at the bottom echelons of society, as tenant farmers or as manual laborers.[14] According to the Japanese Ministry of Foreign Affairs, there were 2,125 people of Japanese descent living in the Philippines as of the end of November 1995, but in reality it is believed there are actually 3,000 or so. There are also roughly 10,000 third-generation Nikkeijin, and if one includes the fourth generation the total figure would climb to 60,000–70,000 people.[15]

In South Korea, it is believed that there are more than 1,000 Japanese women who married Korean men during the period of Japanese colonization, and who term themselves 'Korean resident Japanese wives,' as well as the children of these women. Nearly all of them married Korean men who were living in Japan, and then moved to Korea at about the time of the war.[16] And with regard to Sakhalin, when the Japanese withdrew at the end of the war, people who had married Koreans or who had been adopted by Korean families were excluded from the evacuation orders, and many were left behind.[17] As of the end of 1995, 533 such individuals had been identified, and they also have descendants.

Another notable region with a Nikkeijin population is Micronesia, which was ruled by Japan before World War II. At the height of its rule, in 1940, there were roughly 80,000 Japanese civilians, in addition to soldiers, in contrast to just 50,000 Micronesians. During this period there were many marriages between Micronesian women and Japanese men, and many second-generation Japanese were born. The second- and third-generation Nikkeijin are active in the political and business worlds; among them the most famous are President Kuniwo Nakamura of the Republic of Palau, and Imata Kabua, the first president of the Republic of the Marshall Islands. Both are second-generation Nikkeijin whose mothers were from the chieftain class. The largest population of Nikkeijin resides on Truk Island, with Palau in second place.[18]

In Indonesia, as of 1994 there were 80 surviving former Japanese soldiers who were left behind. It is said that there are some 1,000 descendents of former Japanese soldiers who married local women.[19] It is also reported that Japanese soldiers remained after the War in Thailand, Vietnam, and other places.

Consequently, as long as the current policy, which only lets descendants of Japanese nationals up to the second generation (i.e., grandchildren, but not great-grandchildren) work legally in Japan, remains in place, a limit will eventually be reached to the number of Nikkeijin entering Japan.

In terms of other forms of legal migration, the Japanese government's current policy toward refugees is not to grant official recognition unless there are very strong reasons. The possibility that this policy will change in the near future is close to nil. With regard to college and pre-college students, the number has actually been decreasing, albeit slightly, as they are not allowed to completely rely on part-time work to pay for their tuition and living expenses; it is unlikely that any upswing will come in the short term. However, it seems inevitable that the number of international marriages will increase, given the fact that it is becoming increasingly difficult for some groups of Japanese men to find brides.

In summary, unless there is a change in the economic situation, it appears that the current situation, in which overall migration is increasing at a slow pace, will continue for some time.

2 Migrant Workers Under the Economic Recession

General situation

The 1991 report on 'The reality of foreign workers in the Tokyo metropolis,' released by the Tokyo Metropolitan Institute for Labor, can be seen as a representative survey taken during the period of expansion of foreign labor.[1] It is notable for making the following findings. (1) The role played by foreign workers differs from industry to industry, such as in manufacturing, restaurants, and commerce and services. In manufacturing foreign labor typically replaces or complements Japanese labor; in restaurants it usually involves waiting on customers or providing back-room support; and in commerce and services it is typically either knowledge-intensive or labor-intensive. (2) There were great variations in the way Japanese perceived the work of foreigners depending on whether or not they worked in firms which employed foreigners. In firms which employed foreigners, both the employers and Japanese colleagues tended to welcome foreigners, praised their work, and were generally accepting of the influx of foreigners into Japan. By contrast, Japanese in firms which did not employ foreigners tended to express fear that foreigners might cause various troubles or other problems, and opposed their introduction. (3) Foreigners tended to want the following from government authorities: Japanese-language training, assistance with job searching, and the establishment of consultation services.

In the period of stagnation, the same Institute issued a report (in two parts) in 1995–96 on 'Foreign Workers: Communication and Interpersonal Relations.'[2] Because the amount of research on foreign workers decreased dramatically after the beginning of the economic recession,[3] the Institute's survey has great importance. Part 1 of the report, published in 1995, is composed of a 'Firm

(Workplace) Survey' and 'Survey of Japanese Employees,' both carried out in 1993, and an 'Interview Survey of Employers,' carried out between 1993 and 1994. Part 2 is composed of an 'Interview and Questionnaire Survey of Foreign Workers Themselves,' conducted in 1994. The major findings of the 'Firm (workplace) survey' were first, that there were very few firings or resignations caused by the economic recession, and consequently the recession had little direct influence on the employment of foreign workers. Second, among companies which were employing foreign workers, those which could not find Japanese workers or had poor business performance tended to report that 'the foreigners work harder than Japanese,' whereas other companies tended to say that 'it has been a new experience for our Japanese workers.' Thus, both types had high opinions of the employment of foreigners. The employment of foreigners is becoming stable within the firms which employ them.

Nikkeijin workers

With regard to the employment situation of Latin American Nikkeijin, the survey by the Japanese International Cooperation Agency (JICA), titled *Nikkeijin honpo shuro jittai chosa hokokusho* (Field survey on the employment situation of Nikkeijin in Japan)[4] is a good reference. It is important in that it is a large-scale survey, covers the entire country, and has a broad range of survey contents. It should be noted in particular that this survey was the first to show with some degree of clarity the situation of Latin American Nikkeijin throughout Japan. Some of the important findings were, first, that a majority, or 63.0% of the respondents, had contracts with dispatching agencies or intermediate agencies, showing the involvement of brokers. With regard to residence status, 27.3% of respondents provided no answer, demonstrating that not all Latin American Nikkeijin are staying in the country legally. Furthermore, a full 96.3% of those who were willing to give their residence status said they were 'Long term residents' or 'Spouses of Japanese nationals, etc.,' (with the 'etc.' meaning second generation descendents of Japanese nationals). With regard to Japanese language ability, 43.5% said they could understand spoken Japanese fairly proficiently, whereas 14.1% said they could not at all. For writing, the figures were 11.2% versus 24.6%, showing that reading and writing were difficult. On the issue of their intention to return to Latin America, a relatively large figure (25.7%) said either that they wanted to stay in Japan either unconditionally or with some conditions. The question of generation was made difficult by the complexity of the presence of non-Nikkeijin partners or the generation of spouses, though the survey does give a certain formula.

Following up on this, JICA published *Heisei 4-nendo Nikkeijin honpo shuro jittai chosa hokkokusho* (1992 Survey Report on the Actual Situation of Nikkeijin Working in Japan) in 1993.[5] This report is a compilation and analysis of the contents of consultations given to Latin American Nikkeijin. It is very interesting material as it provides direct understanding of the problems they confront in work and living. From it, one can understand the breadth of these problems. By order of frequency, the consultations involved daily life (28.9%), job-seeking (22.1%), labor problems (17.0%), visa-related (15.0%), insurance and pension (4.4%), Japanese language (learning, interpretation, translation) (4.0%), taxes (2.8%), repatriation (2.1%), medical care (1.7%), help wanted (0.8%), children's education (0.7%), and volunteer activities (0.6%) (the total number of cases of consultations was 3,582). Just under 40% were related to job-seeking or were work-related, showing that employment has become difficult under the economic recession. The next largest category was everyday life-related consultations, making up just short of 30%. A little under 20% of consultations involved immigration matters such as visas and repatriation.

The consultations related to labor reveal some of the problems which have accompanied the employment of Latin American Nikkeijin. Looking at the 609 cases in this area, 'troubles with company or dispatching company' (13.8%), and 'non-payment of wages' (13.1%) were by far the largest complaints. Following these were 'the imposition of fines' (8.4%), 'dismissal' (7.7%), and 'confiscation of passport' (6.6%). This data could be interpreted to indicate that the labor dispatch companies, which are the main employers of Nikkeijin, are passing the negative effects of the economic recession onto the Nikkeijin. With regard to consultations on daily life, the tendency toward settling in Japan is revealed by large number, from among 1,035 cases, of consultations on 'marriage' (7.6%), 'bringing family to Japan' (3.9%), and 'registering the birth of children (2.1%). Furthermore, of the 538 cases related to visas, the top item was 'questions about required documents and procedures for visa renewal' (25.5%), though, on this point, an explanation was added that many Peruvians were unable to renew their visas because the documents to prove that they were authentic Nikkeijin had been lost in the wartime confusion.

In Hamamatsu, where many Latin American Nikkeijin live, the Hamamatsu International Exchange Bureau conducted two surveys, published in 1993 and 1997, which can be used for a time series comparison. I will refer to the 1993 survey as the 'main survey,' and the 1997 survey as the 'follow-up survey.'[6] Points of interest which emerged from the comparison were, first of all, that the process of settling in Japan has moved forward tremendously. The percentage of respondents who had been in Japan for less than two years decreased dramatically between the two surveys, from 73.0% to just 33.6%. Along with this, the number of men living away from their families fell, and many more were living as entire families. In the main survey the percentage of married individuals living without their spouses or families in Japan was 26.8%; by the follow-up survey this figure had dropped to 9.8%. Moreover, the percentage living in families of between 4 and 5 members rose conspicuously, from 15.7% to 25.5%. With respect to the effects of the economic recession on finding employment, the percentage of respondents saying 'it is extremely difficult to find work' decreased to some extent, while those saying 'it is somewhat difficult to find work' rose slightly, indicating that there has been no dramatic effect. By contrast, with regard to wages, the percentage of respondents reporting an hourly wage of less than ¥1,000 (about US$12) roughly doubled, from 22.3% to 44.0%, showing that wages have definitely fallen. Concerning Japanese language ability, the aggregate of 'can understand a little spoken Japanese' and 'can hardly communicate at all' rose from 28.6% to 38.5%. Furthermore, on the question of exchanges with Japanese people in the community, the percentage responding 'only have occasional interactions' and 'have nearly no interactions' increased from 47.9% to 62.7%. This seems to indicate that Nikkeijin society is going through a process of cleavage from Japanese society.[7]

Disguised labor under the training system

The number of trainees, who are in many cases actually people working outside of their residency statuses, surged beginning in 1987, in response to the labor shortage during the expansion period. In both 1991 and 1992, the number of new entrants in this category reached roughly 43,000. This number fell in 1993–94 in response to the economic downturn, but recovered to the 40,000 level in 1995, and then to 45,536 in 1996, resuming its upward trend. In 1990 I conducted a survey on the situation of trainees, on a sample of 597 firms, or roughly one fifth of the population of enterprises accepting foreign trainees.[8] In a large percentage, or 72.2% of the surveyed firms, there were strong suspicions that the trainees were being used as disguised labor. Moreover, this percentage rose as the size of the firm fell.[9]

The policy of tacitly permitting the use of disguised labor in this form was implemented due to strong pressure from industrial associations of small and medium firms. The core of this system is the technical intern training program (*gino jisshu seido*), which was implemented starting in 1992. Under this system, trainees who are nearing the completion of their term and who have passed a certification examination for a specific occupation, are allowed to work legally for a salary as technical interns. However, the total period of study, including training, was originally restricted to two years (in 1997 this was extended to three years). In 1991, the Japan International Cooperation Training Organization (JITCO) was founded to play the central role in the rotation of technical interns. It was originally established to administer or control the entire process, from acceptance to the return home of the trainees, and was a huge body, with 12 local offices throughout the country.

However, the initial expectations of the technical intern system failed, almost completely, to materialize. In 1996, there were only 6,300 technical interns, and the total number between 1993 and 1996 was a mere 15,000. Of all the foreign trainees entering the country in 1996, just 10% came under the technical intern system, with the remaining 90% continuing to be in the gray area between training and disguised labor. Consequently, labor under the guise of training will likely persist to some extent, and it is unlikely that there will be any major expansion in the technical intern system.

An incident which occurred in Choshi, Chiba Prefecture in 1998, and involved the skimming of wages, clearly exposed some of the problems of the trainee and technical intern systems. It involved some 650 trainees and interns dispatched to 215 companies in the marine products processing industry, mainly in Choshi but in other parts of the country as well. They were sent out by one of the country's largest intermediate organizations, the National Fresh Foods Logistics Cooperative Association. The directors of this association, including the executive director, were indicted under the Labor Standards Law for illegally deducting (skimming) the wages of the trainees, to the tune of roughly ¥100 million.[10] They used the following method: companies using interns were made to deposit a monthly wage of roughly ¥125,000 per intern. The association, for its part, only paid the interns ¥36,000 per month while in Japan, and ¥20,000 to ¥24,000 per month upon their return to their home country. They deducted ¥19,000 from the sum for health insurance premiums and taxes, and pocketed the remaining ¥46,000–¥50,000. The association stopped payments of interns in their home countries beginning in 1998, and at the beginning of 1999, failed to honor two promissory notes, and effectively fell into bankruptcy. Many of the trainees and interns, who were Chinese in this case, launched lawsuits against the association and the companies which had employed them, demanding the return of the allowances and wages that had been skimmed.

The first problem which is brought out by this incident is the use of trainees and interns as disguised labor. The aim of trainees and interns is supposed to be the acquisition of skills, but one intern testified in court that her real reason for coming to Japan was to 'earn money.' She also said that the time of her departure she had paid ¥210,000 to the agency in China which was sending her to Japan. I should note, in passing, that the marine product processing industry in Choshi had a previous 'record': in June 1997, the Immigration Bureau refused to extend the visas of 45 trainees, citing the fact that they had not been provided with any real training, including in Japanese language, and that they worked overtime on a regular basis.[11]

The second problem brought out by the Choshi case is that JITCO, which was established with great fanfare, using enormous sums of public funds, and which has acted as an '*amakudari*'[12] receptacle for five government ministries and agencies, is failing in its duty with regard to the normalization of the training and intern systems, as well as to the nurturing and protection of trainees. JITCO itself has tried to evade responsibility by claiming that it has no powers of guidance or supervision, but can merely offer guidance and advice by document. Considering the history of its establishment, however, it is only natural to expect that it should be aware of such situations and should take appropriate measures against such malicious large-scale organizations.

The deterioration of working conditions and the emergence of the dual labor market

In this section, I would like to examine how the job contents and working conditions of foreign workers changed between the expansion period during the economic upswing and the ensuing stagnation period which accompanied the recession. As we saw in the previous chapter, irregular migrant workers continue to occupy a large portion of foreign migrant workers in Japan, and it is clear that because of their irregularity they are more susceptible than others to the effects of the economic downturn. Here, I would like to look at the trends of irregular workers, using mainly data from the Ministry of Justice on violations of the Immigration Law.[13]

Reports on irregular workers released in the period between 1989 and 1991 were inadequate; the first report which contains substantial contents is from 1992. I would note, however, that the year 1992 was the immediate aftermath of the bursting of the economic bubble, and hence has relatively little use as data on the period of expansion. Comparing it with data from 1998, we find that in 1992 a total of 62,161 irregular foreigners were apprehended; this number had fallen to 40,535.

This data allows us to compare daily wages between 1992 and 1998. Looking at Table 2.1, we see that the number of people receiving ¥7,000 or less per day increased significantly, from 25.6% to 34.1%. By contrast, with the exception of a tiny increase in the percentage receiving ¥30,000 or more, the percentages for all categories ¥7,000 or above decreased. Also, the point of divergence at present lies at a level between ¥7,000 and ¥10,000.

Table 2.1   Wages Received by Irregular Workers (Daily wage)

	(%)	
	1992	1998
¥3,000 or less	0.7	1.1
¥5,000 or less	5.5	7.4
¥7,000 or less	19.4	25.6
¥10,000 or less	56.4	48.6
¥30,000 or less	15.3	13.6
Over ¥30,000	0.5	0.6
Unknown	2.1	3.1
Total	**100.0**	**100.0**
Number of cases	62,161	40,535

Source: Ministry of Justice, Immigration Bureau, *Shutsunyukoku Kanri tokei gaiyo* (Overview of immigration and emigration control statistics), Japan Immigration Association (For 1992 figures, see Komai Hiroshi, ed., *Gaikokujin rodosha mondai shiryo shusei* (Compilation of resources on the issue of foreign workers), Tokyo: Akashi Shoten, 1994, Volume 1, pp.93–.

Thus, it appears undeniable, from looking at wages, that working conditions are worsening.

In the past, the image of foreign workers was largely one of people working in the lowest strata of the construction and manufacturing industries. But with the advent of the period of stagnation, there has been a notable shift toward service industries. Looking at the employment of irregular workers as shown in Table 2.2, the percentage of construction workers, among the aggregate of men and women, registered a large decrease from 38.9% to 19.0%. For factory workers, the figure also decreased, from 25.4% to 23.7%. By contrast, the percentage of hosts and hostesses rose from 8.1% to 17.7%, and that of bartenders and waitresses increased sharply from 1.9% to 7.0% for men, and from 7.3% to 14.9% for women. The percentage in other services also rose for women, from 3.3% to 4.3%. In other words, under the economic recession, there has been a notable shift from construction and manufacturing industries into the service sector.

As reasons for this shift, we find, first, that along with the hollowing-out of Japanese industry, the overall capacity of the

Table 2.2   Job Contents of Irregular Workers

(%)

	1992			1998		
	M/F Total	**Male**	**Female**	**M/F Total**	**Male**	**Female**
Construction workers	38.9	50.9	-	19.0	30.5	-
Factory workers	25.4	27.9	17.4	23.7	30.3	13.3
Laborers, etc.	5.3	5.9	3.4	5.0	6.9	-
Hosts and hostesses	8.1	-	34.4	17.7	-	43.0
Bartenders and waitresses	3.1	1.9	7.3	10.1	7.0	14.9
Cooks	2.6	2.2	3.9	5.7	6.6	4.3
Dishwashers	3.8	2.2	9.1	*	3.2	5.7
Services, etc.	2.0	1.6	3.3	*	*	4.3
Porters	1.1	1.4	-	*	*	*
Prostitutes	2.6	-	11.0	*	-	*
Others	7.0	5.9	10.3	18.9	15.6	14.5
Total	**100.0**	**100.0**	**100.0**	**100.0**	**100.0**	**100.0**
Number of cases	62,161	47,521	14,640	40,535	24,808	15,727

* Included in others.

Source: Ministry of Justice, Immigration Bureau, *Shutsunyukoku Kanri tokei gaiyo* (Overview of immigration and emigration control statistics), Japan Immigration Association (For 1992 figures, see Komai Hiroshi, ed., *Gaikokujin rodosha mondai shiryo shusei* (Compilation of resources on the issue of foreign workers), Tokyo: Akashi Shoten, 1994, Volume 1, pp.93–.

Japanese manufacturing sector to absorb employment has decreased. Second, we can cite the fact that due to the large-scale cutbacks in public works spending accompanying fiscal reforms, the ability of the construction industry to absorb employment has also shrunk. Furthermore, this development has been influenced by the increase in demand in the service sector accompanying the high development of industry. Additionally, as legal Nikkeijin workers tend to opt for employment in manufacturing, employers in that sector have tended to replace irregular workers with Nikkeijin. In other words, on top of the hollowing out of industry and the economic recession, irregular workers have been driven out of jobs in the construction and manufacturing sectors by Latin American Nikkeijin, who have spread out into various places throughout Japan, and who are preferable to employers because of their regular status. Consequently, a nationwide phenomenon has emerged where irregular workers have been forced to move from manufacturing and construction into the service sector.

With regard to the employment situation of irregular workers in 1992–1993, there is, in addition to the Immigration Bureau data, a survey report from the Tokyo Metropolitan Council of Social Welfare.[14] One notable finding of this report was that the unemployment rate among irregular workers was as high as 14.7%. Of those who were employed, 40.3% were working in construction-related jobs, 18.5% in factory jobs, and another 27.5 in other miscellaneous jobs. This accords generally with the Immigration Bureau data that many work in field jobs. Incidentally, these workers had three major complaints about their current jobs: 'I receive no bonuses' (47.3%), 'I'm not eligible for social insurance' (45.2%), and 'My wages are low compared to Japanese workers' (42.8%).

I would like to touch upon the role of brokers here. Brokers mediate in the following ways: abroad, they induce and recruit potential workers, and procure travel tickets and visas (including forged documents); and domestically, they meet workers at the airport, and arrange jobs for them. In fiscal year 1995, brokers were of the following nationalities: abroad, they were Thai (40.2%), Filipino (19.8%), and Chinese (12.1%); and domestically they were Japanese (32.6%), Thai (29.3%), and Chinese (15.0%), showing that there was a large proportion of Thais, Filipinos, and Chinese. In the case of Thai female workers, in particular, there was significant involvement by organized crime gangs.

Between 1995 and 1996, a survey team from the Chiba Prefectural High School visited foreigners living in the surroundings of Chiba City, and interviewed roughly 30 people from a variety of countries.[15] Looking at the results, as shown in Table 2.3, we find that 33.3% of the Chinese, 53.3% of the Thais, and 28.1% of the Filipinos said they had had contact with brokers before entering the country. This is a higher figure than the Immigration Bureau data. One can explain this gap by pointing out that Immigration Bureau data is based on individuals who are going to return to their home countries (and hence have been in the country for some time), whereas the Chiba High School data was for foreigners who were currently living and working in Japan. In other words, the results

Table 2.3   Intervention of Brokers at the Time of Enterning Japan

		(%)
	Yes	No
Nikkei	46.7	53.3
Korea	7.4	92.6
China	33.3	66.7
Philippines	28.1	71.9
Thailand	53.3	46.7
Bangladesh	3.6	96.4
Iran	31.3	68.7
Total	**28.0**	**72.0**

Source: Chiba Prefectural Chiba High School, International Social Studies Group, *Gaikokujin rodosha jittai chosa, 1995-nen–1996-nen* (1995–1996 Field survey of foreign workers), 1997, in *Shinrai/teiju gaikokujin shiryo shusei* (Compilation of resources related to newcomer and settled foreginers), Tokyo: Akashi Shoten, 1998, Volume 2, p.31.

appear to indicate that the intervention of brokers at the time of arrival in Japan has increased in the post-bubble period.

In the case of Latin American Nikkeijin, a tendency toward longer periods of stay has been accompanied by a gradual fall in the intervention of brokers and employment agents within Japan. One reason for this is that, with the bursting of the bubble, it has become more difficult for employment agencies to prey on Nikkeijin to make easy money. Not only this, but many foreign workers, as their stay in Japan becomes more extended, come to feel that it is unreasonable to allow brokers to take a cut of their wages.

Looking at the rate of intervention by brokers from available Immigration Bureau data, we find that domestically it decreased from 10.4% in 1992 to 6.5% in 1995. By contrast, it increased outside of Japan, from 9.2% in 1992 to 16.5% in 1995. In other words, the intervention of brokers increased somewhat outside of Japan following the burst of the bubble, but within Japan, partly as a result of the establishment of ethnic networks, the room for this intervention shrunk.

Furthermore, it is worth noting that beginning in about 1996 the signs of a dual labor market began to appear. According to the above-mentioned Immigration Bureau data, the number of foreigners who were working in workplaces with 'no Japanese employees' was 9.9% in 1992 and 6.7% in 1995, but rose to 14.6% in 1996, and to 18.2% in 1997 (recalculated after removing 'unknown' answers). These figures were not included in the 1998 data. These results appear to reflect the fact that there has been an increase in the number of workplaces with absolutely no Japanese employees, particularly in the restaurant and sex and entertainment related industries.

The trend toward rejection in public opinion, and crackdowns

As Japan entered the period of stagnation, public attitudes toward irregular foreign workers changed dramatically compared to the period of expansion. During the earlier period, attitudes toward foreigners were generally positive, and various public opinion surveys showed that roughly two thirds of Japanese were receptive toward foreigners. A representative survey is the 'Public Opinion Survey on the Problem of Foreign Workers' conducted by the Prime Minister's Office.[16] The most interesting result concerned the acceptance or rejection of unskilled foreign workers. The views toward the employment of foreigners in general were: 'It should not be permitted' (7.5%), 'It should be permitted if they possess a certain level of knowledge or skill' (34.0%), 'It should be permitted in occupations which only foreigners can perform' (10.9%), and 'If it is necessary it should be permitted with no distinction toward occupations' (38.8%), showing that there was some form of consensus among Japanese on acceptance. The distribution of responses with regard to unskilled workers was as follows: 'They should be allowed to work within certain conditions or restrictions' (56.6%), 'They should be allowed to work under the same conditions as Japanese' (14.9%), and 'They should not be allowed to work' (14.1%), showing that roughly 70% favored acceptance in some form or another. For those who said they would accept unskilled foreign labor with some conditions or restrictions, the most common restriction they supported was time limits. Among these limits, the most commonly given period was more than one but less than two years.

With regard to the employment of irregular workers, 32.1% said 'It is wrong,' versus 55.0% who responded 'It is wrong, but cannot be helped,' showing that many people saw their presence as inevitable. With regard to measures toward the employment of irregular workers, 40.6% responded, 'They should be dealt with severely only in malicious cases,' 33.6% 'They should all be deported,' and 11.4% 'They should be left alone in areas where there are labor shortages,' meaning that the largest group favored a *laissez-faire* approach within limits. On the question of whether unskilled workers should be able to bring their families with them, 18.6% responded, 'Yes, and they should even be able to settle permanently,' 32.6% said, 'They should be allowed to come for a specified period of time,' and 36.5% said 'No,' meaning that slightly more people approved than disapproved. It appears that the number of people approving was relatively high in this survey partly because it was carried out at the height of the bubble economy, at a time when the labor shortage was a common theme.

Particularly in the post-bubble period, however, there has been an extremely strong backlash in Japanese society against irregular workers. One can easily perceive the strength of this change through the previously mentioned survey conducted by the Tokyo Metropolitan Institute for Labor. In the 'Survey of Japanese employees,' the respondents were almost evenly split between people in favor of acceptance (49.5%) and expulsion (50.5%). The percentage of proponents of expulsion was extremely high, at 78.6%, in companies that did not employ foreign workers, compared to 21.4% at companies that did.

This survey also revealed the demands of Japanese employees and employers toward the government on the issue of foreign employment. What should be noted in particular is their views toward crackdowns against 'irregular' workers. Looking at Table 2.4, which compares views during 1990–1991 to those of 1994–1995, we find that the percentage of Japanese employees at firms employing foreign workers who supported crackdowns against 'irregular' workers increased (though with multiple answers) from 26.1% to 48.4%. For employees of firms that did not employ foreign workers, the already high figure of 46.1% rose further to 60.9%. On the employer side, the percentage for employers who were using foreign workers rose from 18.8% to 26.9%, and for

Table 2.4 Demands Toward the Administration Regarding the Employment of Foreigners (Multiple responses)

(%)

	Japanese employees				Japanese employers			
	Firms with foreign employees		Firms without foreign employees		Firms with foreign employees		Firms without foreign employees	
	1990–91	1994–95	1990–91	1994–95	1990–91	1994–95	1990–91	1994–95
Japanese-language training	(1) 43.1	(2) 44.9	(1) 58.1	(2) 53.7	(1) 43.5	(2) 29.0	(1) 51.8	(1) 49.0
Safety and skill training	(4) 21.0	(4) 29.5	(3) 46.3	(4) 43.0	(3) 22.9	(4) 15.0	(3) 36.3	(4) 32.0
Establishing consultation windows	(3) 25.7	(3) 35.4	(2) 50.4	(3) 48.0	(1) 43.5	(1) 30.1	(2) 45.7	(3) 39.2
Cracking down on illegal workers	(2) 26.1	(1) 48.4	(4) 46.1	(1) 60.9	(4) 18.8	(3) 26.9	(4) 34.5	(2) 42.3

Figures in parenthesis are order.

Source: Tokyo Metropolitan Institute for Labor, *Gaikokujin rodosha no komyunikeshon to ningen kankei* (Foreign workers: Communication and interpersonal relations), Part1, 1995, p.51, introduced in Komai Hiroshi, ed., *Shinrai/teiju gaikokujin shiryo shusei* (Compilation of resources related to newcomer and settled foreigners), Tokyo: Akashi Shoten,1998, Volume1, p.522.

those who were not, from 34.5% to 42.3%. In other words, the percentage of people calling for crackdowns against irregular workers was lower among people who had contact with foreign workers at their firms, and was also smaller among employers than among employees. However, compared to the height of the economic bubble, the number of both employers and employees calling for crackdowns increased dramatically. In short, the stage was reached where six out of ten employees working at firms that did not hire foreign workers supported crackdowns.

Another survey of 3,438 price-of-living monitors commissioned by the Economic Planning Agency (EPA) in Febuary 1999 found similar negative sentiments toward foreign workers. Of the respondents, 51.6% said that Japan's current policy toward foreign workers should be maintained, and 29.8% said the conditions for acceptance should be strengthened even further. Of these people who had negative attitudes toward expanding the acceptance of foreign workers, 68.0% cited concern of rising unemployment and a delay of improvement in working conditions as a reason, and as many as 30.4% cited increasing problems within communities and a deterioration of public security.[17] However, this survey contained some bias; 92.3% of respondents were women, and 56.4% were unemployed, and presumably housewives.

Despite these growing adverse sentiments toward irregular foreign workers, it is still rare for migrants in Japan to become the targets of right-wing groups. There was a period, however, between 1992 and 1993, when scattered groups appeared using the slogan of rejecting foreigners. One representative example was a small group bearing the name 'National Socialist Japanese Workers Party,' which put up posters decorated with swastikas calling for the expulsion of overstayers. Posters calling for the expulsion of 'bad foreigners' were also put up by a small rightist group called Kodo Rengokai ('wide road alliance'). It is likely that these groups were partly stirred up by the fact that during that period, large numbers of Iranians would gather in Tokyo's Yoyogi Park on Sundays. In addition, there was an incident in June 1999, where a dispute broke out between Brazilian residents of the Homi public housing complex in Toyota City, and a group that was believed to be a right-wing organization (this incident will be discussed further in Chapter 6).[18]

Since the era of stagnation began, the actions of public authorities toward irregular foreigners have become harsher. In April 1993, a special survey team was set up within the Immigration Bureau to apprehend people with irregular residence status. In June of the same year, a special campaign to crack down on irregular foreigners was launched, and in some periods concentrated arrests are carried out three times a year. During these campaigns, some 2,000 or 3,000 foreigners were detained. Thus, less than 1% of the irregular foreigners in the country were apprehended during each of these crack-downs.

Looking at the targets of the crackdowns in the past, one finds that they were mainly 'swarms,' meaning gatherings of people. The first examples of this were operations in 1993 at Yoyogi Park, Ueno Park, and the area around Shinjuku Station, which targeted Iranians. In 1995, there were concentrated arrests of Peruvians looking for work in Hiroshima. One of the main focuses of these campaigns was on 'prostitution,' and many prostitutes were arrested particularly in places such as Okubo and Ikebukuro in Tokyo, or Isezaki-cho in Yokohama. More recently, groups of Chinese working *en masse* at fish and marine product markets in Tsukiji and Adachi have been targeted. Other focuses of these raids have been groups of a dozen or more foreigners living together in 'group housing.' In many of these cases, the authorities were tipped off by people living in the neighborhood. In addition, operations have been carried out against 'drugs,' or 'out of status workers,' meaning women who came to Japan on entertainer visas to be singers or dancers but were working in nightclubs and other establishments as hostesses.[19] These have been the six major targets of joint operations carried out by Immigration Bureau authorities and police. Put in a different perspective, however, this means that people outside of these six categories have for the most part been left untouched. Moreover, it appears that a significant portion of these joint operations have originated from 'tips.'

3 The Emergence of Non-Working Immigrants

Categories of non-working immigrants

As we saw in Chapter 2, in spite of the narrowing of the labor market under the economic recession, some portion of migrants have shown no signs of returning to their home countries. If all foreigners had simply come to Japan to make money, the number of returnees should have increased more significantly. It is natural, therefore, to conclude that among foreigners there are people who have come to Japan with greater expectations than just earning money; this exposes the limitations of the use of the category of foreign 'workers' itself. I personally came to this realization while conducting a survey on Iranians in Japan. As I will discuss in the following section, when I asked respondents about their reasons for coming to Japan, it turned out that the number of 'non-migrant workers' exceeded that of 'migrant workers' (or 'money-seekers').

The first category of non-migrant workers I would like to discuss is 'pseudo-exiles.' As one example, after the Iranian Revolution, there was a growing tendency toward Islamic fundamentalism in that country, and in particular in the wake of the Iran-Iraq War, many people came to want to escape from the country. They were people who would say, 'I am dissatisfied with the state of Iran today.' According to an interview with an Iranian youth conducted by Okada Emiko, there was a student movement in the early 1990s against the two-year military conscription system, and when rumors spread that participants would be executed, many people fled abroad after completing the first year of their service. The interviewee said he was one of these people.[1] I will tentatively label them 'pseudo-exiles,' since in spite of having no prospects of being accepted as political refugees, they possess some aspect of exiles in that they have escaped the situation in their home country.

A second category of non-migrant workers is what I call people in search of 'self-actualization.' Iranians in Japan who say 'I want to improve my abilities' or 'I want to broaden my horizons' are, in a broad sense, pursuing this goal. I once conducted a survey of Sikh emigrants from India who were living in Toronto, Canada. Out of 66 respondents, 34 gave as their reason for migrating 'the better opportunities in Canada,' 'adventure or travel,' or 'studying or personal improvement.' This impressed upon me the fact that decision-making on international migration cannot always be put down to economic motives.[2] In this sense, there are similarities among Iranians in Japan and Sikhs in Toronto.

With regard to Nikkei Brazilians as well, there are people among recent young and unmarried entrants who cannot be labeled as money-seekers. According to the observations of Watanabe Masako, there has been a dramatic increase in the number of people saying they came to Japan because 'All my friends are here, and it's lonely in Brazil' or 'I would like to take advantage of this chance to learn about Japan.'[3] At the very least, the people who said they wanted to learn about Japan can be classified within the broad category of 'self-actualization.' On this point, in the survey of Nikkei Brazilians and Peruvians in Hamamatsu City which I introduced in Chapter 2,[4] when respondents were asked about their reason for coming to Japan (with up to two answers allowed)'To learn about Japan' (26.1%) came right after 'To save money' (42.4%) and 'Because the public order and economy are bad in my country' (40.3%). This suggests the existence of a group seeking self-actualization.

According to a survey by Wakabayashi Chihiro, Bangladeshis in Japan tend to be from relatively high social strata and to be well-educated; many came under the mutual visa exemption agreement and to take advantage of the opportunities for study. Accordingly, their situation is closer to that of young people on voyages of discovery than to money-seekers, and they are close to what one would call people in search of self-actualization. However, as the stays of these people, who came to Japan by some form of chance, have lengthened, they have found themselves confronted with a variety of life choices. These choices involve important issues for young people: studies, finding regular employment, love, and marriage. To cope with these issues, some have chosen to return to Bangladesh, and others to remain in Japan. Many found themselves forced to stay in Japan with irregular status, putting them under an immense handicap.[5]

I should add that looking at the 1994 survey by the Tokyo Metropolitan Institute for Labor, which was introduced in Chapter 2, 'Interview and questionnaire survey of foreign workers themselves,' we find that many Koreans came to Japan after failing to achieve success in their own country, or suffering some form of failure, and hence were in search of a new start. Among Thais, as well, an increasing number have been middle-class people from Bangkok or local cities in similar circumstances. Thus, we can see horizontal movements from countries experiencing growth. These people can also be considered to fit into the category of self-actualization.

We have examined three types of motives for foreigners coming to Japan, but there are other, family-oriented reasons, which cannot be ignored. These include people who marry Japanese nationals, who come to join families who are already in Japan, or who move to Japan along with their families. I will call this category the 'marriage/family group.' In addition, there are 'returnees' among Nikkeijin, who feel homesickness for Japan. I will tentatively call them the 'homesick group.'

In this way, newcomer foreigners in Japan can be broadly classified into five types: money-seekers, pseudo-exiles, people in search of self-actualization, marriage/family types, and the homesick group. Nevertheless, human beings must work and earn money in order to survive, so nearly all foreigners have the common attribute of being workers in search of employment. What must be kept in mind is that these five categories are what Max Weber called ideal types. In other words, no individual newcomer foreigner need fit perfectly into any single category. One individual can belong to more than one type. A person might have significant elements of the self-actualization type, but at the same time have smaller proportions of the properties of a money-seeker or person coming to join their family. The category of a single individual can also be fluid over time. For example, a person might enter Japan as a pseudo-exile, and gradually take on the qualities of a person in search of self-actualization.

Of these five categories, it is probably the pseudo-exiles who require the most attention. Myanmar, for example, has long been ruled by an autocratic military regime following undemocratic dictatorial politics. However, as of February 1992, the Japanese government had only recognized three political refugees from that country.[6] It is likely that a significant number of the 6,000 Myanmarese overstayers shown in Table 1.1 would fit into the category of pseudo-exiles. Some Myanmarese people in Japan have formed an organization called The Burmese Association in Japan (BAIJ), and are working here toward the democratization of their country.[7] There is also an important group of pseudo-exiles among the Chinese population. In Section 3, I will further discuss the tendency of Chinese foreign students to remain abroad, but here I would like to point out that one of the factors is the fact that the 1989 Tienanmen Square Incident strengthened distrust among overseas students toward the Communist Party. The same reason can be used to explain the tendency of Chinese pre-college students to become overstayers. In this case, their characteristic as pseudo-exiles plays an important role, along with that of people in search of self-actualization.

An element of the pseudo-exile may be seen in the case of Nikkei Brazilians, though in a different sense than among Myanmarese and Chinese. In the JICA survey of Nikkeijin from five Latin American countries which was introduced in the last chapter, when respondents were asked about their reason for coming to Japan, 30.5% responded 'Because the situation in my home country is poor,' an answer second only to 'To work for a certain period of time, save money, and return home,' with 51.4%.[8] In addition, in the previously mentioned survey of Nikkeijin conducted by Hamamatsu City, 40.3% of respondents said 'Because the public order and economy are bad in my country,' and 21.9% 'Because I have no future in my home country.'[9] According to Fuchigami Eiji, writing on the basis of a field survey conducted in Latin American countries, 'Since the beginning of the *dekasegi* boom, Nikkeijin have increasingly become the targets of burglaries and robberies. Problems of crime have increasingly become concentrated against Nikkeijin, who constitute a form of nouveau riches.' In addition, he quotes one Nikkei Brazilian, whose father had been killed by burglars in Brazil, as saying, 'I don't mind going back to visit relatives, but I don't want to go back to live there.'[10] This case can be seen as a money-seeker turned pseudo-exile.

As shown here, most foreigners in Japan are working, but few came to Japan specifically to work. However, there is very little understanding in Japanese society of the diversity in the life plans of these foreigners. This is one of the reasons why there is 'acceptance' of foreigners as labor power, but 'rejection' as individuals.

Iranians in Japan: Pseudo-exiles and people seeking self-actualization

Many Iranians have been very badly affected by the economic downturn; they are also very far removed from Japan in cultural terms. And yet, there seems to exist among them a strong desire to settle in Japan. Consequently, examining the pattern of settlement into Japanese society of Iranians, who are in some ways a representative group of newcomers, can give important hints for understanding other ethnic groups.

The survey of Iranians in Japan[11] which I conducted in 1993 contained a question on reason for coming to Japan. Looking at the results, 45.7% responded 'To make money,' 18.1% 'Because I am dissatisfied with the situation in Iran,' 9.2% 'To improve my own abilities,' and 20.6% 'To broaden my perspective or experiences,' with 6.3% giving no answer. If those responding 'To make money' are classified as money-seekers, 'Because I am dissatisfied with the situation in Iran' as pseudo-exiles, and 'To improve my own abilities' or 'To broaden my perspective or experiences' as self-actualization types, we find that the money-seekers made up less than half of the population, and that the other categories actually formed a slightly larger percentage.

Incidentally, there are significant gaps between the Iranians who come as money-seekers and those who are pseudo-exiles, in terms of their social statuses in their home country, as well as their desire to settle in Japan. This demonstrates that Iranians in Japan cannot be seen as a monolithic block. Specifically, those who were working in sales/retail or services in Iran, and whose educational attainment is not above the high school level, tend to be money-seekers (the cross-statistics below are all calculated by chi-square test with a significance level of 95% or above). This group is a class who could be called 'bazaar merchants' in Iran, though according to a friend who is familiar with the situation there, they are in actuality closer to bazaar peddlers. By contrast, it is common to find pseudo-exiles among people who worked in socially high positions, such as professionals or managers, and who have high educational attainment, meaning high school or above. However, with regard to the 'self-actualization group,' one does not see any correspondence to any particular social class with regard to occupation and educational attainment. This seems to indicate that there are no class boundaries to people who cross borders in search of self-actualization.

Looking at the distribution of the occupations Iranians in Japan were engaged in before coming, we find that 22.0% were working as professionals, 2.4% as managers, 18.4% as office workers, 18.4% in sales/retail, 7.3% in services, 16.3% as factory workers, 2.0% in construction, 3.7% as drivers, 3.3% as students, 0.8% as soldiers, with 1.2% classified as miscellaneous, 1.2% as unemployed, and 2.9% giving no answer. This means that the share of white-collar workers was large, at 42.8%, versus 25.7% in sales and services, and 22.0% in blue-collar jobs. In addition, it is remarkable that there were practically no unemployed individuals. In other words, Iranians in Japan are not people who had lost their jobs in their home country, but on the contrary people with relatively high social statuses at home. Furthermore, the composition of final educational attainment was: 0.6% for none, 5.4% for primary school, 13.8% for junior high school, 57.5% for high school, and 22.8% for university; high school graduates made up the largest group.

There are also vast differences between money-seekers and pseudo-exiles in terms of their plans to remain in Japan. When asked about such plans, 18.0% responded, 'I want to go home immediately,' 7.3% said 'I would like to return within a year,' 24.1% said 'I would like to go home in one or two years,' 5.3% said 'I would like to stay for more than two years,' 29.8% said 'I would like to stay as long as conditions permit,' and 9.4% responded 'I would like to settle permanently,' with 6.1% giving no answer. Thus, the total of people with short-term plans to stay in Japan ('I want to go home immediately,' 'I would like to return within a year,' and 'I would like to go home in one or two years') accounted for 49.4% of all respondents; however the total of people with long-term plans to stay (the total of 'I would like to stay for more than two years,' 'I would like to stay as long as conditions permit,' and 'I would like to settle permanently') was nearly equivalent, at 44.5%. Roughly 10% of respondents hoped to settle permanently. This shows that there is a very strong desire among Iranians to settle in Japan.

Incidentally, the answers for people who came to Japan as money-seekers were more or less evenly distributed between those who answered, 'I would like to go home in one or two years,' and those who said either 'I would like to stay for more than two years,' or 'I would like to stay as long as conditions permit.' By contrast, for pseudo-exiles the largest answer was 'I would like to settle permanently,' though 'I would like to stay for more than two years' and 'I would like to stay as long as conditions permit' also held considerable weight. In other words, the answers for money-seekers were biased toward short-term stays, while pseudo-exiles showed a tendency toward longer stays. As mentioned earlier, more than 9,000 Iranians returned home in the one-year period leading up to November 1993. Most of these were in the migrant worker group, and it is assumed that the majority of the pseudo-exiles remained behind.

Another difference that can be cited between the money-seekers and pseudo-exiles is the timing of their arrival in Japan. In April 1992, the mutual visa exemption agreement between Japan and Iran, under which vast numbers of individuals had come to Japan, was temporarily suspended. Taking this into consideration, and dividing the periods of stay into 18- and 24-month periods, we find the following distribution at the time of the survey: 17.9% had been in Japan up to 18 months, 60.8% for 19 to 30 months, and 18.0% for 31 months or longer, with 3.3% giving no answer. Thus, roughly 80% had been in Japan for 19 months or longer, meaning they had come before the agreement was suspended. This group of 80% of the respondents was roughly equally divided between those who had been in Japan for up to 24 months and those who had stayed for more than that much time. However, looking at their occupations, we find that the weight of white-collar workers remained high throughout the different periods, but that the weight of people from sales or services dropped as the period extended to over 24 months. This is evidence that the people who returned after the visa exemption agreement was suspended were mostly money-seekers.

The event which divides these two groups is the 1979 Revolution, under which the Pahlavi monarchy was overthrown by a movement led by the Ayatollah Khomeini. Under this Revolution, Western influence was rejected, the United States was considered an enemy, and a theocratic political system was established under the precepts of Shiite Islam. Shiite Islam, unlike Sunni Islam, which accepts the material world, grasps this world as a vulgar one controlled by darkness and evil.[12] Under this form of Islam, freedom and tolerance were increasingly limited, and today the country leans toward a form of perfectionism that is close to what is termed fundamentalism,[13] though in recent years there have been signs the country may be moving away from that tendency.

The religious forces which carried out the Iranian Revolution were supported by clerics, bazaar merchants, and urban lower classes who occupied the traditional sections of the cities surrounding the mosques and bazaars. These people rose up against the monarchy, national elite, and new middle classes who inhabited the modern areas of the cities. These bureaucrats, managers and technicians were expelled from their places of work, and there was a flow of manpower overseas.[14]

The money-seeker types uncovered in our survey, considering their occupations and educational attainment, are perfectly descriptive of the bazaar merchants and urban lower classes. By contrast, the pseudo-exiles correspond to the new middle classes who were deprived of the social basis for their existence by the Revolution. Thus, as a whole the pseudo-exiles are not supportive of the Iranian Revolution (in my survey, 88.5% said they were opposed to it).

The self-actualization group as pre-college students and college students

In the expansion period, when there were shortages of labor, it was very common for pre-college students to hold part-time jobs or for people to do work under the guise of being technical trainees. However, as Japan entered the stagnation period, this situation changed drastically.

The number of pre-college students began to increase when visa restrictions were relaxed in 1984, based on a proposal put out by then Prime Minister Nakasone Yasuhiro to 'accept 100,000 foreign students by the 21st century.' The number of newly entering pre-college students, which was a mere 4,140 in 1984, hit a record of 30,510 in 1988. Of these, the vast majority (80.5%) were Chinese. The government imposed tighter restrictions in 1989, and the number of new entrants fell to roughly 20,000 per year.

Of the pre-college students who entered Japan in 1988, nearly half became overstayers, and this level remained more or less constant in later years. In 1992, the number of newly entering pre-college students began to rise again, hitting a figure of 27,000; this came as a blow to the Immigration Bureau. In 1994, in response, it released a 'Guideline for the Future Acceptance of Japanese Language Students,' which proposed the strict screening of potential students to ensure that they were capable of paying the necessary expenses and that they had the basic scholastic ability to learn Japanese. With these new measures, the number of new entrants began to drop again, falling to 9,436 in 1996. The number of Chinese, in particular, plummeted, falling to the number two position in that year, with Koreans occupying the top spot.

As of the end of 1998, there were 30,691 pre-college students in Japan, with 65.3% coming from China, and 20.3% from South Korea. As a consequence, the number of Japanese language schools, which reached 500 in the boom years, fell dramatically, and it is presumed that only 250 or so are currently functional. Under the revised Immigration Control Law, pre-college students were required to obtain a work permit from the Immigration Bureau before taking a part-time job, and their working hours were limited to no more than four per day. This drastically curtailed the role of the pre-college student system as a source of foreign labor power. Incidentally, pre-college students who have completed their courses at language schools but are unable to enter universities or technical schools are faced with the choice of either returning home or becoming overstayers.

In 1991, the Tokyo Metropolitan Government's Bureau of Citizens and Cultural Affairs conducted a survey on the situation of pre-college students.[15] The results of the survey were separated into college and pre-college students, and it was clear that in general, the study and work situations of the pre-college students were much more difficult than those of the college students. Of the pre-college students, 93.0% were attending Japanese language schools, and a mere 3.0% were receiving financial assistance in some form or another. Consequently, 65.1% were doing some kind of part-time job at the time of the survey. Though this is not stated in the report, calculating the income they received and using the average hourly wage for part-time work, it can be assumed that they worked 35.4 hours per week, meaning nearly six hours a day if they worked six-day weeks. With regard to future plans, a high 71.0% of the pre-college students said they wanted to go on to university or continue their education in some form. In other words, the image that emerges of pre-college students is one of 'struggling students,' relying on part-time jobs to put themselves through Japanese language schools as a preliminary step to going on to a regular higher education. With regard to the kinds of jobs they took, the huge majority were working either in service-related jobs such as waiters and waitresses (61.2%) or in manual jobs such as factory, construction, or cleaning work (22.8%); very few worked in offices or as language teachers. In as many as 56.6% of cases they had been introduced to their jobs by a friend from the same country, showing the importance of compatriot networks.

The trends of Chinese college students are particularly noteworthy within the self-actualization group. Generally most overseas students return to their home countries after graduating, but Chinese are an exception to this rule. Between 1978 and 1989, the percentage who returned to China was a low of 25% among those studying in the U.S., and a high of just 50% among those in France. The figure for Japan was 29%, the second lowest following the U.S. among seven countries. This low number of returnees is a problem that is troubling the Chinese government itself.[16] In this way, a significant number of Chinese studying abroad choose to live overseas, and among them many select Japan. Mo Feng Fu gave the label 'New Overseas Chinese' to the Chinese who left China since the country's opening policy in 1979, and who had a strong desire to settle, in consideration of the fact that they differed significantly, in terms of reasons for leaving and means chosen to attain their goals, from the 'Old Overseas Chinese' who went abroad before the establishment of the People's Republic.[17] Many of the individuals engaged in non-manual labor such as professional and managerial jobs are precisely these 'New Overseas Chinese,' who found work in Japan after studying here.

To get an overview[18] of these 'New Overseas Chinese,' a 1993 reader's survey conducted by *Ryugakusei Shimbun*, the largest Chinese-language media organization in Japan, is insightful.[19] According to the survey, in terms of status of residence, the first largest group was 'company employees,' particularly people working at Japanese enterprises, with 22.7%. This figure was 14.6% in the 1992 survey conducted by the same organization, meaning that it has grown dramatically. The number of overstayers also rose sharply from 4.6% to 13.9% in the same period, as did the number of people married to Japanese nationals also increased remarkably. As a result, the share of students (including pre-college students as well as students at universities, technical schools, graduate schools and research students (*kenkyusei*) at graduate schools) plummeted.

Second- and third-generation descendents of returnees from China as family types

Chinese 'war orphans' refers to Japanese women and children who were separated from their families and left behind in China in the confusion during and after the end of World War II.[20] Most are from the three northeastern provinces of Heilongjiang, Liaoning, and Jilin, and many are the descendants of people who came as colonists. The Ministry of Health and Welfare defines war children as 'people who were less than 13 years of age or so at the time,' and considers women older than 13 to have remained by their own will. The 'war spouses' fit into this category, but in reality many had no choice but to marry Chinese men in order to survive, and ended up staying because they had no way of getting back to Japan. Many of the war orphans, for their part, were adopted and raised by Chinese parents. In 1972, diplomatic relations between China and Japan were normalized, and in 1973 the road was opened for these individuals to return to Japan at state expense. Originally, those who were unable to locate relatives willing to be guarantors had no chance to be repatriated, but after a group of 12 women returned in 1993 on their own, without permission, the Ministry of Welfare decided to repatriate all such individuals who wished to settle in

Japan, at state expense, by fiscal year 1996. In 1994, a 'Law to Promote the Smooth Reentry of Japanese Nationals Left Behind in China, etc., and to Support Their Independence Following Reentry' was enforced. Since 1973, 5,326 people have returned to Japan at state expense (as of November 1998).[21] Also, as of May 1998, some 1,250 Japanese left behind in China had been identified, and 60% to 70% said they hoped to return to Japan someday.[22]

These individuals are all elderly people, over the age of 50, and most are from rural areas of China. Consequently, it is no easy task for them to adapt to life in Japan. Upon arrival, they spend an initial four months in one of eight Readjustment Promotion Centers throughout the country (in 1999 the number was reduced to three), where they are given lessons in Japanese language and customs. After that period, they are half-forcibly sent to the places of their family register (*honseki*) or to where their relatives or guardians are living, and are assigned for eight months to one of 15 Centers for Training in Independence set up around the country. Many have shown great resistance to settling in the designated areas, though, and a significant number have moved to big cities such as Tokyo and their environs.

Among these returnees, the number of recipients of public assistance benefits is extremely high. According to a survey of returnee households conducted by the Ministry of Health and Welfare in 1993, the ratio of recipients was 34.6%, a figure exceeding one third. Even households who had been back in Japan for three to five years had a ratio above 30%, and for those who had been back for more than five years it was still a high 23.6%. Only 60.4% of individuals were working. When asked why they were not, 68.2% responded 'Because of illness.'[23] Iida Toshiro analyzed the living patterns of returnees based on a combination of two axes, namely whether they depended on public assistance or worked, and whether they lived in solidarity with other returnees or were isolated.[24] His analysis demonstrated the extent to which some war orphans have lost the ability to live independently. There is a whole slew of other problems, including the difficulties they find in mastering Japanese language, and the 'culture shock' of trying to adapt to such different lifestyles and values. But even given these problems, they have a strong desire to regain their Japanese nationality.

Partly because the war orphans are now elderly, many have come to Japan along with their spouses or with children and grandchildren (who sometimes have spouses of their own), or have invited them over after a period of time. Under the law, state funds could only be used to bring spouses or unmarried children under the age of 20. There was great dissatisfaction with these restrictions, however, and permission was given, in 1995 for those 60 or order, and in 1997 for those aged 55 and above, to bring with them, at state expense, one child along with that child's family. Children and grandchildren other than this can only come to Japan at their own expense. The children and grandchildren of war orphans and their spouses who have come to Japan along with them are given the aggregate label of second- and third-generation returnees. As of 1999, it was believed that there were 50,000 to 60,000 such individuals living in Japan with Chinese citizenship, and registered as aliens. In addition, it seems there are 20,000 to 30,000 people who have acquired Japanese nationality.

Incidentally, this means that every war orphan who has returned to Japan to settle permanently has brought along, on average, a stunning figure of 10 or more second- and third-generation returnees.

Although there is some information available on these second- and third-generation returnees, it is almost impossible to find data giving an overall picture. This stands in great contrast to the war orphans themselves. In view of this lack of information, I decided to carry out a fact-finding survey to examine their situation. The following is an outline of the information I obtained from these second- and third-generation returnees.[25] The difficulties they face in everyday life and the discrimination they have faced will be dealt with in the next chapter.

The targets of this survey were individuals of at least 15 years of age. Looking at the age composition (setting 147, the total number of respondents minus those who did not answer this question, at 100%, as below), we found that 15.0% were in their teens, 39.5% in their twenties, 29.2% in their thirties, and 16.3% in their forties. Extrapolating for people between the ages of 10 and 14, who were not included in the survey, we can assume that 30% or so were in their teens; the second- and third-generation returnees are thus a relatively young group, with people in their twenties as the core. In terms of generation (145=100%), 77.9% were second-, and 22.1% third-generation, demonstrating that second-generation people made up the vast majority. Looking at marital status (147=100%), 65.3%, or nearly two thirds, were married, and 34.7% were single. Incidentally, when considering the ethnicity of their spouses (96=100%), 3.1% were Japanese, 87.5% Chinese, and 9.4% Chinese of Japanese ancestry. Thus, the overwhelming majority were ethnic Chinese. With regard to number of members in their household (145=100%), 7.6% were single-member households, 30.3% two-member, 31.7% three-member, 22.1 four-member, and 8.3% had households of five or more members. This made the average household size a relatively small 2.99. Many lived in nuclear families, composed of either a couple or a couple and one child.

Looking at their place of origin in China (147=100%), more than half, or 55.1%, came from Heilongjiang Province, 22.4% from Liaoning, 8.8% from Jilin, 7.5% from Inner Mongolia, and 6.1% from other provinces. Needless to say, with the exception of Inner Mongolia they came from the three northeastern provinces (which were colonized by Japan in the 1930s). Looking at the time of their return to Japan (146=100%), 3.4% came in 1980–84, 42.5% in 1985–89, and 54.1% since 1990. More than half had come to Japan within the six years before the survey was carried out. When asked whether they had come to Japan with a war orphan (143=100%), or whether they had been brought over later, 44.1% said they came together, and 51.7% that they had been invited later, while 4.2% had come after the original ancestor had died. Thus, a slightly higher number had come after the ancestor. In terms of payment for their repatriation (147=100%), 70.7% had received no financial assistance at all from the Japanese government, and 29.3% had come at the expense of the government.

The ethnic identity of the second- and third-generation returnees proved to be complex. When asked about where they felt they belonged, (146=100%), 33.6% said they felt Chinese, 24.7% Japanese-Chinese, 11.6% Chinese-Japanese, and 8.9% Japanese, with 21.2% responding 'I don't know/I've never thought about it.' Looking at this, we find that 58.2%, or nearly 60%, considered themselves Chinese, meaning that they answered either Chinese or Japanese-Chinese. By contrast, only 20.5% perceived of themselves as Japanese, answering either Japanese or Chinese-Japanese. Furthermore, more than one third, or 36.3%, chose the intermediate categories of Japanese-Chinese or Chinese-Japanese. What is certain, in any case, is that second- and third-generation returnees have little consciousness of themselves as Japanese.

In this situation, attitudes on the question of acquiring Japanese nationality are ambivalent. When asked their attitude toward becoming Japanese nationals (126=100%), 42.1% said 'I am eager to nationalize,' 16.7% 'I am unenthusiastic/It is unavoidable,' and 41.3% said 'I don't know/I haven't thought about it.' The percentages of both 'I am eager' and 'I don't know/I haven't thought about it' were relatively high. Reflecting these attitudes, not a few respondents (146=100%) had failed to take any action toward acquiring nationality. In contrast to 37.0% who had acquired nationality and 4.8% who were currently in the application process, a full 58.2% said they were not taking any action. In relation to this, when asked 'Would you like to return to China if possible?' (138=100%), 6.5% said 'Definitely yes,' 28.3% said 'Yes,' 48.6% said 'Not really,' and 16.7% said 'Definitely not.' In other words, one third of respondents hoped to return to China.

Regardless of this, it is notable that there are people, albeit a minority, who have taken on the identity of Japanese-Chinese or Chinese-Japanese, thus challenging Japanese society, which draws a sharp distinction between 'Chinese' and 'Japanese' in accordance with the principle of the nation-state.

4 Settlement and the Formation of Ethnic Communities

The progress of settlement

Newcomer foreigners first made their appearance before the Japanese as foreign 'workers.' Japanese society saw them as 'temporary visitors,' since they had come as 'workers,' and the general assumption was that even if a few exceptional foreigners would move their base of livelihood to Japan, the vast majority would eventually return to their home countries. But this belief was erroneous. In spite of the fact that the economic recession has dragged on, and that job opportunities have generally decreased, the foreign population in Japan continues to increase, albeit slightly, and as we saw in Chapter 2, there has been no great drop in the population of irregular workers.

Foreigners generally (with the exception of those who have only one choice forced upon them before they come to Japan) can choose from among the four following patterns with regard to their stay in Japan. (1) Returners: They come to Japan once, and then return to live in their home country. (2) Repeaters: They travel repeatedly between their home country and Japan. This is only possible in cases where travel between the two countries is relatively free. (3) Sojourners: They stay in Japan for a substantial amount of time, though they have not decided whether to settle or not. (4) Settlers: They move their livelihood base from their home country to Japan, and settle here. There is a constant turnover between returners and new entrants, but as some portion of foreign immigrants begin to move the basis of their work and livelihoods into Japan, these individuals begin to choose the course of sojourners or settlers.

As one of the conditions behind the fact that the foreign population has not decreased, one can point to the dual structure of Japan's labor market, which is divided between the large firms on one hand and the smaller ones (sub-contractors and sub-sub-contractors) on the other, and to the fact that as a result of their poor working conditions, the medium, small, and tiny enterprises experience chronic labor shortages, in both times of economic boom and bust. Looking at the Report on the Employment Situation of Foreigners released by the Ministry of Labor in November 1998, we find that the most common size (in terms of number of employees) for business establishments that employed foreigners was 'between 100 and 299 persons,' and that foreigners also tended to be employed in businesses in this same range. If we compare the results of the 1998 survey with the first in the series, which was carried out in 1993, we find there has been a significant decrease in the weight of firms with 1,000 or more employees. By contrast, the share of firms with 300 or fewer employees among those who had foreign employees rose from 78.2% to 81.2%; in addition, the share of foreign employees (direct employees) who were employed at firms of this size rose from 69.4% to 78.0%.[1] This indicates that work establishments with fewer than 300 employees have acted as a receptacle for foreign workers during the period of recession.

A phenomenon has also been seen where, because of stricter control by the Immigration Bureau, foreigners have begun to stay for longer periods of time out of fear that once they return to their home countries, they will find it extremely difficult to enter Japan again. With regard to Korean overstayers, Ko Sonfii reported from a 1992 survey of residents of cheap hotels (flophouses) in Yokohama that 'When it becomes impossible to re-enter the country, foreign workers are pushed into a choice between returning home for good or becoming overstayers. People who have families in their home country will often return, but unmarried men, and especially those with few job prospects at home, will tend to stay.'[2] It is believed that this holds true for people of other nationalities as well, though there may be gaps in scale and patterns.

A survey conducted by the Ethnic Media and Press Coalition (EMPC) provides interesting data, on an ethnic group basis, regarding the desire to settle in Japan, and on positive or negative views of Japan.[3] As shown by Table 4.1, groups in which a majority

Table 4.1   Desire to Settle and Views of Japan

(%)

	Average period of stay (years)	Desire to settle		Views of Japan		
		Yes	No	Like	Dislike	No strong feelings
Filipinos*	3.8	57	43	64	3	34
Chinese*	6.3	51	49	31	19	50
South Koreans	1.8	7	93	29	16	55
Thais	3.2	62	38	27	42	31
Malaysians	5.6	29	71	65	28	7
Myanmarese	4.5	13	87	58	27	15
Indonesians	2.0	42	58	61	3	36
Brazilians	4.5	12	88	35	45	20
Total	**5.0**	**37**	**63**	**49**	**22**	**29**

* Recalculated after excluding no answers.
No strong feelings = No strong feelings one way or the other

Source: Zainichi Gaikokujin Johoshi Rengokai (Ethnic Media and Press Coalition), 'Zainichi gaikokujin shijo chosa/deta shu' (Collection of market surveys and data on foreigners in Japan), 1996, in Komai Hiroshi, *Shinrai/teijyu gikokujin shiryo shusei* (Compilation of resources related to newcomer and settled foreigners), Tokyo: Akashi Shoten, 1998, volume 2, pp.241–.

(excluding blank answers) hope to live permanently in Japan included Filipinos, Thais, and Chinese, while in the remainder this figure did not reach the 50% mark. It was particularly low in the case of Koreans, Brazilians, and Myanmarese. It is notable that in other surveys as well, respondents from Korea have shown an almost complete lack of desire to settle in Japan. According to Ko, no respondents said, 'I would like to stay in Japan forever,' and only 9% responded, 'If possible, I would like to keep staying in Japan.'[4] Similarly, when a group including myself interviewed 10 Korean workers in Kanagawa Prefecture in 1990–91, all of them said they planned to return home within two years.[5]

Next, looking at perceptions of Japan by different ethnic groups (from Table 4.1), more than half of respondents expressed good feelings toward Japan among Filipinos, Malaysians, Myanmarese, and Indonesians; many Chinese and Koreans gave non-committal answers; and many Thais and Brazilians expressed dislike towards Japan. Thus, there are differences in the relationships between desire to settle and feelings toward Japan among the various ethnic groups. The Filipinos had a strong desire to settle and liked Japan; Brazilians had little desire to settle and disliked Japan, and Koreans had little desire and many gave non-committal answers to the question on like or dislike. In these cases the responses matched well. By contrast, Chinese expressed a strong desire to stay but were non-committal on the question of feelings, Thais tended to want to settle, though they disliked the country, and Myanmarese showed little desire to stay, though they said they liked Japan. In these cases the responses seem to be mutually contradictory. This seems to indicate that the Chinese and Thais in Japan face specific problems.

With regard to the Chinese, the reader survey from *Ryugakusei Shimbun*, which was introduced in the last chapter, provides very interesting information.[6] In the 1994 survey, half of the re-spondents, or 53.5%, said they hoped to settle on the Chinese mainland in the future, with only 16.1% saying they desired to settle in Japan. In the 1992 survey, just 24.4% had chosen China. It is believed that positive attitudes toward China's economic growth lay in the background of this leap. When asked to evaluate Japanese people, many wrote 'They are hard-working but are two-faced' in the free space provided for opinions, pointing out a contradiction in behavior; this in itself is a very interesting view of the Japanese. Incidentally, the responses regarding the state of mental life well expressed the positions of the respondents in Japanese society. The three most common anxieties cited in the free space were 'loneliness/boredom' (12.5%), 'anxiety about the future' (11.5%), and 'economic difficulties' (10.4%). We can state that for these Chinese, the struggle against loneliness was a major issue. However, 64.2% of respondents said that they had already become adapted to Japanese society.

M.R.P. Ballescas, in a survey of Filipinos, found that these workers are always considering their homes, and were doing difficult work in Japan to support their families.[7]

Here, looking at the opinions expressed by Iranians about the Japanese in the Survey on Iranians in Japan,[8] categorizing the multiple answers given by respondents in the free space, we find that there was a clear polarization between those who criticized Japan – the 'critical group' – and those who had favorable feelings – the 'pro-Japanese group.' The 'critical group,' which constituted 34.7% of the 150 persons who gave answers in the space provided, wrote about the inhumane treatment and discrimination they had experienced, the coldness of the Japanese, and the lack of humanity and morality in Japanese society as a whole. Naturally, individuals who had experienced discrimination, or who said they had been 'showered with abuse,' were more likely to be in the critical group. By contrast, the pro-Japanese group, which made up 39.3% of the people who had answered in the blank space, cited the diligence of the Japanese, their gentleness and kindness, as well as the good experiences they had had in Japan. Here, in a similar manner, people who had not experienced discrimination tended to be in the pro-Japanese group.

Using the same data, Kura Shinichi conducted an analysis categorizing Iranians into money-seeker types and those who had graduated from university and who had been working in professional or managerial jobs in their home country.[9] Within the money-seeker group, positive views of the Japanese and Japanese society were more common among those who had gained stable employment. By contrast, positive views were uncommon among members of the professional and managerial class. The reason for this appears to be in the relative feelings of deprivation that this group experienced in Japan. However, even within the professional and managerial group, there are significant positive views of Japan among the pseudo-exiles, who are critical of the Iranian Revolution.

With regard to foreigners as a whole, we can gain insight from a study carried out by the Council for Public Policy (Kokyo Seisaku Chosakai), the 'Study on the Situation of Social Non-Adaptation of Foreigners in Japan.' Looking at impressions of Japanese, with multiple responses, the most common answer was 'They are kind' (59.5%), followed by 'They are gentle' (42.2%). Only 21.6% responded, 'They are cold.'[10] Thus, we can conclude that foreigners generally have positive views of Japanese.

Let us now look at the general relationship between migration patterns and the situation in Japan. In the case of money-seeker types, a polarization seems to occur, in times of shrinking employment caused by economic recession, between those who choose to return home and those who decide to stay on until they have earned a projected sum of money. Among Latin American Nikkeijin migrants, because of the relative ease of movement, there are members of all types, including repeaters. Many of the overstayers who make up the main body of the money-seekers are at the stage of sojourners. However, with the exception of Koreans, one can say that quite a few have begun to reach the stage of settlement.

Members of the pseudo-exile group certainly have the choice of returning to their home country when the situation improves at home, or to move to another third country besides Japan, but in reality many seem to tread the path from sojourners to settlers. The few Indochinese refugees and extremely limited number of general refugees who have been granted official status by the Japanese government are exiles in the true sense of the word, and have a strong tendency to settle. Among the pseudo-exiles, it is likely that a portion of Iranians, Myanmarese, Chinese ex-foreign students, and Latin American Nikkeijin will also settle in Japan.

With regard to the self-actualizers, there seem to be various patterns depending on the goals of their search for self-actualization. Some come to study, others to run businesses, and still others simply to wander. Foreigners who come to join families are, among the five groups, the ones who seem to have the strongest desire to settle. Finally, many of the members of the homesick group will likely settle. With regard to people joining families, I will discuss the cases of partners in international marriages and Chinese of Japanese ancestry in later sections. The Nikkei Chinese, in particular, find it difficult to return to live in China once they have left and experienced life on the outside, so in many cases they settle in Japan despite their initial intentions. Latin American Nikkeijin who come along with family members or who are brought over by family members tend to settle along with the homesick types.

In the following section, I would like to examine the phenomenon of settlement by looking at the lengthening of periods of stay and the increase in international marriages. As seen in Table 4.2, in 1992 only 6.2% of overstayers had been in Japan for at least three years, the minimum period necessary for acquiring Japanese nationality (normally it take five years), by the time they left. But by 1998, this figure had reached 45.6%, or

Table 4.2   Period of Work of Irregular Workers

		(%)
	1992	**1998**
6 months or less	23.1	14.1
1 year or less	35.7	11.1
2 year or less	24.9	14.3
3 year or less	9.6	12.9
5 year or less	5.3	19.9
Over 5 years	0.9	25.7
Unknown	0.5	1.9
Total	**100.0**	**100.0**
Actual number	62,161	40,535

Source: Ministry of Justice, Immigration Bureau, *Shutsunyukoku Kanri tokei gaiyo* (Overview of immigration and emigration control statistics), Japan Immigration Association (For 1992 figures, see Komai Hiroshi, ed., *Gaikokujin rodosha mondai shiryo shusei* (Compilation of resources on the issue of foreign workers), Tokyo: Akashi Shoten, 1994, Volume 1, pp.93–.

nearly half. The previously mentioned 1996 survey by the EMPC also found that the average period of stay, as can be seen in Table 4.1, has already reached five years. Chinese had the longest periods of stay, with over six years, followed by Malaysians (over five years), Brazilians and Myanmarese (over four years), Filipinos and Thais (over three years), and Indonesians (over two years). Koreans had the shortest average length of stay, at approximately two years.[11]

For Chinese, the above-mentioned readers' survey from *Ryugakusei Shimbun* gave information from a form of panel survey. In the 1994 survey, 19.1% of respondents had been in Japan for 5–6 years, and 16.9% for 2–3 years. These figures were higher than those in the survey taken two years earlier, when the top answer was 2–3 years, with 30.9%. This reflects the fact that a significant portion of the people who came Japan during the Japanese language school boom of 1988–89 stayed on and followed the road toward settlement. For this reason, the largest age group among respondents was 30–34 years, making up 36.4% of the total, and a large number (65.6%) were aged 30 or older.

Moreover, 60.1% were married, and 80% of the married people were living in Japan with their spouses.[12]

Along with the lengthening of periods of stay, the number of international marriages has increased dramatically. Up until 1980, the yearly number of international marriages never rose above 10,000. However, the figure surged between 1985 and 1990, surpassing 25,000 per year. In 1997 it hit 28,251, or 3.6% of all marriages that year. Since 1975, the number of marriages with foreign brides has exceeded that with foreign grooms; by 1997 by a factor of nearly three. An increasing number of Japanese men, particularly in rural villages, are finding it difficult to find marriage partners, and there are public agencies as well as profit-oriented private companies that introduce them to Asian brides. This is one factor behind the increase in international marriages.[13]

Looking at the nationality of foreign wives, in 1995 the top position, which in 1992 was held by Koreans, was taken over by Filipinas, and in 1997 the Filipinas were overtaken in turn by Chinese. In terms of grooms, Americans, who held the top position in 1970, were overtaken by Koreans and relegated to second place. However, in 1997 they were again in the top position, with Chinese in second place. The divorce rate, which is calculated by dividing the number of new marriages by divorces, was 32.4% in 1997, a figure not all that different from that of Japanese couples, which was 28.6%. In 1998, foreign wives gave birth to 13,635 children. The ratio of births to marriages, the fertility ratio, was a low 61.5%. This hints at the widespread existence of fake marriages. Looking by nationality, the figure was 84.1% for Filipinas, versus just 38.9% for Chinese wives.[14]

According to the survey by the Tokyo Metropolitan Council of Social Welfare which was introduced in the last chapter, 37.5% of irregular workers were married. Of them, 9.4% were living with a non-Japanese spouse who was also in Japan, and 14.1% living with a Japanese spouse, meaning that a larger number were married to Japanese. Of the total of 45 individuals who were married, 23.5% were living with their families in Japan. In addition, 20 of the 509 people surveyed had children. However, the vast majority of these children were preschoolers, and most were in daycare centers, kindergartens, custodial care homes for infants, or child care institutions.[15] This survey took place at the beginning of the period of stagnation, so it can be inferred that the number with Japanese spouses has increased since then, as has the number of children who are in primary, junior high school, or even senior high school.

With regard to ethnic groups for whom information is available, Okada Emiko, who was mentioned earlier, wrote the following about Iranian men: 'Among foreign workers in Japan, at least 5% of Iranians are said to be married, or at least engaged, to Japanese women,' and she also stated that some of them might have done this as a way to get a residence visa.[16] In our survey of Iranians, 29.0% of respondents said they had experienced dating in Japan. Needless to say, all of the people surveyed were men. Incidentally, 26.5% of the respondents were married.[17] It is certain that a significant number of these men have gone on to cohabitation and marriage, and have had children.

From 1992–93, Sugiyama Katsumi and colleagues interviewed 22 Thai women working in sex and entertainment related businesses in Tochigi Prefecture. Of these women, 14 had domestic partners, and three were married. Nine of the partners were Japanese, four were Thai, and in one case the respondent gave no answer. Seven of the women were living with their partners in Japan (one was married), and all of the partners in Japan were Japanese. In cases where the partner 'actually helped with their livelihood,' in most cases he was the manager of the woman's place of work, but in some cases he was a lover or customer.[18]

Also, the Islamic Center, Japan, in Tokyo, which has the authority to grant Islamic-style marriage licenses, issues such licenses to 70 to 100 people a year. Nearly all of these couples are men from Islamic countries and Japanese women. The Isezaki Mosque, which can also grant marriage licenses, holds approximately 20 wedding ceremonies per year. In the area where it is located, many of the marriages are between young Nikkeijin women from Brazil or Peru, and men from Islamic countries.[19]

The 'Kawasaki City Field Survey of Attitudes of Citizens with Foreign Nationality,' which will be introduced in more detail in Chapter 6, provides interesting information on Filipinas, for which there was little quantitative data in the past. Eighty-six percent of the Filipino respondents were females, and 81% of these women were married to Japanese men. Although 48% were living with

Table 4.3   Families Coming to Japan

	Valid responses	At least one family member in Japan	Spouse or parent in Japan
Nikkei Brazilians	30	19	8
Koreans	27	7	5
Chinese	24	19	17
Filipinos	30	17	5
Thais	15	3	1
Bangladeshis	28	6	3
Irarians	31	9	2
Total	**185**	**80**	**41**

Note: 'Others' are excluded from family members.

Source: Chiba Prefectural Chiba High School, International Social Studies Group, *Gaikokujin rodosha jittai chosa, 1995-nen -1996-nen* (1995-1996 Field survey of foreign workers), 1997, in *Shinrai/teiju gaikokujin shiryo shusei* (Compilation of resources related to newcomer and settled foreigners), Tokyo: Akashi Shoten, 1998, Volume 2, p.185.

their children, 24% were separated from their husbands, a much higher percentage than for other ethnic groups. In other words, the vast majority of Filipinas in Japan are married to Japanese men, but seem to experience many problems in their family life. Also, Europeans, Americans, and people from Oceania make up a large portion of the foreign men living in Kawasaki (67%) and as many as 43% of them are married to Japanese women.[20]

As a result of the increasing number of international marriages and the bringing of families from home countries, foreigners are steadily forming families in Japan. In a survey I conducted in Kanagawa Prefecture in 1990–1991, I found that only five out of 91 newcomer foreigners were living with families, including spouses or parents.[21] However, as shown by Table 4.3, according to the 1995–96 survey carried out by Chiba High School as many as 80 out of 185 respondents had brought at least one member of their family to Japan. Looking by ethnic group, the largest groups of foreigners who had brought family members were Chinese, Brazilians, and Filipinos. Among these three groups, more than half had come to Japan with at least one other family member. Of the 80 individuals, a full 41 had brought their spouse or parents with them; this number was particularly high among Chinese and Brazilians. By contrast, among Koreans, Thais, Bangladeshis and Iranians, relatively few had brought family members along.

Identity crisis

Immigrants who come to the foreign land of Japan sometimes experience a continuing emotional tug-of-war between their home country and culture and Japan; this can lead to an ethnic identity crisis. The Study Group on the Problems of Chinese Returnees carried out a survey on 105 returnees, and found that the psychological process of adjustment could be divided into the six steps listed below.[22] Though the list is somewhat long, I would like to reproduce it in its entirety as it is very suggestive.

(1) Period of immigration (honeymoon period): When people have just returned (or first come) to Japan, they tend to experience many joys, feel great freshness, and find themselves completely absorbed in adapting themselves to rapid changes.

(2) Period of maladjustment (first period): As they become accustomed to life in Japan, they face a harsh reality where everything is unfamiliar to them and betrays their predictions and expectations. They can become emotionally unstable: they get easily angry, are often irritated, and can feel helpless.

(3) Superficial adaptation: As their life in Japan grows longer, they learn how to cope with this problem. This is a period when they come to accept Japanese society from a sense of resignation (in the case of returnees) characterized by thoughts such as 'I can't go back to China, so have no choice but to live in Japan' and 'So this is what kind of a place Japan is.'

(4) Period of maladjustment (second period): They become tentatively adapted to Japanese society, but more aware than ever about its bad aspects; they come to think of their overall experience living in Japan as disagreeable. The higher the original expectations of Japan, the greater their disappointment tends to be. Those who did not really want to come to Japan tend to compare their lives with the contentment they felt in

China, and regret having come to Japan at all. In this period, they become vulnerable to depression or to other physical and psychological ailments.

(5) Period of stable adaptation: As they accumulate positive experiences of surmounting difficulties and solving problems, their life in Japan becomes stable. This is a period where they overcome 'resignation,' and rather become able to 'enjoy life in Japan.'

(6) Period of homesickness: In this period, their minds become filled with affection for Chinese culture and of their relatives back in China. It is a time when, after achieving 'success and fame,' they 'yearn for their homeland.'

In terms of conditions for determining these different stages, the report proposes the importance of whether the individual has been successful in acquiring Japanese language skills and the ability to overcome problems that arise from differences in lifestyle and customs. However, the heart of the problem can be seen as arising from their identity, which sways between China and Japan.

Kuwayama Norihiko, a psychiatrist in Yamagata Prefecture who has treated Filipina brides of Japanese, offered a list of phases to indicate the degree to which foreigners have adapted, based on a different perspective. According to Kuwayama, foreigners experience stress in the five following stages:[23]

(1) First month crisis: Loss of bearings and confusion. Because they are in a state of nervous tension, problems do not usually emerge (first period of physical stress).

(2) Third month crisis: anxiety, anger, and dissatisfaction with the need to adapt to this area. At this point they are able to perceive the situation around them (period of psychological stress).

(3) Sixth month crisis: The Japanese people around them who have helped them up to that time begin to press them to be independent, and the foreigners experience 'fatigue' from having to do everything for themselves (second period of physical stress).

(4) Second year crisis: They become more relaxed from becoming capable of doing the jobs they are supposed to do, and become less nervous about the people around them. They can understand most customs, but begin to make a

distinction between 'what they can accept and what they cannot' (first period of comparison).

(5) Fifth year crisis: They begin to seek their identity in Japan, and using their 'life' as a unit, begin a deep comparison of the country where they are living (Japan) and their home country, and find they cannot accept the differences (second period of comparison).

In this model, like the one proposed by the Study Group, a process is described where a shift of identity between the home country and Japan gradually become apparent in a substantial way.

In some cases, identity problems are at the root of mental illnesses suffered by foreigners. This underscores the importance of identity for people living in foreign countries. Psychiatrist Ebata Keisuke has introduced the case of a 35-year-old female returnee from China.[24] From her childhood, she hated her Chinese father, and when she arrived in Japan began an attempt of what could be called excessive assimilation. As a result, she became ill with an acute form of confused identity. Kuwayama Norihiko has also presented cases of serious psychogenic reactions in Filipina brides caused by 'conflicts between their attempts on one hand to adjust to this closed society, and on the other their great efforts to protect their own ethnic identity.' Considering that children also begin to go to school, he stated that 'If we demand that the children become 'perfectly assimilated Japanese,' as we did for the Filipina brides, these children will become more distressed and confused than their mothers...and at some point they may feel hatred toward their mothers.'[25] Consequently, in order to ensure that the settlement of foreign immigrants proceeds smoothly, it is necessary to deal with issues involving identity.

The formation of ethnic communities

Increased settlement has been accompanied by the formation of ethnic communities. In the following section I would like to give an overview of this trend, focusing on ethnic businesses, ethnic media, religious facilities, and ethnic networks.

Ethnic businesses have the following typical features. They tend to be funded and operated by members of minority groups; they are originally founded based on their own ethnic markets, but gradually come to target the general market; and in most cases their employees are made up of members of the ethnic group. The major forms they take include: retail shops offering foods, sundry goods, newspapers, and magazines from their home countries; video rental shops; restaurants and bars offering food and drink from their home countries; travel agencies which sell air tickets and carry out paperwork for people traveling between Japan and the home country; beauty salons; publishing companies issuing newspapers or magazines targeted at their ethnic groups; and computer programming companies.[26] Tajima Junko carried out a diligent examination of the creation of such ethnic businesses in Tokyo. She found that media and businesses have a cooperative relationship as advertisers and mediums of advertising, and because of this, Japanese often played an important role as owners or business partners. She also found that having powerful connections in the home country was helpful for the development of businesses. Furthermore, depending on the ethnic group, religious factors could be very important.[27]

With regard to Chinese, Ito Yasuo conducted a survey on the management of ethnic business by 'New Overseas Chinese.'[28] Looking at the results, we find that there were few examples of 'outside assistance' types, which receive capital assistance but are not closely related to the ethnic group. With regard to 'ethnic-group types,' whose businesses and capital assistance are both tied to fellow compatriots, there was one case of a major chain store. By contrast, there were many cases where 'joint management' types, where there are strong ethnic bonds and capital is provided on an equal basis between compatriots and Japanese. There were also examples of 'de-ethnicification' types (where there are weak ethnic bonds and capital is provided equally between compatriots and Japanese) becoming joint management types. In addition, there were businesses run by individuals. Ito stressed the importance of the joint management-type businesses.

Moving to ethnic media, this can be defined as print or broadcast media which regularly transmit information within Japan with ethnic minorities as their main audience, using mainly that group's language but sometimes using Japanese or English as well. According to Shiramizu Shigehiko, media targeted at foreigners, in the form of newspapers, magazines, broadcasting, and telephone lines as means of communication, began to appear gradually in the late 1980s, and blossomed in the 1990s. Thus, media aimed at newcomer foreigners emerged in the period of expansion, showing particularly vigorous growth at the beginning of the 1990s and the late 1990s. Many of these organizations did not have strong business bases, and eventually went out of business. Ethnic media, while cultivating a sense of belonging to a particular ethnic group, communicate information on what people need to know to live in Japan, news from the home country (or countries), as well as information on Japanese society. In addition to this, they play a mediating role in transmitting information from ethnic groups toward Japanese society. In the period of expansion, they tended to carry mainly information on living, but during the period of stagnation have gradually come to focus more on understanding Japanese society and relations between Japan and the home country.[29]

Limiting the discussion to information newspapers and magazines, more than 200 such media were being published as of 1998. Of them, half were independently managed with a full-time editorial staff. The main languages they used were English (36), Chinese (27), Korean (12), Portuguese (11), Tagalog (6), and Spanish (6). Other languages included French, Thai, Myanmarese, Malay, Vietnamese, Indonesian, Urdi, and Persian. In total, 15 languages were being used. Representative print media were *Ryugakusei Shimbun*, the longest-running newspaper aimed at Chinese, *Jornale Tudobem* and *International Press*, both newspapers for Brazilians, *Aliran*, a magazine for Koreans, and *Kaibigan*, a newspaper for Filipinos. Thus, printed media existed for each of the major ethnic groups. All of them had circulations above 20,000 copies, with the largest at 90,000. In addition to these, there were nearly 100 newsletters and mag-azines, put out by local governments, as well as others aimed at multicultural exchanges issued by NPOs.

With regard to broadcast media, there were, in addition to programs for foreigners on regular radio stations, two stations targeted specifically at foreigners, and nine satellite channels.[30]

The importance of ethnic media can be confirmed from surveys related to media contact behavior. In the 1993 Hamamatsu City survey introduced in Chapter 2, respondents were asked, 'What media do you depend on most?' (with up to three answers allowed). The most common answers were 'A newspaper in my own language published in Japan' (49.0%), 'Newspapers or magazines sent to Japan from my home country' (48.7%) and 'What I hear from my friends and relatives' (34.7%).[31]

Moving on to religion, the increase in immigrants in Japan has been accompanied by an increase in attendance by foreigners at the established institutions of various religions, such as Christianity and Islam, but new institutions are also being built. These religious establishments provide religious relief to immigrants living in a new land full of stress, give them a sense of stability by meeting with compatriots, and allow them to exchange information on work and housing, as well as shopping. Many immigrants visit religious facilities more frequently than they did in their home countries. In the following paragraphs, I would like to discuss the situation of particular religious groups.

First, with regard to Catholicism, it appears that many Filipinos become more devoted after arriving in Japan. The Akabane Church (in Kita Ward, Tokyo) plays an important role in this regard; on the third Sunday of every month as many as 1,000 Filipinos go to attend mass.[32] With Akabane at the top, there has been a rapid increase in the number of foreign worshippers at Catholic churches in various parts of Japan, including mainly Filipinos and Latin Americans, but also Koreans, Vietnamese, and Nigerians. Some of these churches conduct masses not only in Japanese but in English, Tagalog, Portuguese, and Spanish. There are even churches that have special masses for Filipinos, separate from those for Japanese. A number of priests are known to have been involved in activities to protect the rights of their foreign followers, some of whom are irregular, and to protect their livelihoods.

With regard to Protestant churches, Koreans play an important role. Roughly 30% of the population of South Korea is Protestant, and it is believed that this figure is as high as 60% for newcomer Koreans in Japan. There are at least four Protestant churches that conduct services in Korean in the Okubo Street district in Shinjuku Ward, Tokyo, the greatest concentration of newcomer Koreans.[33] Early on, newcomer Koreans tended to go to the churches established by the old-comers, but they gradually began to build churches for their own denominations in Korea. One special feature of Korean Protestants in Japan is that they usually worship at different churches depending on their social statuses. For example, business people sent by companies and diplomats or embassy staff rarely worship at the churches frequented by migrant workers.

Incidentally, the Chinese, who are the largest ethnic group in Japan, hardly participate in religious activities at all. In Shinjuku Ward, Tokyo, which I mentioned earlier, there is only one small Taoist shrine.

Islam, like Christianity, is developing rapidly in many places.[34] The oldest official mosque is the Kobe Mosque, which was built in 1935. Approximately 100 people gather there each Friday for worship. In Tokyo, the Islamic Center Japan began its activities in 1977. It is mainly operated by Pakistanis, though Japanese are involved as well. It not only provides space for people to worship, but also serves as a center of propagation activities in Japan, through the publication of pamphlets and magazines. Every Friday, between 50 and 100 people gather there. It is said that in all there are some 40 mosques in Japan, big and small, including these two major ones. There is no centralized organization, but they have emerged spontaneously in former pachinko parlors or as prehab buildings in parking lots, using donations.

The Tobu Line, which runs through the northern Kanto region, an area populated by many Muslims, is sometimes known as the 'ethnic line.' Several large mosques are concentrated along its tracks. In 1992, the Ichinowari Mosque was established in a rented three-story building in Kasukabe City that had previously been a prep school. It has two rooms that can hold approximately 50 people each, and another smaller room, so that in all some 100 individuals can worship at one time. Like the Islamic Center, it is mainly operated by Pakistanis, though there are some Japanese who converted to Islam in the 1980s. Every Friday, some 60 to 70 Pakistanis, Bangladeshis, Malaysians and Egyptians go there to worship.

The Isezaki Mosque, the largest in Japan, was built at the initiative of Pakistanis in Isezaki City, at the northern end of the Tobu Line. It is near Ota City and Ooizumi Town, which will be mentioned in the next section, both of which are home to large numbers of Pakistanis and Bangladeshis. Every week, 150 people regularly attend worship there. In 1997, the members were able to bring over an 83-year old Turkish *imam*, who had been through ascetic practices in Mecca, and was thus a qualified man of great respect. There are other smaller mosques in the area, and in fact Isezaki City has become known as Japan's 'Islamic city.' There are five '*halal* shops' (Islamic food shops) in the center of the city.[35] The Sakai-machi Mosque, which is along the Tobu Line and close to Isezaki City, is also quite large.

In this way, the largest concentrations of Islamic residents can be found in the Tokyo metropolitan region, centered around the capital, but there has also been a remarkable dispersal into other areas. There are now mosques as far north as Sendai and as far west as Hiroshima. They can be found in all the major cities along the Tokaido Shinkansen (the bullet train line that runs west from Tokyo), such as Yokohama, Shizuoka, Nagoya, Kyoto, Osaka, and Kobe. There are also mosques in the cities of Toyama, Niigata, and Mito. Along with the mosques, approximately 30 *halal* shops have been opened in various places. Furthermore, with the cooperation of a Buddhist temple called Monjuin in Enzan, Yamanashi Prefecture, it has become possible to conduct Islamic-style burials in Japan.

Touching briefly on how Muslims secure time for worship, many ask their employers to give them a long lunch break on Fridays, and in exchange work past their regular working hours. Therefore, the number of worshipers is usually twice as great when a Friday falls on a holiday. Incidentally, Japanese police and immigration authorities have never entered any mosque to look for overstayers. Neither has any mosque yet encountered organized interference to its activities. In only one case, a poster was put up in opposition to one local mosque.

The Islamic Center Japan's fundamental stance on proselytizing toward Japanese is that they should never be forced to convert to Islam, but that Japanese who have an understanding of Islam should not be rejected. At present, small numbers of Japanese, who are typically employers or fellow employees of Muslims, have begun to be converted. It can thus be said that the target of proselytizing activities in Japan has expanded from people from Islamic countries to the Japanese. It is surprising to note that the relationships between mosques and neighborhood residents tend to be very warm. The mosques participate actively in local activities, and offer food to neighborhood people. In response, local leaders may not go as far as participating in worship, but have tended to show a warm acceptance of the worshipers.

With the progress of settling, ethnic networks have formed both between people in Japan and in their home countries, and among people from the same ethnic group who are living in Japan. For example, in many cases where Bangladeshis are working in a certain workplace, one individual going home introduces a friend to the employer, and the friend then comes to work. Such networks are particularly well developed among Filipinos, who often maintain close relations with relatives and acquaintances from their own regions. These relationships are mediated by ethnic businesses, and especially by restaurants and religious institutions.

In many cases, ethnic businesses such as shops, restaurants, and beauty salons form the center of wide networks within ethnic groups, with their owners serving as loci. Ethnic businesses are particularly well developed among Latin American Nikkeijin, Chinese, and Koreans. Needless to say, a multitude of ethnic businesses often develop in areas where specific groups are concentrated. Restaurants are particularly important in the sense that they serve the double function of confirming identity, since eating is a basic human activity, and of offering a place where people of the same ethnic group can meet.

In the case of Japanese-Chinese, there is a report of one Chinese restaurant, which was established both to support the economic independence of returnees through work and to provide a place for them to maintain and expand networks with other returnees. It has served as a gathering spot for second- and third-generation returnees.[36] In the Hamamatsu City Survey, which was mentioned earlier, 45.7% of the responses were collected at Brazilian restaurants.[37] A survey of Chinese Malays, which was conducted by Ishii Yuka, was carried out mainly by Malaysian Chinese restaurants in Tokyo.[38]

Next, I would like to review the status of networks in the various ethnic groups. In the case of Iranians, when we asked respondents to our own survey about who had introduced them to their current workplace, 26.9% said a friend, 26.1% a family member or relative, 17.6% an Iranian broker, 6.9% a Japanese broker, 6.1%

a broker of some other nationality, 5.7% they were hired directly, and 0.4% a support organization, with 6.5% not responding.[39] This means that in more than 70% of cases the introduction was from a member of an Iranian network, including friends, family, relatives, and Iranian brokers.

At the beginning of the 1990s, Iranians were very conspicuous in Japan, as they tended to cluster in large numbers on Sundays around stations and parks, where they made friends and exchanged information. In this sense they were very different from other groups of irregular workers. Up until about 1992, the largest gathering spot was Ueno Park in Tokyo, but partly because of stricter police control, Yoyogi Park, which is also in Tokyo, became a larger gathering spot around 1993. In a survey conducted by the University of Tokyo Health and Social Science Research Institute, Iranians were asked why they had come to Ueno Park. With multiple responses allowed, 60 said they had come to look for work, 43 to perform work, and 22 to meet friends or compatriots (out of a total of 138 respondents). Thus, it appeared that many had come to look for work, and often from quite far away.[40] This can also be seen as an indication of the effort they put into forming networks.

Regarding the relationships between Iranians and Japanese, the 'Survey on Iranians in Japan' found the following distribution: 24.5% said 'I have no close friends among Japanese,' 15.9% 'I greet some people when I meet them, but that's about all,' 12.2% 'I make small talk with them,' 18.4% 'I go out with them,' and 20.2% 'I consult them over worries and other matters,' with 9.0% not responding. Roughly 40% responded either 'I go out with them' or 'I consult them over worries and other matters,' a far larger number than the slightly more than 20% who said 'I have no close friends among Japanese.' It seems thus that their networks with Japanese were much further developed than might have been expected. In addition, considering the fact that many of the 'non critics of Japan' (meaning people who were not critical of Japan, but not necessarily pro-Japanese) had Japanese friends, it seems that having networks with Japanese helps to decrease feelings of animosity toward Japan.

Iida Toshiro, in his survey of returnees from China, asked the question, 'Have you gotten any help from anyone when you were ill?' Assistance through networks of friends stood out, especially among war orphans, but among second- and third-generation returnees as well. Iida stated that, 'Because the category of those living in Tokyo is larger in number than others, and because many of them are studying or working, it is easy for them to form networks of friendship with other second- and third-generation returnees.'[41]

Enari Miyuki and colleagues, who conducted a survey of Latin American Nikkeijin living in Kanagawa Prefecture, found that many people in this group made use of personal networks formed with other Nikkeijin when they did not rely on brokers to solve problems related to their living.[42] I would like to add here that in contrast to the strength of these ethnic networks, many Nikkeijin have only weak links with their Japanese relatives. In the Hamamatsu City survey, when Brazilian Nikkeijin were asked about the frequency of their relationships with Japanese relatives, 11.3% said 'They are active,' 17.7% 'Occasional,' 10.8% 'Very seldom,' and 60.2% 'Practically none.' The overwhelming majority said they had practically no relations with their Japanese relatives. The survey report explained this point as follows: 'For postwar immigrants in Brazil, who held the goal of 'returning to their homeland in glory,' it does not appear easy to meet relatives even when they want to.'[43]

With regard to Koreans, we can gain insights from a survey by Ko Sonfi of Korean workers living in cheap dwellings in Kotobuki-cho, Yokohama, one of Japan's four largest *yoseba* (a place where day laborers go to find work). Many of the people living there came from village K on Cheju Island. The flow of Korean workers into Kobobuki-cho began by chance in about 1988, a time when it had become impossible for newly arriving Koreans to depend on relatives among old-comer Korean residents. The news that there were jobs to be found and housing in Kotobuki-cho spread by word of mouth from village K to the whole island of Cheju, and then throughout South Korea, by word of mouth. The Korean inhabitants of Kotobuki-cho can be divided by people from Cheju and people from the peninsula; mutual assistance networks are particularly well developed among those from Cheju, and are especially strong among the residents of village K.

When asked, 'Do you have anybody to consult when you have emotional problems?' 53.1% of the people from Cheju, and 31.7% of those from the peninsula, said 'Yes, somebody from the same village or province.' Similarly, when asked who had introduced them to their current job, 50.0% of the people from Cheju, and 36.6% of those from the peninsula, said 'A person from the same province.' When asked what relationships they had with oldcomer Koreans, 20.5% said 'I greet them when coming to and leaving Japan, but do not do much more than that,' and 16.4% said either 'I consult with them when I have a problem' or 'I visit them often,'[44] showing a similar tendency to Nikkei Brazilians. In other words, the relationship between oldcomer Koreans and the people from Cheju Island can be seen as a cool one, such as the typical relationship between employer and employee.

Looking at Ishii Yuka's survey of Chinese Malaysians, 24 out of 96 respondents, when asked why they came to Japan, said 'Because I had relatives or friends here.' Ishii concluded that the presence of the networks of overseas Chinese was a major factor behind the increase in migration from Malaysia to Japan.[45]

Wakabayashi Chihiro has published notable findings on networks among people from Africa, particularly those from Ghana and Nigeria, noting that they are formed on the basis of religions or hometowns, and are used to maintain identity. People from Africa first confront the fact that they are 'black' when they come to Japan, and they form networks to build pride in being Africans. At the root of this problem lies the fact that Japanese people have certain stereotypes of Africans. For example, they perceive them as sexually powerful, or as refugees and primitive people.[46]

In her survey report, Ballescas discussed the existence of networks among Filipinos linking the home and host countries. Within these, she focused on the personal networks Filipinos have with friends, neighbors, and relatives. Of the 60 respondents, 17 said they were currently working with the person who introduced them to their jobs, and 23 said they had relatives in Japan.[47]

Patterns of housing

Next, let us look at types of housing used by foreigners in Japan. According to the previously mentioned survey by the Tokyo

Metropolitan Social Welfare Council, 38.9% of irregular workers were living in rented apartments, 27.3% in housing prepared by their employer, 15.1% with an acquaintance or friend, and 9.4% at dormitories attached to the factories where they worked. Moreover, as many as 40.5% were living together with at least three other people who were not family members. Their most frequent complaints about housing were 'It's too small,' 'I couldn't find what I wanted,' and 'The rent is too high.'[48] With regard to differences between specific ethnic groups, the Chiba Prefectural High School data showed that many Filipinos lived in apartment houses, and that Thais and Bangladeshis tended to live in dorms or other company-arranged housing. In the case of Iranians, it was common for one person to rent a house and then share it with others.[49] In the aforementioned survey of Iranians in Ueno, the respondents were asked where they slept at night. There was a slight concentration of answers in metropolitan Tokyo, but they were spread out among the six prefectures in the Kanto region, in a pattern similar to their jobs.[50]

As foreign workers have settled in Japan, several areas of concentrated inhabitation have begun to form. We already touched upon the concentration of Muslims in the environs of Isezaki City. As we saw earlier, Shinjuku Ward, Tokyo is well known as a zone of concentrated inhabitation for Asian newcomers, and particularly Koreans. It is close to Kabuki-cho, one of Japan's largest amusement quarters, where there are many sex industry establishments. Apartment houses intended specially for foreigners have been built, and there is also a lot of old and low-rent housing that Japanese tend to avoid. For foreign workers, the area thus has advantages in terms of both work and housing. Many ethnic businesses are now operating in the area, beginning with grocery stores that cater to the various ethnic groups. For Chinese, the area around Ikebukuro, Tokyo has become a major area of concentration. It has one of the largest concentrations of old ramshackle houses left in Tokyo, and has a large amusement quarter, though it does not rival Kabuki-cho. Again, there is convenience both in terms of work and housing. However, in neither Shinjuku nor Ikebukuro have ghettos emerged where foreigners live in isolation. The living pattern is rather one of foreigners mixed with Japanese.

Latin American Nikkeijin are concentrated in the area near Ota City and Ooizumi Town in Gunma Prefecture, as well as the Tokai

Region, which is located between Tokyo to Nagoya, and includes the cities of Hamamatsu, Toyohashi, Toyota, and Kosai. The area around Ota City and Ooizumi Town is host to Sanyo Electric Co. as well as Fuji Heavy Industries, a major automaker which came out of Nakajima Aircraft. Hamamatsu City is home to motorcyle manufacturers such as Honda and Yamaha, and Toyota is the base of Toyota Motor, Japan's best-known automaker. As a result, all of these areas are the sites of many sub-contractors and members of the *keiretsu* of these large firms, and many of the towns are what are known as 'company castle towns.' Nikkeijin are employed in many of these sub-contractors and affiliated firms. In Gunma Prefecture and the Tokai Region, it is projected that as comm-unities of Latin American Nikkeijin develop, they are becoming increasingly isolated from Japanese society. Grocery stores and restaurants are becoming gathering places for people within the ethnic groups, ethnic media are providing necessary information in their own languages, they are showing a tendency to live in groups of families in adjacent rooms of huge apartment complexes, and they are often under the management of the dispatching companies. As a result, they no longer face the need to have any contact with Japanese society. In fact, as previously mentioned, the Japanese language ability of Latin American Nikkeijin is apparently deterioration.

Though there are such concentrations in places such as Gunma Prefecture and the Tokai Region, it is notable that in the period of stagnation, the population of newcomer foreigners has generally become concentrated in Tokyo. Table 4.4 shows data from the Immigration Bureau on the places of work of foreigners. I used this figure because it includes data from 1991, during the period of expansion; other data is only available starting in 1992. We see that the percentage of irregular workers working in Tokyo, which was 28.2% in 1991, had risen to 32.4% by 1998. With the exception of Saitama Prefecture, which remained constant, the percentage fell in all other parts of the country, including Kanagawa, Chiba, and Osaka. Thus, we can say that irregular foreign workers, at least, are becoming increasingly concentrated in Tokyo, and that their numbers are generally decreasing in other regions. By contrast, in 1991 there was one prefecture, Saga (in Kyushu) where there were no irregular workers, but in 1998 there were none, meaning that

Table 4.4   Place of Work of Irregular Workers

	1991	1998
		(%)
Tokyo	28.2	32.4
Saitama	10.7	10.5
Kanagawa	10.6	8.9
Chiba	9.2	8.1
Osaka	8.2	7.4
Others	33.1 (excluding Saga)	32.7
Total	100.0	100.0
Number	32,908	40,535

Source: Ministry of Justice, Immigration Bureau, *Shutsunyukoku Kanri tokei gaiyo* (Overview of immigration and emigration control statistics), Japan Immigration Association (For 1992 figures, see Komai Hiroshi, ed., *Gaikokujin rodosha mondai shiryo shusei* (Compilation of resources on the issue of foreign workers), Tokyo: Akashi Shoten, 1994, Volume 1, pp.93–.

irregular workers were spread throughout all prefectures of the country.

It appears that the increasing concentration of irregular workers in Tokyo is connected to a shift away from construction and manufacturing and into the service industry. This indicates, conversely, that there are now fewer opportunities for irregular workers to be employed in construction and manufacturing. Specifically, legal Nikkeijin have been driven by industrial hollowing and the recession to seek jobs around the country, and in this process have taken jobs that were previously occupied by irregular workers.

Here, I would like to make some mention of Kotobuki-cho, a section of Yokohama which has unique features as an area of concentration. Why has Kotobuki-cho alone, of Japan's four major *yoseba*, become the home to many foreign workers? The conventional response is that up to 90% of the landlords there are resident Koreans, and thus have sympathy for foreign workers. However, whereas most of the newcomer foreigners living there are from Cheju Island, the owners of the flophouses are not. According to Ko, the majority of the flophouses do not admit foreign workers, and seem to have a very cool attitude toward them.[51]

If this is the case, then what caused the pattern of concentration of foreign workers into Kotobuki-cho, a phenomenon unusual even for *yoseba* in Japan? It turns out that in Kotobuki-cho, a very strong non-governmental organization called Kalabaw no Kai has taken a strong stance in opposition to police crackdowns. As a result, the authorities have been reluctant to take forceful actions there. In other *yoseba*, partially because of the crackdowns on gatherings, there has been a breakdown of the pattern that was common in the period of expansion, where brokers assembled foreign workers in the morning and loaded them into microbuses to take them to workplaces. In this sense, it can be said that the concentration in Kotobuki-cho was the result of a combination of circumstances.

In summary, foreigners have begun to settle in Japan with their families, networks have developed along with the activities of ethnic businesses, media, and religious facilities, and areas of concentrated population have begun to appear among different ethnic groups. I think it is worth emphasizing that at the present time, no major animosity can be seen between these communities and Japanese society. Perhaps it is due to indifference, but it appears certain that Japanese people are generally tolerant of the existence of these ethnic communities.

Part Two
Structural Inequalities and Responses

5 The Human Rights of Immigrants

The international trend toward human rights

In this chapter, I will present an overview of the human rights of immigrants in Japan. As we saw in Chapter 1, foreigners have generally been seen in Japan as objects to be monitored and controlled; at least as the policy level, there has essentially never been an awareness that they should be seen as partners in society. This situation remains fundamentally unchanged. However, international conventions on human rights have the potential to break this state of affairs. The points of departure are of course the International Declaration of Human Rights, as well as the United Nations Convention on Human Rights, which emerged as a concrete embodiment of the Declaration. There are in addition two conventions of particular importance, as they relate to foreign immigrants. The first is the Convention on the Elimination of All Forms of Racial Discrimination, and the second the United Nations Convention on the Rights of Immigrant Workers.

The first, the United Nations Convention on the Elimination of All Forms of Racial Discrimination, originated in the barbarous crime of genocide against the Jews that was carried out during World War II in fascist Germany. In order to prevent the recurrence of this kind of act, recognition was given to the principle that racial discrimination was a crime against humanity. This treaty, along with the Convention Against All Forms of Discrimination Against Women and the Convention on the Rights of the Child, forms one of the three pillars of the United Nation's framework on human rights.

It was adopted in 1965 by the General Assembly of the United Nations, and has the most signatories of the three U.N. conventions on human rights, with over 130 countries. All the world's major nations have ratified it. In 1960 the United Kingdom passed race-related legislation based upon it, and in 1972, also in relation to the Convention, France passed a law banning racial discrimination.

West Germany has enacted similar legislation. The United States has not ratified the Convention, claiming that it would contradict the 'freedom of speech,' but has enforced various civil rights bills in its place. It can thus be said that the spirit of the Convention on the Elimination of All Forms of Racial Discrimination is alive in the U.S. as well.

In Japan's case, the ratification of this Convention came much later than that of the Convention Against All Forms of Discrimination Against Women and the Convention on the Rights of the Child. Japan finally signed it in 1995, but under the condition that it did not accept sections which conflicted with the freedom of expression. In the Convention, racial discrimination refers to discrimination on the basis of race, color, descent, national origin, or ethnic origin. Signatories are obliged to establish measures to abolish racial discrimination, and to report on these measures to the Commission on the Abolition of Racial Discrimination. In concrete terms, the Convention is violated if people are discriminated against in employment, housing, or various services on the basis of being foreign. It also prohibits acts of violence or insult for racial reasons.

The second international treaty, the International Convention on the Protection of the Rights of All Migrant Workers and Members of Their Families, focuses on both legal and irregular workers, as well as their families. Beginning from the premise that irregular movements of migrant workers must be prevented, it sets the goal of protecting the human rights of workers and their families. It emphasizes rights including the equal treatment of migrant workers and national in terms of working conditions and social security; the rights of children including those to a name, registration, nationality, and education; the respect for cultural autonomy through, for example, ethnic education; and the right to maintain cultural unity with one's home country. In other words, it can be said that it recognizes the significance of maintaining cultural autonomy as a fundamental component of human rights. It was adopted in 1990 by the General Assembly of the United Nations, but few nations have yet ratified it. Japan is not among them. However, this Convention is still the focus of attention as a set of guidelines for policies toward foreign workers.

In connection to this, there are two ILO conventions which deal mainly with migrant labor: No. 97, which was adopted in 1949, and

No. 143, which was adopted in 1982. Convention No. 97 stipulates that migrant workers should get equal treatment to nationals in terms of working conditions, including access to public services, wages, and the right to join unions. Convention No. 143 calls for the granting of labor rights to all migrant workers, including those who are irregular. In terms of social security, Convention No. 118, which was adopted in 1962, calls for equal treatment for nationals and foreigners, and Convention No. 157, adopted in 1982, stipulates that migration should not lead to a loss of benefits such as pensions. Japan has not ratified any of these four conventions, however, so they have no force in Japan's domestic laws.

Destitution and discrimination

Destitution in living

Among Japan's foreign migrants, it is the second- and third-generation Chinese returnees, Peruvians, and Iranians who have experienced the greatest destitution in everyday life. We already examined the family types of Chinese returnees in Chapter 3, and in this section I would like to provide an overview of the financial difficulties they face, based on my survey which was introduced in that chapter. In essence, they have faced tremendous hardship since returning.[1] I would like to examine their situation in terms of income, employment, public assistance, and housing.

For second- and third-generation returnees from China, both household and individual incomes are low. Looking at the distribution of monthly household income (121 individuals = 100%), 4.1% received ¥100,000 or less, 25.6% between ¥110,000–200,000, 43.8% between ¥210,000–300,000, 20.7% between ¥310,000–400,000, and 5.8% over ¥410,000. Thus, nearly 30% received ¥200,000 or less. The average figure was just ¥183,000. With regard to individual income (87 = 100%), 34.5% received ¥100,000 or less, 41.4% between ¥110,000–200,000, 18.4% between ¥210,000–300,000, and 5.7% over ¥310,000, meaning that three fourths received 200,000 or less. The average income was a low ¥147,000.

Next, looking at employment, we found that many were unemployed, and on top of this, that there was a strong tendency among those who did have jobs to be employed in manual labor.

The labor force participation rate was 67.8%, a figure similar to that for Japan as a whole, but the unemployment rate among those in the total labor force (99 = 100%) was a high 12.1%. Looking at the occupations of those for whom we were able to get data (85 = 100%) (with the last occupation listed for those who were unemployed), 57.6% were doing manual labor, 28.2% sales and services (including transportation and security), and 14.1% non-manual labor. Thus, the overwhelming majority was performing manual labor. Of those who were not in the labor force (47 = 100%), 53.2% were students, 25.5% full-time housewives, 17.0% people studying Japanese language or other miscellaneous, and 4.3% ill or disabled.

Looking at the receipt of public assistance (136 = 100%), 13.2% said they were currently receiving assistance, 37.5% had received it in the past, and 49.3% had never received such assistance. Thus, the numbers of recipients and non-recipients were roughly equivalent, demonstrating the tough living situation they faced upon their return to Japan. In terms of the period of time for which they had received assistance, 65.2% of those who had received assistance (69 = 100%) answered less than two years, 18.8% at least two years but less than four years, and 15.9% at least four years. This shows that many returnees were cut off from public assistance at around the time of their second year in Japan.

With regard to the possibility of future receipt (136 = 100%), 30.9% said they hoped to receive assistance. Of these, just 1.5% (two individuals) were receiving assistance at the time of the survey. This points undeniably to the existence of a group of impoverished people who do not have access to welfare. Moreover, when asked about the notice informing them they were no longer entitled to public assistance (33 = 100%), 33. 3% said they thought it was unfair, compared to 66.7% who said they felt it was reasonable. Thus, fully one third of the recipients felt it was unjustified, showing that there are problems with the measures used for cutting people off public assistance. Incidentally, looking at housing, 40.3% were living in public housing, 50.6% in private rental housing, and 9.0% in other forms of housing. Only one individual was living in housing owned by that person.

Another issue that cannot be disregarded is the existence of second- and third-generation returnees who are completely isolated.

Looking at responses to the question of whom they consulted about troubles (139 = 100%), 22.3% said they had nobody at all. Of those who did have people to consult with, nearly half, or 47.5%, consulted with other returnees; this points to the existence of networks among returnees. Only 11.5% said they consulted with Japanese. In the rest of cases, they consulted with non-returnee Chinese (5.0%) and others (13.7%). With regard to relations with their Japanese relative in Japan, 54.7% of respondents said they had very little or no relationships at all, showing a form of estrangement.

Along with the economic hardships, second- and third-generation returnees face prejudice and discrimination in Japanese society. When asked whether they had faced such experiences (135 = 100%), 11.9% answered 'frequently,' 54.1% said 'from time to time,' and 34.1% said 'never.' Two out of three said they had felt discrimination or prejudice.

When those who answered affirmatively (76 = 100%) were asked whether they had experienced discrimination at work, 73.7% responded 'yes' versus 26.3% 'no.' For school (64 = 100%), the figures were 42.2% versus 57.8%, for living (70 = 100%), 55.7% versus 44.3%, and for housing and community (67 = 100%) 47.8% versus 52.2%. A relatively large number of respondents felt discrimination or prejudice in their jobs.

Incidentally, the respondents were also asked whether they had felt discrimination in China because of the fact that their parents or grandparents were Japanese (130 = 100%). 'Frequently' was given by 8.5% of respondents, 'sometimes' by 33.1%, and 'never' by 58.5%. Thus, roughly 40% of respondents had experienced discrimination because they were of Japanese ancestry. In other words, a significant portion of the respondents had experienced discrimination both in Japan and China.

When looking at second- and third-generation returnees who faced hardships in terms of living, two factors could be cited: low educational background and poor Japanese language ability.

First, looking at educational background in China (147 = 100%), 2.7% had received no schooling, 18.4% were elementary school graduates, 31.3% junior high school graduates, 32.7% senior high school graduates, 6.8% had graduated from junior college or university, and 8.1% had gone to technical schools or other institutions. Approximately one half of respondents were junior high school graduates or lower. This reflects the fact that many of these returnees grew up in hinterland areas of northeastern China, where they had few educational opportunities. Furthermore, looking at those who had done their schooling in Japan (52 = 100%), 44.2% were junior high school graduates, 19.2% senior high school graduates, 7.7% junior college or university graduates, and 28.8% graduates of technical schools. This shows that it was difficult for them to go on not only to university, but even to senior high school. Looking at the reasons people couldn't attain a satisfactory education in Japan (26 = 100%), 38.5% cited their Japanese language or scholastic ability, 34.6% financial difficulties, 19.2% said they had no time because of full-time or part-time jobs, and 7.7% gave other reasons. More than half said they had to halt their education because of poverty.

In terms of Japanese language ability, the answers could be divided into those on 'listening comprehension' (147 = 100%), 'speaking' (146 = 100%), 'reading' (146 = 100%) and 'writing' (145 = 100%). The answers 'My ability permits everyday living with almost no difficulty' and 'I don't feel any handicap' were given by 46.3% of respondents for 'listening comprehension,' 43.8% for 'speaking' and 'reading,' and 40.7% for 'writing.' Thus, the number of people who felt no handicap gradually fell in the order of 'listening comprehension,' 'speaking' and 'reading,' and 'writing,' with only 40% or so of respondents feeling no handicap with writing. By contrast, the answer 'I am practically incapable' was given by 8.8% for 'listening comprehension,' 13.7% for 'speaking,' 23.3% for 'reading,' and 26.2% for 'writing.' In this case the percentages gradually rose, with roughly one fourth of respondents being unable to write.

When asked where they had studied Japanese (140 = 100%), 35.7% said a Japanese language school, including volunteer organizations, 25.7% said a Japanese class in a public school, or at a resettlement promotion center, 30.7% said they had not studied, and 7.9% gave other answers, meaning that 30% had never done any real studies. It should also be noted that a high percentage studied at language schools or volunteer organizations, which do not receive public funding. Considering, on top of this, the fact that people who return at their own expense are not given the chance to learn Japanese language at resettlement promotion centers, it can be said that inadequate language instruction is given to second- and third-generation returnees. This has led to their lack of Japanese language skills.

There are many problems confronting these second- and third-generation returnees, in particular those who are still minors. Because of their poor Japanese ability, they find it difficult to follow their lessons in school. Entrance examinations at various levels are only given in Japanese language, so their prospects for advancing to higher levels of education are grim. Higashizawa Yasushi, a lawyer who worked on a case involving the murder of a third-generation returnee, explained the situation as follows. 'These third-generation children tend to be silent and to hide their identity, fearing cruel bullying from their peers, being outcast, or being subjected to discriminatory taunts such as "Go back to China!" "Pauper!" or "Stupid!"'[2] As a result, some end up forming motorcycle gangs composed solely of second- and third-generation returnees, and getting into fights with Japanese groups of juvenile delinquents.

Thus, second- and third-generation returnees from China have been pushed into the lower strata of Japanese society, and appear to be alienated and isolated from Japanese society. It is difficult for them to escape from this situation because of their low educational levels and lack of Japanese language skills. At the root of this is the fact that unlike other ethnic groups, they did not come to Japan after a period of preparation for some definite goal, such as working or studying.

Another group which stands out for its impoverishment is irregular Peruvians. Many are what are commonly called 'fake Nikkeijin.' They buy documents to prove that they are of Japanese ancestry, and come to Japan believing that they can work legally. However, in many cases they are caught by Immigration officials during the screening process, or else lose their courage and become overstayers without even going through the process. Within a tightening employment situation, many of these irregular Peruvians have lost their employment to legal Nikkeijin, and fallen into an extremely tough economic situation.

Next, moving on to Iranians, the major influx took place after the bursting of the bubble economy, and their status as irregular workers made their employment prospects very tough. At one time they stood, along with irregular Peruvians, at the bottom strata of foreign workers. Moreover, looking at the results of the survey on 'Ueno and Iranians' which was introduced in the last chapter,[3] they seem to have been hit by the economic recession to a remarkable degree. Among the 143 respondents, 78 said they had found employment during the previous one month, whereas a full 50 said they had not. This indicates an unemployment rate of 39.1%. Moreover, of those who had found employment, two thirds had worked for fewer than 20 days during the previous month. With regard to Japanese language ability, which is one condition for finding work, 76.2% responded 'I'm not very good at it' or 'I'm not able to communicate at all,' pointing to the existence of a significant language barrier.

For Iranians, the situation began to improve slightly in 1993. The results of my own 'Survey on Iranians,'[4] gave the following picture: 21.2% were unemployed, 24.9% in unstable employment (meaning they worked for 20 days or less a month), and 51.0% in stable employment (meaning they worked 21 days or more), with 2.9% not responding. Thus, though the figures were lower than for the survey in Ueno, nearly half of Iranians were either unemployed or in unstable employment, and as many as one in five was jobless. As mentioned previously, the survey by the Tokyo Metropolitan Council of Social Welfare found that the unemployment rate among irregular workers was 14.7%;[5] the rate for Iranians was much higher. In addition, Iranians had an average monthly income of ¥187,000, the lowest level among foreign workers in the Tokyo metropolitan area.

As a result of this situation, many Iranians became homeless. In the 'Ueno and Iranians' survey, when asked where they stayed at night (with multiple answers), 14 said in a park and 3 in a sauna or movie theater. These figures accounted for a total of 14.2% of answers. In the same survey, 54 people said they had had negative experiences since coming to Japan, involving (with multiple answers) the coldness of Japanese, etc., in 24 cases; 11 cited unfair treatment at their jobs, etc., 8 that there were no jobs, and 3 complained of not having housing. This shows the difficult economic situation that they faced.

Iranians have also come face-to-face with problems of discrimination. In the survey of 'Iranians in Japan,' 60.4% of respondents said they had experienced discrimination by Japanese, a percentage almost double that of those (35.5%) who said that they had not (with 4.1% not responding). In terms of the contents of the discrimination (with multiple answers), 32.7% said 'I was called names,' 16.3% 'I was refused housing,' 15.5% 'I was questioned by police when I was doing nothing wrong,' 15.1% 'I spoke to someone but was ignored,' and 13.9% 'I was stared at.' In addition, when asked about gaps with Japanese workers or discriminatory treatment at their workplaces, 61.2% said that such gaps existed.

Changes in the disparities between ethnic groups

With the transition from the period of expansion to stagnation, major changes took place both in the level of economic hardship as well as in the differences in income between ethnic groups. Originally, in terms of income, it was said that there was a 'principle of westward progression,' where wages fell progressively, starting from Latin America and moving to East Asia, Southeast Asia, South Asia, and West Asia. In other words, Latin American Nikkeijin held the top wages, followed by Koreans and Chinese, then further down by Filipinos and Thais, then by Bangladeshis and Pakistanis, and finally by Iranians, who held the lowest position.

This same tendency was seen in a survey that I conducted from 1990–91 in Kanagawa Prefecture.[6] On the other hand, the previously mentioned Chiba Prefectural High School survey gives insight into wage level differentials between ethnic groups in the post-bubble period. As shown in Table 5.1, Nikkei Brazilians had the highest wage levels of the six listed ethnic groups, followed by Iranians, Bangladeshis, and Chinese. The fifth and sixth places were held by Filipinos and Thais, both of which were 30% to 40% women. In other words, if one ignores the gender composition, the 'principle of westward progression' has lost its validity. In particular, there was a phenomenal rise in the status of Iranians and Bangladeshis, and the Filipinos and Thais ended up at the bottom. This may indicate that in the period of economic recession, Japanese language ability has begun to count.

With regard to Thais, most are not proficient in English, and also tend to have poor Japanese language ability even when they have lived in the country for some time. Filipinos, for their part, are good at English, which ironically may be an impediment to their

Table 5.1   Monthly Income by Nationality

	<¥200,000	≥¥200,000	≥¥300,000	≥¥400,000	Unknown	Total	Average
Nikkei							
Brazilians	6	8	11	1	4	30	¥261,000
Koreans	11	9	2	-	5	27	¥159,000
Chinese	9	9	4	1	1	24	¥199,000
Filipinos	15	12	1	-	4	32	¥182,000
Thais	9	5	1	-	-	15	¥180,000
Bangladeshis	6	19	2	-	1	28	¥214,000
Iranians	9	20	2	-	1	32	¥219,000
Total	65	82	23	2	16	188	¥205,000

Source: Chiba Prefectural Chiba High School, International Social Studies Group, *Gaikokujin rodosha jittai chosa, 1995-nen–1996-nen* (1995–1996 Field survey of foreign workers), 1997, in *Shinrai/teiju gaikokujin shiryo shusei* (Compilation of resources related to newcomer and settled foreginers), Tokyo: Akashi Shoten, 1998, Volume 2, p.179.

learning Japanese. By contrast, Iranians and Bangladeshis tend to have high levels of educational attainment, and many are young and ambitious. For the Bangladeshis who came during the period of expansion, as well as of course for the Iranian youths who came at a time whether it was unclear whether Japan's economic bubble would last or not, it was no easy task to live in Japan. However, as their stays lengthened, they acquired Japanese language skills, and began to achieve more stable lives.

Foreign crime

As mentioned earlier, it has been among irregular workers that we have seen the greatest tendency toward committing criminal offenses because of difficulty in finding work in the midst of the recession. In the case of Chinese, who make up the bulk of irregular workers, the amount of money paid to 'snakehead' gangs, which smuggle people into Japan, has risen to ¥300,000 per person. In many cases, the families of the smuggled individuals borrow money, and then pay the fee to the gang after confirming that the family member has safely arrived in Japan. Consequently, people who are unable to get work in Japan find themselves burdened with a large sum of loans, and in many cases have no choice but to become involved in criminal activities. The main criminal offenses committed in Japan by Chinese include thefts of clothes and automobiles, forging *pachinko* (gambling) prepaid cards, 'hacking' machines to get pachinko balls, and becoming 'snakehead' smugglers themselves. Very few are individual criminals; group crimes are becoming predominant. Also, the number working along with Japanese, including members of *boryokudan* (yakuza) groups, is increasing.

Among Iranians, though relative income levels are rising, one can find individuals who have been forced into delinquency or crime. As Iranians became economically strapped, they are sometimes used by organized crime in Japan. Okada Emiko, in her interview survey, reported the story of a young Iranian who was accosted by a yakuza in Ueno Park, and given work selling forged telephone cards in Osaka. This particular youth told her, 'Recently, a lot of people have suddenly lost their jobs...Many Iranians are working with the yakuza. After all, the yakuza are very kind.' He continued, 'The number of bad Iranians has been growing so much that we have begun hating to get together. It's rumored that up to 60% are involved with something bad.' He also said, 'Iranian people feel many kinds of stress in Japan. As a result, their personality becomes rough and they lose their cultivation.'[7] In other words, some Iranians, albeit a minority, have become involved in the production and selling of forged telephone cards, trading in narcotics and firearms, or in pimping. As many as 1,000 individuals are involved in drug peddling.[8]

Incidentally, Iranians in general are hurt by the fact that Japanese tend to identify them with the portion of Iranians who are criminals. The 'Survey on Iranians in Japan' included a space where respondents could write their opinions freely. A majority of the answers in this space involved either views of Japanese people and requests to be treated equally by Japanese, or responses to Iranian crime. As many as 150 (61.2% of the total) respondents provided answers in this space, and the responses were generally quite long. One characteristic of the responses was that they called criminals who sold forged telephone cards or narcotics 'bad Iranians,' distinguishing them from 'good Iranians' who were working and living in a proper manner. They expressed the earnest desire that Japanese not lump the 'bad Iranians' and 'good Iranians' together. Up to 28.7% of the people who wrote answers in the free space expressed this type of opinion. Many of them called for the 'bad Iranians' to be deported from Japan or prosecuted. In connection to this, a large number of answers (from 36.0% of respondents) expressed strong resistance to the stereotype in the Japanese media that all Iranians were criminals. Moreover, this type of opinion tended to become predominant along with rising Japanese language ability, which gave them the ability to understand the contents of Japanese media reports.

Crime has also begun to emerge among Nikkei Brazilians in spite of the fact that they are able to live in Japan legally. In the first half of 1998, Nikkei Brazilians were arrested for 1,502 counts of burglaries or robberies, a figure three times higher than the same period one year earlier. It can be assumed that this is an effect of the recession.[9]

How should we interpret the emergence of this phenomenon? First, with regard to irregular workers, I would like to point out that the policy of total rejection of undocumented workers has had the effect of pushing people into a corner. Thus, the phenomenon of foreign crime serves to underline the importance of granting some form of phased legality, based on the degree of settlement. With regard to the legal Nikkeijin, it demonstrates that the initial assumption that they would assimilate easily into Japanese society because they were the descendents of Japanese was flawed. Although they are of Japanese descent, the fact is that they are in essence foreigners.

Incidentally, there is a very important study by Hashimoto Kohei on the issue foreign crime.[10] He conducted time series regression analysis using the National Police Agency's 'Criminal Statistics.' His findings can be summarized as follows. (1) It is certain that crime is increasing among newcomer foreigners, including Filipinos and Thais. (2) By contrast, the crime rate is falling among Korean residents, who are long-term residents of Japan. (3) The crime rate for foreigners as a whole has been falling for the last three decades, and since 1976 the rate of arrest for Japanese between the ages of 20 and 64 has surpassed that for foreigners. (4) There is a tendency for the number of crimes committed by members of certain ethnic groups to fall as the number of people from those groups increase. His conclusion was that 'With regard to newcomers, such as Filipinos and Thais, the crime rate and scale of crimes committed are not problems worthy of any urgent focus.'

The right to life, the right to residence, civil liberties, and social rights

Overall responses of government organs

A 1992 report by the Administrative Inspection Bureau of the Management and Coordination Agency, which monitors other government organs, gives important insights into the neglect and violation of the human rights of foreign migrants by governmental organs.[11] Some points of interest in the survey included: (1) the reality of the obligation of government organs to report irregular foreigners to the Immigration Bureau; (2) the general disorder that reigns in immigration and emigration control; (3) the poor state of workers' accident compensation and unemployment insurance; (4) inadequacies regarding health care and pensions; and (5) problems with education.

With regard to the first point, government workers are obligated under the Immigration Control Law to report the presence of irregular workers. This acts as a major barrier to protecting the human rights of foreign workers. However, in reality, 70.9% of such reports come from prosecutors or the police, and very few from other types of government employees. In fact, since 1988, there have only been 116 reports filed by labor-related organs from 16 prefectural governments. The report, however, offered no recommendations on this point.

With regard to the second point, the report revealed that there are a host of problems relating to immigration control, and the situation has deteriorated to a point where it can no longer be ignored. There are cases of people being refused entry into the country even when they have valid visas,[12] and it has been noted that it is very difficult for people whose native language is not English to pass immigration inspections or file complaints. Applicants are sometimes told, during pre-entry inspections, to collect enormous numbers of documents which are not required under regulations. There have been cases when people applying for changes in status of residence have been forced to 'wait long periods because of the time-consuming process of deciding whether or not to grant the permission.'

On the third point, the report stated that efforts should be made to apply worker's compensation insurance in an adequate way. Unemployment insurance, which is becoming more important under the economic recession, is supposed to be applied as an obligation to both Japanese and foreigners, but the Ministry of Labor lacks a firm grasp of how many foreigners are enrolled versus how many are not.

On the fourth point, health care, the report noted that 56 medical institutions which were surveyed said that 744 of the 1,396 foreign patients they had treated had no public health insurance, and 34 people had failed to pay their medical bills. On the issue of pensions, the report found that many foreigners failed to enter the national or employees' pension insurance systems because they included an old-age pension system, which subscribers cannot receive unless they are enrolled in the scheme for more than 25 years.[13]

In terms of the fifth point, education, the report found that insufficient information was being given to foreign residents on compulsory education and on kindergartens and nursery schools.

The report made the following recommendations based on its survey findings. (1) There should be a better grasp of the working situation, etc., of foreigners. (2) Systems and operations related to immigration and emigration control should be improved. (3) The application of various other systems and operations to foreigners should be improved. (4) Other miscellaneous recommendations. The greatest number of pages was given to improvements in immigration and emigration control systems, showing an awareness that the urgency of this need. (1) In terms of grasping the employment situation, proposals were made to use the data collected from various systems related to immigration control and alien registration, to allow administrative organs such as the Ministry of Justice, Ministry of Labor, and Ministry of Construction to work to grasp the situation, and to ensure better linkages among the organs involved. (2) In order to improve immigration control, problems were listed with criteria for landing inspections, immigration and residence status control such as landing and pre-entry inspections and residence status control, the technical intern system, and the pre-college foreign student system. (3) With regard to improving systems and operations regarding foreigners, it raised problems related to labor, medical care, pensions, education, and housing. (4) Finally, as miscellaneous recommendations, it raised the issue of employing foreigners as government workers, etc., and setting up and improving consultation windows for foreigners.

As can be seen from the above, the administrative stance toward foreigners in Japan continues to be one based on the idea of control. Moreover the policies themselves are merely reactive, and represent attempts to catch up with changes.

The right to life: medical issues

Although they pay income taxes, it is almost impossible for irregular workers to receive any form of legal protection. A good example of this occurs when they experience a life-threatening illness or injury. Even at such times, their human rights are ignored. One Filipina living in Adachi Ward, Tokyo, filed a suit in Tokyo District Court against the Ward Office, demanding the cancellation of the Office's decision to refuse to issue her a National Health Insurance Certificate on the basis that she was an illegal resident, claiming that 'It was unjust.' This particular woman had children (the Japanese father had died) who had Japanese nationality, and was in the process of applying for special permission to stay. A judgment was handed down on September 27, 1995; it essentially closed the door for so-called illegal residents to enroll in National Health Insurance, finding that the ward's actions were 'not unjust.' Not being able to enroll in health care insurance programs means that people staying in Japan irregularly must pay the full costs of treatment for illnesses or injuries themselves. This obviously prevents them from receiving medical care. This can be seen as a violation of the right to life, which is one of the fundamental human rights, and is a problem that should not be overlooked.

The previously mentioned survey by the Chiba Prefectural High School provides data on illnesses and injuries suffered by foreigners in Japan.[14] It was carried out on 43 foreigners living in Chiba Prefecture. None of the respondents were enrolled in health insurance programs. However, a full 40 of the 43 had experienced some illness since coming to Japan; the report quoted a doctor as saying this was an extraordinarily high figure. Some of them had become ill on more than one occasion, so the total number of cases reported in the survey was 73. In decreasing order of frequency, they suffered from fevers (14 cases, with 7 being treated as outpatients), coughs or phlegm (13, with 2 outpatients), headaches (10, with 1 outpatient), contusions or sprains (6, with 6 outpatients), eye, nose or ear problems (6, with 4 outpatients), toothaches (5, with 4 outpatients), fractures (3, with 3 outpatients), and others (16, with 8 outpatients), meaning that in a total of 35 cases they had been treated by doctors. The report also mentioned that 27 brought medicine from their home country, 7 bought medicine in Japan, and 4 got over their illnesses without medicine or going to a doctor, by resting at home.

The report classified the illnesses into three major types. First, 19% were conditions such as headaches, muscle aches and fatigue, which were likely caused by the stress of living in Japan. Next, 18% were work-related injuries such as contusions, sprains, fractures, bruises, and cuts. Third, 18% were common illnesses such as colds and coughs. In the report, a physician commented that with the exception of the work-related injuries, they were generally not serious ailments, which was natural given that many of them were young. Regarding the high frequency of colds, the doctor stated that it reflected not only the fact that Japan is a cold country, but also that working conditions tended to be very severe.

With regards to the problem of AIDS, there is one analysis of clinical records from a medical facility in Ibaraki Prefecture, where many Thai women came to be treated.[15] Looking at it, we find that in 1990, 3.0% of the women tested positive for HIV, and that this number rose to 3.6% in 1991 and 5.0% in 1992, giving an average HIV infection rate of 4.6%. The situation regarding condom use by Thai women working as prostitutes can be gleamed from an interview survey of 154 people who had been detained in the suburbs of Tokyo for overstaying.[16] In this survey, 49.3% of the women said they did not use condoms (not counting 19 whose answers were unclear). Another survey was conducted on Thai women working in the sex industry in Utsunomiya City, Tochigi Prefecture.[17] When asked about condom use, the women responded that only an average of 3 out of 10 customers would agree to use one even when they asked, and 7 out of the 22 respondents said that none of their clients ever used condoms.

We have looked at the situation of illnesses and injuries among foreigners, but it is important to mention that the requirement that irregular foreigners must pay the full cost of their medical treatment is a great obstacle to their access to medical institutions. The previously mentioned survey by the Tokyo Metropolitan Council of Social Welfare included among its subjects people with 'no status of residence/unknown,' which corresponds to people staying in Japan irregularly, and provided data on their behavior toward medical care. According to the survey, only 61.8% of such individuals who experienced illnesses or injuries (other than work-related) that required examination in a medical institution responded that they had actually gone to see a doctor, and 20.3% had not done so because 'It would have cost a lot.' Only 2.2% of people with 'no status of residence/unknown' were enrolled in health insurance. However, a huge majority (87.9%) said they wanted to enroll.[18] Incidentally, in the survey by the Chiba Prefectural High School, 29 out of 30 respondents said that ¥10,000 was the upper limit they could afford for one visit to a doctor. Also, 26 of 28 respondents said that they could not pay more than ¥500,000 if they had to be hospitalized for a serious ailment.[19]

It is common that, when an irregular foreigner becomes ill enough to finally decide to visit a doctor, the resulting bill is so high that the individual is unable to pay. However, in October 1990, the Ministry of Health and Welfare issued a guideline that 'It is not appropriate to provide public assistance to individuals staying in Japan illegally.' It is likely that in the background of this guideline lay a decision by the Ministry of Health and Welfare to follow the Immigration Bureau's policy of driving irregular foreigners out, but in addition it was probably part of an attempt to suppress the country's rapidly-rising national medical costs. Before the guideline was issued, it was possible to supplement some portion of high-cost medical fees incurred by people with no ability to pay by applying for public assistance, and as a result many medical institutions were willing to treat irregular foreigners who were seriously ill. After the guideline was applied, however, medical institutions began to face the problem of unpaid medical bills left by foreigners who had no ability to pay, bills which could no longer be supplemented by public assistance. I will touch upon this issue in more detail in the next chapter, but as a result of this change, medical institutions have become reluctant to treat irregular foreigners, especially when their condition is serious, and thus many people have been abandoned by the medical care system.

The right of residence

In spite of the increasing trend toward settlement among irregular foreigners in Japan, the policy stance taken toward them has been one of complete exclusion. The authorities' stance is that amnesties, a form of relief mechanism that has been adopted in the U.S. and European countries, are not even an option. At present, the only route open for irregular foreigners to make their residence in Japan legitimate is to receive a special permission from the Minister of Justice. These permissions have almost exclusively been granted in cases where the foreigner was married to a Japanese or was raising children of his/her own with Japanese nationality. It is worth noting, however, that in recent years the framework for acceptance seems to have been expanded slightly.

One of the major reasons for violations of the human rights of irregular foreigners is that the Immigration Control Law requires government employees to report the presence of irregulars to the Immigration Bureau. In cases of work-related accidents, foreigners can apply for workers' accident compensation insurance benefits even if they are irregular. However, filing the application carries the inherent risk that the individual will be reported to the Immigration Bureau and deported. For this reason, foreign workers hesitate to apply. In cases of unpaid wages, which have become more common in recent years, filing a complaint with a public organ engenders the same danger.

In addition, the provision of general public services is in principle limited to foreigners who have carried out alien registration, a fact which excludes irregulars. A few municipalities have begun to accept alien registration applications from irregular foreigners, from the perspective of protecting their human rights. As can be seen from the column on 'visa-less' in Table 1.1, there were 9,297 such individuals as of January 1998. However, these individuals are forced to live in constant danger of being reported to the Immigration Bureau.

Also, with the 1999 revision of the Immigration Control Law, the 'waiting period' during which people deported as overstayers are ineligible for re-entry into Japan was extended from one year to five years. For people smuggled into the country, a new criminal offense, 'illegal residence,' was also instituted.

Civil liberties

The stance of total exclusion toward irregular foreigners has led to frequent violations of human rights against such individuals by immigration officials. When irregular foreigners are arrested but cannot afford the price of a plane ticket home, they can be detained indefinitely. Incredible acts of brutality by guards within detention centers have occasionally been reported.[20] One center in Kita Ward, Tokyo, lacks even an outdoor exercise yard, as stipulated by regulations.

Social rights

Most foreign workers are employed in medium-, small- or tiny-sized enterprises, where working conditions are poor. As a result, there have been many cases of sudden dismissals, unpaid wages, wage gaps with Japanese workers, and non-application of the workers' accident compensation insurance system.

This insurance exists to guarantee wages during periods of medical treatment, and in some cases covers the treatment expenses as well. However, the rate of payment of such benefits to foreign workers is far lower than that for their Japanese counterparts. This is because it is quite common, when a foreign worker gets injured on the job, for the incident to be 'hidden'; reports are not filed, and no insurance is applied for. For the employer, filing such reports carries the danger of being reprimanded by Labor Standards Inspection Offices or the police for employing irregular workers. For the worker, it carries the danger of being reported to immigration officials, and subsequently being deported. According to the previously mentioned survey by the Tokyo Metropolitan Council of Social Welfare, 36.3% of respondents had experienced workplace-related sickness or injuries, but in only 19.5% of these cases had applications been filed for workers' accident compensation insurance. Irregular workers are not recognized by the labor administration system, and hence cannot ask for mediation when labor disputes arise. They must bear their situation in silence.

Housing discrimination is a major form of human right violation in everyday life. Many real estate agents require potential renters to produce a *juminhyo* (resident card), and this is used as a basis for rejecting foreigners, who are not have such documents.

The right to assume public service is another social rights issue that has created much controversy. In the past, the Japanese government maintained the unwavering stance that foreigners could not become government employees. The sole basis for this was an opinion issued arbitrarily by a director at the Ministry of Justice in 1957, that 'It is a natural legal principle that the right to become civil servants cannot be granted to foreigners.' Thus, there is no legal basis for the exclusion. Subsequently, the 1957 opinion was set out in the so-called Nationality Clause, which restricts the right to become government employees to people with Japanese nationality. As a result, foreigners were excluded from civil service not only at the national level, but at the local level as well.

In recent years, there have been considerable changes in terms of local public employees, which I will mention in more detail in the next chapter. It was a 1996 ruling, by the Tokyo District Court, which did much to open the door for the future employment of foreigners in managerial positions in local governments. The court ruled that the Local Government Law does not preclude foreigners from being employed in managerial positions in local governments. As of 1999, this ruling was still in appeal at the Tokyo High Court, so it is not yet firmly established. With regard to national government employees, there has been no debate at all on employing foreigners either as field or non-field workers, with the exception of professors at national universities and similar positions.

Cultural rights

Looking at cultural rights, a major issue involves the use of language in areas where many foreigners are living. According to a survey by the Ministry of Education,[21] the number of children at public elementary and junior high schools who needed Japanese language instruction rose sharply from 5,463 in 1991 to 16,835 in 1999, and the number of schools which were being attended by such children from 1,973 to 5,061. In addition, as of 1997, 461 senior high school students who needed Japanese language instruction were enrolled in 148 schools. In 1997, the distribution of mother tongues of the non-Japanese speaking children enrolled in elementary and junior high schools was as follows: Portuguese (44.2%), Chinese (29.7%), Spanish (10.2%), Tagalog (3.6%), and others (12.3%). This means that Latin Americans made up just over one half, and Chinese close to a further third of the total. Comparing to the figures for 1991, the ratios held by Korean, Vietnamese, and English dropped, with their positions taken up by a mild increase in Portuguese, Spanish, and Tagalog. In 1997, 53 mother tongues were represented.

Reflecting the trend toward settlement, the periods of enrollment of children requiring Japanese language education are becoming longer. In 1991, 68.5% of these children were enrolled for periods of less than one year, 18.4% for at least a year but less than two years, and 12.1% for at least two years. In 1997, the figures were 45.8%, 22.3%, and 31.9%. Looking at data from 1995 by grades, we find that the increase was largest in the lower grades, with the exception of the first grade of elementary school. The number of third year junior high schoolers (ninth graders, the final year of compulsory education in Japan) was 1,237, versus 2,231 in the second grade of elementary school. Looking at the regional distribution of children in elementary and junior high schools who needed Japanese language instruction, the most common prefectures in 1991 were Tokyo, Kanagawa, Aichi, Osaka, Shizuoka, and Gunma, in that order. In 1997, the order was Aichi, Kanagawa, Shizuoka, Tokyo, Osaka, and Saitama. The increase was particularly striking in Aichi and Shizuoka prefectures, which are home to large concentrations of Latin Americans.

The data from 1991 makes it clear that long enrollment does not lead to improvement in Japanese ability. In the case of junior high school students, only 36.2% of children who had been enrolled for three or more years could 'generally read' Japanese, and just 28.7% could 'generally write.' This suggests that there are problems with

Japanese language education at public schools. Furthermore, the wide distribution of these children in schools makes any resolution very difficult: as of 1997, 44.9% of schools with children who needed Japanese language instruction had only one such student, 40.0% had between 2 and 5, and 15.2% had 6 or more. Thus, the overwhelming majority had 5 or fewer such children.

In a very limited number of municipalities, measures are being taken, which include dispatching teachers who are proficient in the mother tongues of children to schools, or assembling children from different schools in one place where they can be taught Japanese. However, in most municipalities, nothing at all is being done. According to the earlier mentioned survey by the Ministry of Education, the most common measure adopted by municipal boards of education is 'dispatching people who can cooperate with Japanese language instruction.' However, in 1993 only 19.6%, and 21.1% in 1997, of boards of education in areas where such children were enrolled had adopted this measure. There has been hardly any increase at all in this share.

According to research by a group headed by Nakanishi Akira,[22] there are a considerable number of foreign children who are in danger of dropping out of school because they are not able to keep up with their studies. It appears that the biggest reason for this is their lack of Japanese language ability. It takes several years to gain proficiency in Japanese, and it is very difficult for children who have just arrived in the country or whose parents do not plan to stay for a long period of time. Moreover, Japanese language teaching is still taking place on a trial-and-error basis, and it seems that it is often dependent on individual teachers bearing extra burdens on themselves.

Lacking Japanese language ability leads directly to difficulty in making friends. Foreign pupils tend to congregate with children from their own country, apart from the regular, Japanese children, and can become completely isolated. The fact that many drop out of club activities only strengthens this tendency. The difficulty they have in understanding classes taught in Japanese, and in finding friends, creates hardships for them in the junior high school years, when the course subjects become more difficult. They often find themselves at the bottom of their classes. As a result, even if they have a strong desire to go on to senior high school, many abandon these plans because of the difficulty of undergoing entrance examinations in Japanese. At present, as there are very few special quota systems for foreign children, these children tend to do poorly in educationally-conscious Japan. There is also a tendency for them to forget their mother tongues as they master Japanese. It seems that a system needs to be created to protect the rights of these children through organizational measures.

In the case of Nikkeijin Brazilians who come to work along with their families, the children have a stronger tendency to drop out. They cannot bring themselves to learn Japanese when their parents lack clear plans regarding whether or not they will return to Brazil and when they will do so. According to a survey by JICA,[23] as many as 18.1% of Nikkei Brazilians come to Japan with school-age children. For these children, the problem of entrance into high school is a major one. Introducing an example from interviews done by Watanabe Masako at a junior high school in Hamamatsu City, one respondent said that, 'Under the current system, with their Japanese language ability, their only real choice is to enter night school, even if they hope to go to day school. But the entrance examination for night school consists solely of essays and interviews, so it's possible for them to enter if we focus our instruction on essay writing.'

One teaching assistant who helped with Portuguese said, 'There are some parents who don't want to send their school-age children to school because they think they will only be in the country for one or two years...Even if they send their children to school in Japan, the children will have to start again from scratch when they get back to Brazil...If they study in Brazil, they might have the chance to become a lawyer or a doctor, but the parents worry that if they go to school in Japan, they might give up after junior high school, and even if they can find work it would be as manual laborers.' In these junior high schools, there are major problems involving school refusal and dropping out among Brazilian pupils.[24] The problems faced by Latin American Nikkeijin children, like those of Nikkei Chinese which were introduced in this chapter, are an indication that Japan, like other countries, is beginning to confront the problem of 'second generation immigrants.'

One survey conducted on newcomer foreigners living in Saitama Prefecture provided important information on the demand for education.[25] An incredible 42.8% of respondents had children aged 18 or under, showing the degree to which settlement has taken place. Among Filipinos, the ratio was over 60%; it was also high among Chinese and other Asian foreigners. The majority of these parents were sending their children to Japanese schools. Incidentally, the biggest complaint they had about schools was that 'The communication from teachers is all in Japanese, and there are things which I cannot understand.' This complaint was most often cited by Latin Americans who were not Brazilians, followed by Brazilians and North Americans or Europeans. This is to some extend related to Japanese language ability. In other words, Japanese language ability tends to be high among Chinese and Koreans, less so among Brazilians and non-Chinese/non-Korean Asians, and lowest among non-Brazilian Latin Americans.

I would like to add here that in Japan, ethnic schools are not recognized as ordinary schools. Thus, efforts for ethnic education are generally inadequate as well.

Political rights

Summing up the situation of political rights for foreigners, these rights do not exist either in terms of voting or standing for office, for any type of foreigner, at either the national or local level. However, Japanese society has been forced to confront the issue of political rights of settled foreigners due to the presence of many old-comer foreigners from the Korean Peninsula, many of whom have chosen not to adopt Japanese nationality even though nearly 90 years have passed since they began settling in Japan. On this issue, there is a 1993 ruling by the Supreme Court regarding voting rights at the national level. It found that the Public Officers Election Act, which restricts the right to vote for Diet members to Japanese nationals, was not unconstitutional. With regard to the right to run for elections, the Supreme Court ruled in March 1998 that it is not unconstitutional for the Public Officers Election Act to make Japanese nationality a requirement for becoming a member of the National Diet. Thus, at present no foreigner of any type can be granted political rights at the national level.

However, with regard to the local level, the Supreme Court issued an epochal ruling in June 1995, stating that 'It cannot be said that it would be forbidden to grant voting rights, through law, to foreigners, such as permanent residents, who have strong ties to their municipalities.' In other words, it would be constitutional for the National Diet to enact a law granting foreigners political rights at the local level. The powerful Metropolitan Tokyo Government has formally asked the state to grant local political rights to foreigners. Moreover, a bill to give local voting rights to long-term residents was submitted to the ordinary Diet session in the autumn of 2000, but was tabled, due mainly to opposition from within the ruling Liberal Democratic Party. On the issue of granting foreigners the right to stand in local elections, however, there has been no debate to date.

6 The Role of Local Governments and NGOs

The international policies of local governments

In the early 1980s, a group of progressive local bodies began pioneering efforts in the area of international activities, with a proposal for '*minsai gaiko*,' or 'people's international diplomacy.' It was based on the idea that people's diplomacy organized by local governments could be more effective than state diplomacy for solving issues of a global nature, such as peace, human rights, environmental preservation, and the eradication of poverty.[1] This proposal was eventually absorbed by the state, and in 1987 the Ministry of Home Affairs issued 'Guidelines on International Exchanges Conducted by Local Public Bodies,' for local governments. In 1989, it issued a set of 'Guidelines on Formulating Plans to Promote Regional-level International Exchange,' and in 1995 'Guidelines on Formulating Principles for Policies to Promote International Cooperation by Local Governments.' These guidelines were aimed at prefectures and to designated cities. According to the Ministry of Home Affairs, this constituted a move from 'international exchange toward international cooperation.'[2] In other words, the Ministry was hinting at the fact that it was no longer enough simply to increase international understanding and promote exchanges of people and information, but that there was a need to carry out international cooperation based on the needs of foreign countries.

However, the influx of newcomer foreigners, which grew rapidly beginning in the 1970s, gave local governments a whole new set of tasks in the area of international policy. These new foreigners lived and worked, naturally, in specific areas under the jurisdiction of local governments.[3] Consequently, whether willingly or not, the local governments found themselves forced to deal with foreigners as part of their administration. This became a passive condition pushing the 'internal internationalization' of local governments. However, there was also a positive condition demanding internal internationalization. The accepted view is that the Japanese Constitution only recognizes Japanese nationals as enjoying various rights, and excludes foreigners in principle from its protection. Under this Constitution, therefore, as incredible as it may seem, foreigners are basically not recognized as having human rights, beginning from the right to life, and extending to the various social and economic rights. It seems that the emphasis placed by the Ministry of Home Affairs on international exchange and cooperation, in contrast to its lack of regard for internal internationalization, is partly a reflection of this basic stance of the Japanese nation-state.

However, the Local Government Law stands on a clearly different perspective than the Constitution. Under its provisions, local governments have the responsibility to protect the safety, health, and welfare of their residents, and 'residents' here naturally includes foreigners whose livelihoods are based within their jurisdictions. The philosophical underpinning for this law, which is open to universal human rights, can be found in the last century's tradition of local autonomy, related to the Jiyu Minken Undo (Freedom and People's Rights Movement), which set people's rights in opposition to state rights. In other words, local governments have the potential to develop international policies that are independent from those of the state. Thus, internal internationalization, which involves the question of how to cohabit with the newcomer foreigners, has emerged as a positive task for local governments. Its ultimate goal is the creation of local cultures filled with rich individuality. The different cultures brought by foreign migrants can, in synergy with the historical and endemic atmosphere of different regions, contribute toward the regions' own development.

An outline of the international policies[4] of local governments was given by a 1994 report by the Tokyo Metropolitan Government Bureau of Citizens and Cultural Affairs, 'Survey on Measures for the Internationalization of Local Governments in Japan,' a systematic compilation of information at the national level.[5] Looking at very interesting items revealed by the report, one is surprised to find that there are major gaps among the levels of awareness of different local governments. While some are making consistent efforts to solve the problems faced by settled foreigners, others have practically no awareness of these problems. One major method for distinguishing these two types of local bodies is to look at their policies toward irregular workers. Whereas some are seriously considering ways to protect them, from the standpoint of defending their human rights, many others go beyond simply ignoring them, as they are illegal and hence not subject to their measures, and intentionally report them to immigration or police officials. In the Kanto area, where many newcomer foreigners have settled, a relatively large number of local governments are of the former type. In terms of irregular workers, Ibaraki Prefecture, Hyogo Prefecture, Yokohama City and Kawasaki City have taken the stance that it is important to respect their human rights as well as their labor rights. Many local governments that do not take this stance follow the policies and guidelines of the central government. They seem to have forgotten the historical circumstance in which local autonomy was established in a tense relationship with the central government, and to be content with their position as mere sub-contracting entities.

An epochal event in the international policies of local governments came in 1993, when the Kawasaki City Study and Research Committee on Policies Toward Foreign Citizens came up with a proposal entitled 'A Proposal for Creating Guidelines for Kawasaki City's International Policies.' It was a concrete proposal for how a local government could implement international policies.[6] The aim of the proposal was to 'promote measures toward foreign citizens from the standpoint of respecting human rights and eliminating discrimination, based on the policy principle of "coexisting within the community,"' on the basis of the 'prospects for international policies centered around "coexistence" and "cooperation".' In the background of this was the fact that many Koreans, who had been forcibly brought to Japan to maintain Japan's military industry during the war, had settled in the southern part of Kawasaki City. Thus, mainly as a response toward the old-comer foreigners, Kawasaki City conducted various social and educational practices, including the establishment of the Council to Promote Policies Toward Foreign Citizens, experiments in school education, and the establishment of the Fureai Hall (international exchange hall) and citizen halls.

The contents of the proposal were divided into five parts: establishing civil rights for foreign citizens; building communities where foreigners could live easily; medical care and welfare; creating linkages between organs promoting internationalization in communities; and tasks to be solved. In terms of civil rights for foreigners, it proposed improving alien registration procedures and creating ways for foreigners to participate in the city government. In terms of community-building, it included items on school education, culture, housing, community-building, career searching, and foreign students. The section on organs promoting internationalization mentioned international exchange associations, international exchange centers, volunteers, and the city. Finally, in terms of remaining tasks, it cited 24 items which the Council to Promote Policies Toward Foreign Citizens failed to solve in its December 1990 report, as well as alien registration, the International Convention Against All Forms of Racial Discrimination, and the Nationality Clause.

One particularly important item that was raised by this proposal is the idea of civil rights for foreign citizens. It suggested that alien registration, which is a form of citizen registration, should be used not simply for control but as basic data for the provision of administrative services. The resulting proposal, that 'There is a need to create a system where people can register without anxiety, including for example providing consultations to unregistered people, and investigating the possibility of accepting people whose registration form is incomplete,' was of great significance for local government administration. However, a problem remained as to whether the direction taken by this proposal would be sufficient for the treatment of irregular foreigners. The basic direction of the proposal can be understood as a conversion from 'alien registration' to 'citizen registration,' and hence the provision of civil rights for unregistered irregular foreigners, with services given to them as necessary. However, as it appears nearly impossible at the ground level to get around the clause in the Immigration Control Law that gives government employees the duty to report irregular foreigners, completely separating the treatment given by local governments to irregular foreigners from registration could be considered.

On the issue of participation in city affairs, another pillar of civil rights for foreigners, the report included proposals for the abrogation of the Nationality Clause, the enlargement of participation by foreigners in monitoring and advisory councils of city government, and lobbying toward the central government to grant local voting rights to foreigners. It also suggested increasing the number of non-Japanese government employees to a ratio commensurate with the makeup of the population. This appears to be a new idea for future direction. In the area of community-building, a notable proposal was to set up bases for international exchange, taking into consideration community structures. Since the Oohin district, in the south of the city, is an area where Japanese and Korean residents live in a mixed pattern, the proposal found the potential for development as 'communities of coexistence' through citizen participation, using ideas such as the 'Korean Town Plan,' based on the accumulation of different cultures. In terms of linkages between organizations working on international exchanges, it found the relations with volunteers to be particularly important. In this area, it called for a system to provide subsidies to volunteer groups, and to get feedback from people working in the field into the city administration. In relation to this, it seems essential for administrative bodies to create links with NGOs working to support newcomer foreigners, but the proposal did not specifically mention support groups. And in the area of culture, it included a proposal to respond to the needs of foreign residents by having a book selection committee at each library, with the participation of foreign citizens.

Issues facing local governments and current efforts

Demands for administrative services

When searching for and identifying demands on international policies for both foreign and non-foreign residents, two surveys on the demand for administrative services, conducted by Kawasaki City and Saitama Prefecture, can be of reference.[7]

Kawasaki City's 'Report on a Field Survey of the Attitudes of Citizens of Kawasaki City with Foreign Nationalities' (1993), was an unprecedented comprehensive survey of foreign residents, including newcomers, carried out by a local government.[8] The impetus for this survey was clear: it was planned as the foundation for administrative policies for the internationalization of the local government of Kawasaki City. The report included several interesting points of analysis, and can well serve as a model for future surveys of the same type.

However, there are also points of reservation, beginning with the fact that it was only targeted at people with legal status, and failed to include irregular foreigners. At the time of the survey, nearly one half of newcomer foreigners were irregular, and it is certain that there were many living in Kawasaki as well. Consequently, it may be that measures implemented on the basis of this survey would neglect or downright ignore the needs of irregular foreigners, who according to the spirit of the Local Government Law should naturally form a constituent group of these bodies. It is of course very difficult to carry out surveys on irregular foreigners, but it would have been desirable for the survey to attempt by some method to compensate for this.

In connection to this, the survey took the stance of looking at old-comer and newcomer foreigners in an aggregate way, but it is debatable whether this is valid or not. Though a significant portion of newcomers have begun to tread along the path toward settlement, they are very different from the old-comers, for whom a return to their homeland is no longer even conceivable. It may well be that these differences should lead to different measures toward the two groups. With regard to this issue, the report merely presented data on whether people from the Korean peninsula have been in Japan for less than ten years or for ten years or more, a clearly inadequate criteria for resolving the problem.

The survey was composed of seven main pillars, including attributes, life within the community, work and living, medical care and welfare, children and school education, culture and study, and demands toward the city government and national government. As mentioned earlier, the points of departure for the survey were the 24 items for examination based on the city's guidelines for international policies. In particular, in the area of cultural exchanges, when asked what type of facilities they would like to have near their homes, 47% of respondents said 'places to learn Japanese language and culture,' 43% 'places to have deeper relations with Japanese,' 38% 'facilities where I can borrow books and videos concerning my home country' and 25% 'facilities where I can deepen exchanges with other foreigners.' The demand was highest first for Japanese language and culture, and next for contact with the culture of their home countries.

Next, the 1997 'Report on a Survey of the Attitudes of Foreigners Living in Saitama Prefecture,' by the prefectural government, is valuable for its careful analysis of the demands of foreign residents for administrative services and for the volume of information provided.[9] The aim of the survey was given as, 'To grasp the daily living situation of foreign residents, and their own voices toward the administration.' The survey's contents included housing, present job, medical care and insurance, education and child-rearing, exchanges within the community, disaster preparedness, information services from the administration, and attributes.

One interesting finding was that different ethnic groups have different demands for administrative services. There were huge differences in terms of the first demand they had for information from the administration. For people from China and other Asian countries, it was 'employment'; for Filipinos 'education,' for Koreans 'housing,' for Brazilians and Europeans/North Americans 'measures in time of emergency,' and for other Latin Americans 'medical care and insurance.' The background for this can be understood through the fact that in terms of occupation, Chinese tended to be professionals and technicians, and people from Brazil and Asian countries other than China to be factory workers, whereas Filipinos had a strong tendency to be housewives. In the same way, the demand to display 'various signs in foreign languages' was particularly strong among Filipinos, Brazilians, other Latin Americans, and Europeans/North Americans. The demand for 'more Japanese language courses for foreigners' was also high among people from Latin Americans other than Brazil, European/North Americans, and Brazilians. This, again, is related to Japanese language skill.

Efforts on the tasks facing local governments

In the following section, I would like to look at efforts toward internal internationalization in a series of places. First, I will look at four local governments that have taken an active stance toward foreign workers: Hamamatsu City in Shizuoka Prefecture, Gunma Prefecture, and Ota City and Ooizumi Town in the Tomo region of that same Prefecture. Second, I will look at one region and three local governments that face specific problems. The Mogami region of Yamagata Prefecture confronts the issue of foreign brides, Kobe City suffered from the Great Hanshin Earthquake of 1995, Tsukuba City, Ibaraki Prefecture, is home to a large number of foreign students, researchers and professors, and Okinawa bears the heavy burden of the U.S. military bases.[10]

The major turning point for Hamamatsu City, Ota City, and Ooizumi Town came with the 1990 revision of the Immigration Control Law. As a result of this revision, as seen in Chapter 4, many of the Nikkei Brazilians and others whose immigration and employment were liberalized came to concentrate in these areas. For these local governments, coping with these newcomers turned into a major issue. In 1994, Hamamatsu City became the first organization to be decorated by the Minister of Home Affairs for being 'A town open to the world.' Ota City and Ooizumi Town are also areas that are well known for the good relations of coexistence between their foreign and local populations. The policies of these local governments to date toward foreign residents can be deemed to have been highly successful.

As a major factor behind this success, one can cite the fact that in both of these regions it was people rather than local governments who took the initiative. In Hamamatsu, the Hamamatsu International Exchange Association acted as the core of activities for internal internationalization; the city administration contributed less than half of the funds for the organization, and very few people from the city government acted as officials. In Ota City and Ooizumi Town, an organization called the Council to Promote Stable Employment in the Tomo Region was formed by owners of small- and medium-sized companies that were sub-contractors or affiliates of major firms. This organization played a leading role in systematically bringing in Nikkei Brazilians, and in assuring them stable livelihoods.

The local governments not only gave indirect support to these organizations, but also provided administrative services for foreign residents. Looking at the contents of these services, there were many similarities between the two regions. They included the provision of information in Portuguese and other foreign languages, consultation services in foreign languages, Japanese-language classes at elementary and junior high schools, and the holding of Japanese language classes or courses in the communities. It is particularly noteworthy that in both regions there were efforts to nurture and use volunteers to give Japanese language courses and lectures. I would also add that in Hamamatsu City, guidance is now being provided on preserving the mother tongues of foreign residents. These measures can be valuable references for other local governments with foreign residents within their jurisdictions.

One major feature common to both Ota City and Ooizumi Town is that there was a significant level of organization among the foreign residents themselves. The 'Nikkei Brazilian Chamber of Commerce,' organized by Nikkeijin shop owners, and the 'Japan-Brazil Center,' where one returnee from Brazil began accepting consultations on daily living, functioned as nodes for community networks of Nikkei Brazilians. As a result, for example, samba teams began to participate in the Ooizumi Festival, to the great enthusiasm of local residents. In Hamamatsu City, it was mainly commercial employment brokers that took charge of the introduction of labor power, but in Ota City and Ooizumi Town it was mainly the Council to Promote Stable Employment in the Tomo Region. Undoubtedly in the background for this was the development of labor-management relations and livelihood stability for foreign residents, as well as citizens' organizations, in Ota City and Ooizumi Town. Looking at the historical experience of Gunma Prefecture, in which the two municipalities are located, a major role was played by the Gunma Prefecture International Exchange Association, which was formed jointly by the government and private citizens. It receives approximately 2,000 cases of questions or requests per year for advice by foreign residents, and partly as a result, there have not yet been any major troubles between foreigners and Japanese residents.

Next, turning our focus to regions and local governments that confront specific problems, we can look at Okinawa Prefecture, which has 60,000 foreign residents, of which 50,000 are American military personnel and their families. These individuals, under the Status of Forces Agreement which accompanies the U.S.-Japan Security Treaty, are exempted from alien registration, and thus are not subject to immigration control. Partly because the U.S. bases are out of the jurisdiction of the local governments, the military personnel are not considered subjects of local administration. In Tsukuba City, there remains a strong traditional local political structure, and just as newcomer Japanese residents are alienated from it, foreign residents do not have an active position within the administration. In these two areas, the foreign residents are nearly non-existent as subjects of the administration. In pre-earthquake Kobe there were, in addition to the resident Koreans, increasing numbers of newcomer foreigners, such as Vietnamese, but the city administration paid very little attention to them. However, because the effects of the earthquake were particularly devastating to the foreign residents, the city administration found itself forced to switch to a stance of internal internationalization.

In Tsukuba City, because of the virtual absence of any visible international policies, it is natural that the foreign residents are essentially invisible to the city administration. In Okinawa Prefecture, by contrast, international policies were in place but in the totally opposite direction of internal internationalization, which began from the perspective of international exchanges. Specifically, Okinawa had set up offices abroad and held conventions for 'Uchinanchu' (Okinawans) spread out throughout the world (many of the Japanese who went abroad during the late 19th and early 20th century were from Okinawa), and had accepted students and trainees from among people who had migrated abroad. Kobe City, for its part, had maintained the image of an international port city since its opening in the Meiji Era, and was carrying out development projects aimed at transforming it into an information-oriented and international city. Thus, in the case of these two local governments, the existence of these outward-looking international policies may have actually focused attention away from internal internationalization.

In the Mogami Region of Yamagata Prefecture, in contrast to other cases, individual local governments were involved from the very beginning in 'internationalization,' which took the form of the acceptance of foreign brides. Consequently, the administrations had to provide diversified care to assist in the settlement of these women. Two noteworthy developments emerged from this process. The first was the creation of a network centered around private individuals, among the foreign brides, local governments, and local residents. The second was the organization of volunteer activities by the foreign brides themselves. Meanwhile, in Okinawa, the opposition to U.S. military bases has not been translated into hatred toward Americans, and hence could be used in a positive way. In Tsukuba City, as well, the impetus for change could come from the foreign residents themselves, who have a feeling that they have rights as citizens. Both locations may have positive, albeit latent, conditions which may be able to promote internal internation-alization in the future, but they have yet to be used.

The problem of unpaid medical bills

As we saw in Chapter 5, there are limits to the ability of foreigners without health insurance, both regular and irregular, to pay medical bills. As a result, a problem of unpaid bills has arisen, imposing serious burdens on the financial health of medical institutions. Because foreigners are often treated in emergency rooms, the bills they leave behind tend to be very high. The reason for this is that individuals without health insurance often wait until their condition is serious before they go to see a doctor, and thus many of them end up in emergency rooms. In one Tokyo hospital, 70% of unpaid bills come from emergency room patients, and in Kanagawa Prefecture, 95% of the ¥37 million in unpaid medical bills in fiscal 1991 came from emergency medical facilities.[11]

The financial difficulties of medical institutions make the situation more serious through the phenomenon known as 'patient selection.' It refers to the behavior through which medical institutions try to avoid patients who are 'unprofitable,' and to accept those from whom a profit can be made. As a result of this 'selection,' private hospitals, which are more business oriented, tend to turn away foreigners who do not have health insurance, who end up being concentrated at public facilities, which are relatively treatment-oriented. As a result, the budgets of public medical facilities, in particular, have been squeezed by unpaid bills. Dividing medical institutions into local government hospitals (operated by prefectures or municipalities), other public hospitals (operated by organizations such as the Japanese Red Cross Society or Saiseikai), private hospitals, and national hospitals, we find that in 1990 only 20% of local government hospitals were operating in the black, and that this figure rose to barely 50% for other hospitals, in the order of private, then national, and finally other public hospitals. In the same year, private hospitals made up 81% of all hospitals.[12]

A variety of measures have been used to provide relief to medical facilities from the problem of unpaid bills. The first was a revival of the 'Law for the Treatment of Ill Travelers and Deceased Travelers,' which was established in the Meiji Era. Some prefectures, such as Tokyo, Gunma, Saitama, Chiba, and Kanagawa, have made budgetary allocations, reviving this law. It was abolished in practically all local governments during World War II, but Ibaraki Prefecture never took the steps to formally end it, so it is still in force there. However, this law can only be applied to people who have fallen ill or died on the road, and who have no fixed abode. Hence, there are limits to applying it to foreigners who have a fixed address.

There have also been attempts by local governments to directly compensate hospitals for unpaid medical bills. The forerunner in this area, Kanagawa Prefecture, initiated measures in April 1993 through which it defrayed the entire cost (or shared it equally with a designated city) in cases of 'tertiary emergency care' (which indicates that the patient either requires emergency surgery or is in danger of dying), and shared the cost with the municipality in cases of other types of emergency care such as 'secondary emergency care' where the patient required hospitalization. In July of the same year, Gunma Prefecture instituted a policy under which 70% of the costs of unpaid bills would be defrayed, with the prefectural government bearing 70% of this burden and municipalities and companies the remaining 30%. In fiscal 1994, Chiba and Saitama prefectures began to adopt similar policies, and in October 1994, Tokyo began to compensate 70% of unpaid medical bills. It is certain that these systems are a step forward both for foreign patients and for medical institutions. However, they do not constitute a fundamental resolution of the problem. Not only do they impose an unfair financial burden on local governments with such policies compared to others, but inequalities also develop in terms of the access of foreign patients to medical care.

In the midst of these developments, it became clear in May 1995 that the Ministry of Health and Welfare was prepared to finally take a step toward changing its stance on the issue. A report submitted by the Advisory Council on Medical Care Relating to Foreigners, chaired by Kato Ichiro, recommended that it would be appropriate to apply the health insurance system even to irregular foreigners, as long as they had regular employment, and if the employer filed an application. It also called for the establishment of a national system to provide assistance to local government compensation systems for unpaid medical bills. In response to this recommendation, the Ministry decided to launch a system in fiscal 1996, targeted at roughly 130 specially designated emergency medical centers throughout the country, under which the state and the prefectural government would defray 30% of the portion of unpaid medical bills beyond ¥500,000 per case.

How should we appraise this policy? As we saw in the last chapter, the survey by the Tokyo Metropolitan Council on Welfare found that there was very high demand among irregular workers for access to health insurance systems.[13] Thus, the recommendations can be valued for contributing to the possibility of irregular workers to enroll in health insurance. However, the vast majority of irregular foreigners are working in unstable employment in tiny business operations, many of which lack the stability themselves to file applications for enrollment into the system. In other words, the way to solve the problem of unpaid medical bills would be to allow these individuals to enroll in the National Health Insurance system, which is managed by the state. And with regard to compensation for unpaid bills, the Ministry's decision must be deemed insufficient as it only covers the approximately 130 designated emergency medical centers.

Most foreign workers are young, with strong bodies, and their enrollment into health insurance systems would be a benefit rather than a burden to the finances of the schemes. It should be added, though, that even if the door is opened, there is still a problem of whether or not foreigners will actually enroll in health insurance schemes. Many Nikkeijin have legal residence status, and thus can enroll in health insurance schemes, but looking at the JICA survey, it is notable that the enrollment rate was quite low, at just 54.2%.[14]

Attempts have also been made to deal with the problem of the medical expenses of foreigners through the creation of mutual aid systems. In the case of the 'Minatomachi Mutual Aid Association,' which organizes several thousand individuals, members can receive significant discounts on outpatient treatment with only a small membership fee. The 'Bright' system in Ikebukuro is similar. These can be recognized as having significance as initial measures, but they are limited to outpatient visits and thus cannot contribute to the main focus of the problem, which is emergency medicine.

The problem of the medical expenses of foreigners is of course an issue of human rights, but it is also one that has the potential to trigger the collapse of the Japanese health care system. Unpaid medical bills have placed a particularly heavy burden on local government hospitals and hospitals run by other public bodies, which are treatment- rather than business-oriented. It is likely that the only way to solve the problem will be to allow the application of public assistance to irregular foreigners, and to permit their enrollment into health care insurance systems, including the National Health Insurance scheme.

The problem of appointment to civil service and measures toward housing discrimination

Let us now look at efforts made by local governments to appoint foreigners to positions as government employees, as was outlined in the previous chapter. First, during the 1980s, a significant number of local governments in the Kansai area (near Osaka and Kyoto), where many resident Koreans are living, began to abolish the Nationality Clause, in defiance of the Ministry of Home Affairs, for field jobs which did not involve decision-making. In spite of the opposition of the Ministry, this process continued; in the early 1990s, many began to allow foreigners to work in non-field positions in areas such as medical care, which did not involve public decision-making, and in the late 1990s began to open the door to foreigners taking non-field positions which *did* involve public decision-making.

In 1996, for example, Kawasaki City completely abolished the Nationality Clause with the exception of managerial positions, and other local governments such as Kochi Prefecture and Osaka Prefecture are considering its total abolition. It is also notable that in many areas of Western Japan, which are home to many old-comer foreigners, efforts have been made to develop concrete measures against employment discrimination toward foreigners. A number of local governments are trying to interpret the Ministry of Home

Affairs' opinion, that foreigners cannot 'participate in the exercise of public authority or in the formation of public decisions,' in a limited way. They include Kanagawa Prefecture, Aichi Prefecture, Yokohama City, Kawasaki City, as well as Osaka Prefecture, Kobe City, Hiroshima City, and Fukuoka City.

Also, some local governments that are actively considering concrete measures to abolish housing discrimination against foreigners, including Kawasaki City, Kyoto Prefecture, and Osaka Prefecture.

Conditions for coexistence within local communities

In his classic study of ethnic problems, *An American Dilemma*, Myrdal stated that prejudice toward blacks tends to increase when whites see them only as an anonymous group, when they pass them on the street, but to decrease when they recognized individuals by name and face.[15] Naturally, the same thing should be true for Japan.[16]

With regard to the overall situation in this country, the survey conducted by the Institute of Public Policy introduced in Chapter 4 can be of reference.[17] Of the Japanese respondents, 56.6% said they felt anxiety toward foreigners, and when categorizing this according to how close they lived to foreigners, the amount of anxiety increased in the order of (1) those who lived in neighborhoods with no foreigners, (2) those who lived in neighborhoods where foreigners also lived, and (3) those who lived in close proximity to foreigners. The same trend could be seen among the 46.4% who said 'I have experienced troubles with foreigners.' Despite this, when they were asked who ought to solve such problems, 41.1% said the city or ward office, 29.5% some other public body, 17.3% the police, versus only 6.5% who said the problems ought to be resolved by talks between the parties involved, and 2.6% by some third party within the community. In other words, community residents have given hardly any thought to the need for direct contact as a means to resolve conflicts. Furthermore, the number of people who said they 'exchanged greetings' or 'had relations' with foreigners was 10.5% for the respondents as a whole, and 22.2% for people who lived in close proximity to foreigners. Of the foreigner respondents, 45.7% said they had Japanese friends, but in most cases these relationships did not go beyond 'exchanging greetings.' However, even among those who said they had no Japanese friends, roughly 70% said they wanted to have relations with Japanese. In other words, it can be concluded that when Japanese live in close proximity to foreigners, the lack of actual contact can lead to increased anxiety among them.

A survey in Tokyo carried out by Watado Ichiro supports this hypothesis. When asked how they had perceived increases in foreign residents in their neighborhoods, feelings of anxiety or resistance had risen among those who 'had no relations with foreigners,' and the number who said they 'don't mind' or were 'tolerant' had decreased.[18]

Sugiyama Katsumi, Mita Yuko et al. have examined how ideas of 'acceptance' and 'exclusion' are formed at the level of residents. In Tochigi Prefecture, following the murder of a Japanese woman by a Sri Lankan man, an individual incident expanded into anxiety regarding foreigners as a whole, and people came to hold a fear that went beyond rational understanding. Moreover, since they had no ties with the employers of foreigners, a feeling in favor of 'exclusion' arose. By contrast, in the Tomo region of Gunma Prefecture, people tended to see foreigners in their neighborhood as 'the foreigner working for Mr. so and so,' and as a result prejudice has not increased. In this region, there are strong links between firms and workplaces, and information about individual foreigners is widely shared.[19] We can interpret from this that, unlike when people see foreigners as an anonymous group, the idea of 'acceptance' is formed when people recognize them as individuals, even if it is in the form of 'the foreigner working for Mr. so and so.'

Incidentally, it is worth mentioning that in one notable case, at the Homi Housing Complex near Toyota City, troubles between foreign and Japanese residents have become quite serious. Through employment brokers, 3,100 Nikkeijin Brazilians now live in the complex, which houses a total of 11,000 people. In addition to problems such as noise and illegal dumping of garbage, incidents have occurred one after another, including robberies, arson, retaliatory violence and group threats, leading to troubles between the Brazilians and Japanese residents. Some of the residents have been forced to leave the complex. The problem is partly related to a specific feature of the community, namely that the brokers have been allowed to do as they please, but it is a striking incident in that problems which were not given consideration when newcomer foreigners began to flow into Japan have begun to emerge. One of the factors behind the trouble is the fact that many single foreigners came to live in a housing complex that was originally intended for families, and another is that there was a lack of contact between the two groups.

Originally, the problem at the Homi Housing Complex was not very serious. According to the research of Tsuzuki Kurumi, a long-time observer of the complex, the relationship between the Nikkei Brazilians and Japanese residents went through a three-stage process. First, there was a 'period of breaking out of problems,' then a period of 'watching each other,' a quiet time with tensions, and finally an 'initial period of coexistence,' which was a first step toward getting along together. At the beginning, the arrival of the Nikkei Brazilians caused major friction, as they had appeared suddenly in an 'enclosed' way, in order to make corporate mass management possible. However, the feelings of incompatibility and anxiety among the residents began to abate when the Brazilians participated in the yearly Bon Odori festival. Tsuzuki found that a variety of Japanese in the community, who served as contacts or communication points with the Brazilians, played a major role in the movement toward coexistence.[20] As of 1999, the situation was growing worse.

For foreigners to be seen as individuals, what is of crucial importance is the role placed by key people who act as bridges with the ethnic community. According to Enari Miyuki et al., with regard to the relationship between Latin American Nikkeijin and Japanese residents, a small number of volunteers with respective strengths emerged who tried to create equality between the groups in various fields, and in doing so became links.[21]

The importance of NGOs

NGOs, along with local governments, are expected to play a very important role. I would like to begin by looking at support groups who provide advice and assistance to foreigners, on labor and living issues such as unpaid wages and workplace accidents. Some representative groups, which have long histories, include the HELP

Asian Women's Shelter in Tokyo, Kalabaw no Kai, which works in the flophouse district of Kotobuki-cho, Yokohama, and A.L.S. (Asian Laborers Solidarity) in Nagoya. In addition, the Asian People's Friendship Society (APFS), which has its headquarters in Itabashi Ward, Tokyo, is a group organized by irregular workers themselves. Starting in 1999, this organization began a campaign to obtain special residence permits for long-term overstayers who had established livelihoods in Japan. These support groups have achieved some progress by holding negotiations with central government organs such as the Ministries of Labor, Health and Welfare, and Justice. The activities of community-based unions are also very important.

Another notable organization is the International Movement Against Discrimination Based on Race (IMADR), one of very few 'UN NGOs' based in Japan that have deliberative status in the United Nations Economic and Social Council (ECOSOC). This organization, which inherited the tradition of international solidarity developed over the years by the *buraku* liberation movement (the *buraku* are a caste in Japan who have been victims of discrimination), that began with the Zenkoku Suihei-sha, was founded in 1988 as an international human rights organization aiming to defend human rights both abroad and at home. It has links with similar groups around the world. In terms of activities, in addition to working to abolish *buraku* discrimination and to defend the human rights of women and children, it has placed an important focus on opposing racism and racial discrimination, and dealing with problems of migrant workers, minorities and indigenous peoples, refugees, as well as specific human rights problems in specific countries. It has an office in Geneva, and has actively lobbied the United Nations Committee on Human Rights. It has also held a variety of international symposiums. In terms of the problems of migrant workers in Japan, it has focused particular attention on violence by the Immigration Bureau and the arrest and deportation of irregular workers.

In addition, there are volunteer groups teaching Japanese language to foreigners, which have been very active in recent years. They exist principally in the Kanto region, centered around Tokyo, but are spread throughout the country. According to a survey by the Cultural Affairs Agency, as of November 1998 there were a total of 336 private organizations (which are neither controlled nor protected by law), with a total of 6,511 volunteers working as teachers.[22] There were a total of 83,086 foreigners studying with them, including overstayers, with the number of students per group ranging from a few dozen to more than 100. In the following few paragraphs, I would like to outline the organizational development and activities of these Japanese language networks.[23]

They are inevitably organized around a small number of key people. In many cases these organizers are middle-aged women, with high educational background, who have experienced living abroad. This is because these individuals have experienced the difficulty of using a foreign language abroad, have sufficient free time to carry out such activities, can teach Japanese, and feel the significance of international activities. In terms of the contents of activities, one major decision that volunteers are forced to make is whether they will limit their activities to teaching Japanese language or whether they will conduct consultations on life problems as well. This choice must be made because the students often ask the volunteers, who are their points of contact with Japanese society, for advice or help with a range of daily problems that go beyond just Japanese language. The emphasis placed on each area differs from group to group, but it is certain that responding to consultations on life problems not only requires significant time, but can also be psychologically stressful.

With regard to the method of teaching Japanese, it is common for volunteers to begin with a form of 'professional complex,' believing that there must be a standardized teaching method using appropriate textbooks, and that they are not 'professionals' themselves. However, they eventually realize that teaching Japanese depends on the human relations between the learners and volunteer teachers, and that there is no 'panacea' teaching method. The reasons for this, first, are that the students end up studying for very few hours, such as an average of two hours a week, or 80 hours a year, and second that the students have completely different needs depending on whether they are workers, foreign brides, or returnees from China.

Turning our focus to organizational problems, conflicts occasionally emerge within the organizations regarding leadership. In particular, conflicts tend to emerge between autocratic-type leaders and those who value equality, or between people with a strong sense of mission and those who see it as a hobby. As a result, in many cases splits occur or new organizations are founded, and the number of networks ends up rising. Close cooperation with local government administrations is indispensable for the success of these networks. Receiving subsidies can strengthen the weak financial foundation that they typically possess, and access to public facilities can be a major benefit. In addition, through public relations materials issued by the local governments, the group's social significance can be recognized by general citizens.

Part Three
The Cultural Contribution of Migrants

7   Foreigners Will Change Japanese Society

Everyday culture and high culture

The 'old-comer' foreigners are already a part of Japanese society, but with the increasing rooting of 'newcomer' foreigners, the phrase 'society of multicultural coexistence' has come into ever more frequent use. The phrase sounds beautiful, but one cannot say that a general consensus has yet emerged on its precise meaning. If it simply means a society where people with different cultures live together without friction, there is no reason to use such a contrived term. In fact, it is believed that the phrase was coined using as a hint the term 'multiculturalism,' which is used in many Western countries. In those countries, multiculturalism is often justified by the idea of the 'mutual enrichment of cultures.' Even in this case, however, one cannot say that a concrete image necessarily exists of precisely what is meant by 'culture' and 'enrichment.' In this Chapter, I would like to examine, using survey data, the positive significance of a 'society of multicultural coexistence.'[1]

At the time of this writing, Japanese society has come to an impasse in many areas. One can point to silent group pressure in decision-making processes and the submission of the self to the group, as well as senses of superiority and inferiority that have no basis in reality. The accumulation of these traits has led to a centralized structure of authority which is totally controlled by state bureaucrats. This is at the root of the feeling of suffocation that permeates Japanese society today. In the following sections, I intend to show that foreign residents of Japan should be seen not simply as subjects of management and protection, but rather as precious catalysts with the potential to reform Japan's culture. This reform should be directed toward what can be called global culture, which transcends national culture as specified by the nation-state. The meaning of global culture is a culture on a global scale which can, to the greatest extent possible, allow varied cultures to co-exist, mutually interact with one another and develop together. It can also be seen as a single tapestry with elaborate and complex interwoven patterns.

Incidentally, in past debates on multiculturalism, there has been little consensus on the meaning of culture itself, and this seems to have caused unnecessary confusion. In this sense, I would like, in consideration partly of the tradition of anthropology, to divide the concept into 'everyday culture' and 'high culture.' Everyday culture refers to the way that people feel, think, and act in their everyday lives, whereas high culture refers to highly systematized symbolic modes of life, such as philosophy, art and religion.[2] Whereas high culture permeates everyday culture and sets its direction, everyday culture creates the foundation for high culture to exist and develop.

The reason for dividing culture into these two categories is that because high culture is formed on the premise that every culture is an absolute and accomplished system, the co-existence of different cultures is essentially impossible. Consequently, the question of whether or not to accept a certain form of high culture is ultimately a problem for an individual or group. Not only can society not become involved in its potential existence and in the choice, but it *must* not. By contrast, everyday culture is universal; it is shared by all humanity. Here there is a major difference between the two. In order to create high culture, everyday culture must above all have unrestricted freedom and be able to accept others and format dialogues with them. Thus, debates up until now have been inadequate in that they have discussed culture as a general concept, in spite of the fact that it is in actuality made up of these two strata.

Everyday culture can be generalized as values. The best-known theory of values is Parsons' pattern variables.[3] Because the five value variables are based on a modern European-type model, they can be labeled modernism theory-type values. At present, when the concept of modernism has lost its historical validity, we need a conception of global citizen-type values that meet the needs such as freedom, tolerance and dialogue, as listed above.

In determining such global citizen-type values, I received many hints from the Dutch sociologist G. Hofstede.[4] He prepared a questionnaire for employees of IBM in 50 countries and three multinational regions throughout the world, with questions on feelings, ways of thinking, and patterns of behavior. He performed factor analysis on the answers, and discovered four dimensions of culture. He called the first dimension power disparities; this concerns the degree to which members with little power accept inequalities of power. The second dimension expresses individualism versus collectivity. Collectivity here indicates, in behavior, whether the priority is put on the collective interests of the family or organization, or whether it is put on individual interests. The third dimension is termed masculinity versus femininity. Masculinity is represented by strong self-assertiveness and competitiveness, and femininity by humility and by paying attention to the quality of daily living. The fourth dimension involves the avoidance of uncertainty. In some cultures, uncertainty leads to a high level of anxiety, and dependence upon laws and regulations emerges as a way to cope with this.

However, the questions that became the bases for this classification were made on the premise of Western values; Hofstede himself conceded that there were doubts as to whether they had universal validity. Given this, he went on to analyze Confucian-type culture, and added a fifth dimension to his analysis, namely a long-term orientation (placing weight on the future) versus a short-term one (placing weight on the present or past). He claims that this actually is a question of whether virtue or truth is the fundamental standard, but his analysis is not very clear in this regard. As seen by the addition of this fifth dimension, his dimensions of culture are not definite categories, and there is still a need to improve and expand on them.

What must be kept in mind here is that Hofstede maintains a neutral position regarding the desirability of these values. For example, he does not speak on whether it is better for cultures to have strong power disparities or weak ones. However, looking from the point of view of global citizen-type values, these dimensions sometimes have universality, and at other times do not.

First, on the issue of power disparities, global citizens would surely assert that interventions based on power positions cause a loss of the freedom necessary to create culture. On the other hand, from the side of aristocratic conservatism, a powerful argument could be made that without aristocratic ranks, which carry with them the responsibility and ability to protect and develop culture, culture is bound to fall into vulgarity. On this issue, I would like to point out that since culture inevitably becomes manneristic, cultural reform has always come not from aristocratic conservatism but rather from people at the periphery. It is important, in order to create the basis for cultural creativity, for power disparities to be small. Hence, one can say that a culture with small power disparities is more desirable than one with large gaps.

With regard to individualism versus collectivism, an insurmountable boundary is established if individual autonomy, which should be respected, is subjugated to the group. This inhibits the openness to mutual stimulation which is essential for the creation of culture. (In the rest of this section, I will call this dimension individualism.) On the issue of masculinity versus femininity, it is clear, when considering war and ecological issues, that the importance of femininity is growing. And with respect to the avoidance of uncertainty, global citizens would likely find that excessive control through rules and regulations severely limits the acquisition of originality and inspiration. This thinking can be found in current Japanese thinking which concludes that regulations must be relaxed. Furthermore, with regard to long-term versus short-term orientations, the need for a long-term orientation based on virtue is growing.

According to Hofstede, Japan outranks other countries by far in terms of its degree of masculinity, and also ranks very high in the dimension of avoiding uncertainty. Following Hofstede's interpretations, these represent weak points of Japanese culture. If this interpretation is correct, then these flaws in Japanese culture could be rectified through contact and exchanges with other cultures where femininity is strong and the orientation of avoiding uncertainty weak. Conversely, if an ethnic group living in Japan has strong power disparities, for example, the weakening of this element under the influence of Japanese culture may expand the universality of that culture.

However, Hofstete's description on the two dimensions of masculinity versus femininity and long-term versus short-term

orientation, are ambiguous, and lack a clear conceptual pre-
scription. As a result, I did not use these dimensions in my survey.
Hofstete's discourse also fails to include dimensions of values that
relate to demands for acceptance and dialogue, which are global
citizen-type values. Therefore, I added them, labeling them
'tolerance' and 'trust.'

First, tolerance seems to be necessary to create the social
conditions in the public sphere to allow for the coexistence of
various forms of high culture, a coexistence which is in principle
impossible without conflict. These conditions actually mean
intolerance for the type of exclusivism expressed in forms such as
religious fundamentalism. This is because fundamentalism, in its
ultimate meaning, attempts to obliterate all principles other than
its own. Put in other words, tolerance for the existence of other
high cultures is the starting point for multicultural coexistence. It
approves of the existence of the 'rational contradiction' of
accepting in a rational manner the existence of other high cultures,
and of not trying to expel them.[5] In concrete terms, this means the
acceptance of otherness and of diversity. Trust, for its part, can be
defined as the strength of the expectation that social contracts that
have been made will be observed. In cases when tolerance and trust
are high, the conditions are ripe for acceptance and dialogue.

In this way, I came up tentatively with five dimensions for
global citizen-type values. I do not have a great deal of confidence
that they are fully adequate, but it was necessary to start some-
where. It is likely that their theoretical flaws will be gradually
corrected with time.

In terms of the specific method used for the survey, a
questionnaire was prepared with questions asking the respondents
how they assessed themselves, their home country, and Japan on
the five dimensions at three levels, namely the state and politics,
companies and the economy, and the family. They were asked to
rate each item on a five-point scale. On the question of trust, they
were not asked to rate themselves; this would be meaningless.
Consequently, the questionnaire was composed of a cover sheet
and 42 questions. In addition, of course, Japanese nationals were
not asked to assess their 'home country.'

Simplifying the contents of the questionnaire, the section on
power disparities for the state and politics asked respondents

whether the state should be governed by a small group of capable people or through the participation of many; for companies and the economy about their acceptance of the orders of superiors; and for the family whether they would need their parents' approval to marry. On individualism, for the state and politics they were asked about the properness of the state training individual Olympic athletes; for companies and the economy whether they would be willing to work overtime even if it meant breaking a family promise; and on the family whether they would be willing to go and care for a sick parent who lived faraway. On the avoidance of uncertainty, for the state and politics they were asked whether they would support an ambitious economic plan that might end in failure; at the company and economic level whether they would change jobs to do something they wanted to do, but which was risky; and at the family level whether they would force their child to go to college against the child's wishes. On the dimension of tolerance, for the state and politics they were asked whether they would agree to granting the same rights as nationals to foreigners who had lived in their country for five years or so; for companies and the economy whether it would be acceptable that more than half of the managers of their company be foreigners; and for the family whether they would allow their daughter to have premarital sex. Finally, on the dimension of trust, at the state and politics level they were asked if it was likely an escaped heinous criminal would be captured; for the company and economy whether it was likely that a promise a bankrupt company had made to find new jobs for its workers would be met; and at the family level about the probability that money lent to a close friend would be returned.

The subjects of the survey were ten ethnic groups, made up of the largest newcomer groups in Japan, i.e. Chinese, Brazilians, South Koreans, Filipinos, South Asian Muslims (Bangladeshis and Pakistanis), Thais, Peruvians, and Americans, in descending order, plus Vietnamese and Japanese. It was carried out from November 1997 to January 1998, and was principally done through questionnaires printed in the native languages, distributed at places throughout Japan where members of the different ethnic groups tended to congregate. There were gaps in the numbers of valid responses recovered from each group, ranging from 30 in the case of Thais to 94 for South Koreans.[6]

Data on alien registrations was not available for public viewing, and there is of course no official data on irregular foreigners, so no sampling was done. For Japanese, the respondents were selected among acquaintances of students at Tsukuba University.

Japan: not an easy place to live for foreigners

In the following sections, I will analyze the data obtained in the survey, but should begin by mentioning that they are expressed as averages for the different ethnic groups. These averages, for which 5 would indicate perfect global citizen-type values, and 1 a state very far from such values, were obtained by dividing the total number for each group by the number of respondents. Thus, figures above 3 are in theory close to global citizen-type values. The average for foreigners as a whole was obtained by averaging the figures for the different ethnic groups, and hence the numbers of respondents was abstracted. The figures are all shown in Table 7.1. I will examine the data on the dimension of trust separately from the four others.

First, looking at the aggregates for all foreigners on the different dimensions, the scores given to themselves were, in descending order, power disparities (3.4), tolerance (3.3), avoidance of uncertainty (2.9), and individualism (2.3), showing that their values in the areas of power gaps and tolerance were fairly close to global citizen levels, but that those for the avoidance of uncertainty were intermediate, and they tended to have values close to collectivity. Next, looking at the aggregate scores for how foreigners saw Japanese society on each dimension, the order was power gaps (3.1), tolerance (3.0), avoidance of uncertainty (2.6), and individualism (2.2), giving the impression that they did not think that levels of global citizenship were being reached. Comparing the appraisals the respondents gave to themselves with those they gave to Japanese society, the scores for themselves were 0.3 higher for power gaps, 0.3 for tolerance, 0.3 for the avoidance of uncertainty, and 0.1 for individuality, revealing that values in Japan lag behind those of foreigners in Japan.

Incidentally, foreigners gave the following appraisals to their home countries: power disparities (3.2), tolerance (3.0), avoidance of uncertainty (2.8), and individualism (2.4). In all the dimensions

Table 7.1 Value Consciousness of Foreigners in Japan (average value)

(1) The scores are 1.0 to 5.0 points.
(2) The higher the score, the higher the orientation toward global citizenship.

	State/politics			Company/economy			Family			Total		
	Self	Home country	Japan	Self	Home country	Japan	Self	Home country	Japan	Self	Home country	Japan
Disparities in Power Relations												
United States	4.1	4.0	2.9	3.3	3.4	2.2	3.7	4.0	2.3	3.7	3.8	2.5
Vietnam	3.7	3.1	3.6	3.0	3.6	2.9	3.3	2.8	3.6	3.3	3.2	3.4
Philippines	3.1	3.4	2.9	3.1	2.9	2.7	3.6	3.4	3.1	3.3	3.2	2.9
Brazil	3.3	3.1	3.3	3.0	3.3	2.7	3.7	3.8	3.4	3.3	3.4	3.1
Peru	4.1	3.5	3.4	2.7	3.1	2.5	3.6	3.7	3.1	3.5	3.4	3.0
Islamic countries	3.5	3.5	3.5	2.7	3.0	2.8	2.6	2.3	3.6	2.9	2.9	3.3
South Korea	3.8	3.1	2.7	3.8	3.5	2.6	3.2	2.9	3.7	3.6	3.1	3.0
China	3.9	3.3	3.6	3.7	3.6	2.9	2.7	2.5	3.6	3.4	3.1	3.4
Thailand	3.3	3.3	3.0	2.9	2.8	2.9	3.3	2.9	3.3	3.2	3.0	3.1
Simple average	3.7	3.4	3.2	3.1	3.2	2.7	3.3	3.1	3.3	3.4	3.2	3.1
Japan	3.6		3.3	4.2		2.7	3.7		3.3	3.8		3.1
Individualism												
United States	2.7	2.6	2.5	3.0	2.4	2.2	2.2	3.4	2.0	2.6	2.8	2.2
Vietnam	2.6	2.8	2.7	3.1	3.2	1.9	2.0	2.5	2.7	2.5	2.8	2.4
Philippines	2.1	2.3	1.7	2.7	3.3	1.9	2.8	2.1	3.8	2.5	2.6	2.4
Brazil	2.2	2.3	2.2	3.3	3.1	2.1	1.5	1.7	1.8	2.3	2.4	2.0
Peru	1.5	2.5	1.5	2.9	3.4	1.8	1.9	1.8	3.4	2.1	2.5	2.2
Islamic countries	1.7	1.9	1.8	2.4	3.1	2.1	2.9	2.1	3.0	2.3	2.4	2.3
South Korea	2.0	2.0	2.1	2.7	2.2	1.7	1.9	2.0	3.3	2.2	2.1	2.4
China	2.1	2.1	2.1	1.7	1.8	1.7	2.0	1.9	3.1	1.9	1.9	2.3
Thailand	1.5	1.6	1.9	1.9	2.3	1.3	1.9	1.7	2.5	1.8	1.9	1.9
Simple average	2.0	2.2	2.0	2.6	2.8	1.9	2.1	2.1	2.8	2.3	2.4	2.2
Japan	3.1		2.7	2.8		1.7	2.3		2.6	2.7		2.3
Avoidance of Uncertainty												
United States	2.8	3.0	2.5	3.1	3.1	2.4	3.3	3.2	2.0	3.1	3.1	2.3
Vietnam	3.0	2.6	2.1	2.7	3.0	2.7	3.4	2.9	2.7	3.0	2.8	2.5
Philippines	3.0	2.9	2.7	3.1	3.0	2.6	3.1	3.1	2.4	3.1	3.0	2.6
Brazil	2.9	3.1	3.0	1.8	2.0	1.7	2.7	2.7	2.2	2.5	2.6	2.3
Peru	2.0	2.4	2.4	2.3	2.7	2.5	3.4	3.1	3.0	2.6	2.7	2.6
Islamic countries	2.5	3.1	2.8	2.5	2.7	2.4	3.2	2.7	3.6	2.7	2.8	2.9
South Korea	2.3	2.5	2.2	3.3	2.8	2.1	3.5	1.8	2.7	3.0	2.4	2.3
China	3.5	3.2	2.9	3.7	3.3	2.9	3.4	2.7	3.0	3.5	3.1	2.9
Thailand	2.4	2.1	2.3	2.4	2.1	2.2	3.4	2.8	3.0	2.7	2.3	2.5
Simple average	2.7	2.8	2.5	2.8	2.7	2.4	3.3	2.8	2.7	2.9	2.8	2.6
Japan	2.4		2.3	3.2		2.2	3.6		2.4	3.1		2.3

Table 7.1 Value Consciousness of Foreigners in Japan (average value)...continued

	State/politics			Company/economy			Family			Total		
	Self	Home country	Japan	Self	Home country	Japan	Self	Home country	Japan	Self	Home country	Japan
Tolerance												
United States	3.5	3.6	2.5	3.4	3.1	2.6	2.1	3.6	3.0	3.0	3.4	2.7
Vietnam	3.9	3.6	3.0	3.2	3.0	2.7	2.5	2.2	3.4	3.2	2.9	3.0
Philippines	3.7	3.4	2.2	3.2	3.0	3.0	2.5	2.2	3.8	3.1	2.9	3.0
Brazil	4.2	4.1	3.8	3.9	3.7	3.2	3.5	3.6	3.4	3.9	3.8	3.5
Peru	4.2	4.4	2.7	3.3	3.0	2.0	3.0	2.5	3.8	3.5	3.3	2.8
Islamic countries	3.9	3.7	2.4	3.3	3.0	2.9	2.1	1.7	3.0	3.1	2.8	2.8
South Korea	4.0	2.8	2.3	3.0	2.2	1.8	2.5	2.1	4.5	3.2	2.4	2.9
China	4.6	4.2	3.7	3.2	3.0	3.1	2.4	2.2	3.5	3.4	3.1	3.4
Thailand	3.4	3.3	3.4	2.8	2.8	1.6	2.6	2.1	3.8	2.9	2.7	2.9
Simple average	3.9	3.7	2.9	3.3	3.0	2.5	2.6	2.5	3.6	3.3	3.0	3.0
Japan	3.6		2.5	3.3		1.8	3.9		3.8	3.6		2.7

	State/politics		Company/economy		Family		Total	
	Home country	Japan	Home country	Japan	Home country	Japan	Home country	Japan
Trust								
United States	3.9	3.8	2.9	3.7	3.6	3.8	3.5	3.8
Vietnam	3.5	4.1	2.9	3.5	3.4	3.4	3.3	3.7
Philippines	3.9	4.3	2.9	3.6	3.3	3.4	3.4	3.8
Brazil	3.8	3.8	3.0	4.0	3.2	3.3	3.3	3.7
Peru	3.7	4.7	2.3	3.8	3.3	4.2	3.1	4.2
Islamic countries	4.2	4.5	3.8	4.3	4.0	3.8	4.0	4.2
South Korea	4.0	4.1	3.1	3.4	3.9	3.7	3.7	3.7
China	4.4	4.4	3.5	3.5	4.2	3.8	4.0	3.9
Thailand	4.3	4.8	2.8	3.8	3.1	3.3	3.4	4.0
Simple average	4.0	4.3	3.0	3.7	3.6	3.6	3.5	3.9
Japan		4.0		3.0		3.1		3.4

but tolerance, they gave slightly higher scores to their own countries than to Japan. This shows that foreigners in Japan rate their home countries as slightly closer to global citizen values than Japan.

One of the main factors behind this negative assessment can be found in the realities of Japan's companies and economy, and in its state and politics. Comparing the appraisals respondents gave to themselves and to Japan at the level of companies and economy, they gave themselves higher scores, with the following gaps: tolerance (0.8), individualism (0.7), power disparities (0.4) and avoidance of uncertainty (0.4). This creates the impression that Japan's companies and economy are intolerant, have strong collective pressure, and are quite authoritarian, with strict rules. Comparing the respondents' appraisals of themselves with those of Japan with respect to the state and politics, the gaps were tolerance (1.0), power disparities (0.5), avoidance of uncertainty (0.2), and individualism (0.0). This reflects the fact that foreigners see the Japanese state and politics as overwhelmingly intolerant and authoritarian.

On the dimension of tolerance, where the gaps between self-appraisals and appraisals of Japan's companies and economy were the highest, I would like to take a closer look at the answers separately by ethnic group. Ethnic groups where the gap was over 0.7 were Peruvians (1.3), South Koreans (1.2), Thais (1.2) Americans (0.8), and Brazilians (0.7). Thus, Peruvians had the strongest feelings about the intolerance of Japan's companies and economy, followed by South Koreans and Thais. This likely reflects the fact that the ratio of irregular foreigners is high among Peruvians, that Koreans also include a large number of irregular workers, and that many Thais work in the sex and entertainment industry. They all face negative workplace environments.

Next, let us look at gaps between self-appraisals and appraisals of Japan's companies and economy in the dimension of individualism, which were second largest after tolerance. The ethnic groups for which the gaps were at least 0.8 were Vietnamese (2.2), Brazilians (1.2), Peruvians (1.1), South Koreans (1.0), Americans (0.8) and Filipinos (0.8). In other words, there is strong resistance to collectivist pressure (which is said to be a special feature of Japanese-style management) among people from the Asian countries of Vietnam and South Korea, Latin American, and the United States, as well as Filipinos, who were influenced by the U.S.

The gaps between self-assessments and assessments of Japanese state and politics were highest in the dimension of tolerance. Ethnic groups for which the gap was at least 0.9 were South Koreans (1.7), Filipinos, Peruvians and Muslims (1.5), Americans (1.0), and Vietnamese and Chinese (0.9). Thus, South Koreans to the greatest extent, but also Filipinos, Peruvians and Muslims, felt that Japanese state and politics were very intolerant. Irregular foreigners make up significant portions of each of these groups, and the responses are likely a reflection of this.

Good points of Japanese society

The data introduced in the previous section shows that foreigners who have either chosen or found themselves forced to live in Japan have a strong consciousness that Japanese society is a very difficult place to live. However, in the dimensions of trust and views of the family, they assessed Japan as closer to the values of global citizens than their own self-assessments or the situations in their home countries. It appears that both of these are factors which lead foreigners to make the decision to settle in Japan.

First, looking at the dimension of trust, the overall assessment of Japan by foreigners was a surprising 3.9; Japanese respondents also gave their own country a rating of 3.4. On the three other dimensions, with the exception of tolerance, foreign respondents gave slightly higher ratings to their own countries than to Japan, but with regard to trust they only rated their own countries at 3.5, an assessment 0.4 lower than that of Japan. Ethnic groups for which the evaluation of Japan was at least 0.4 higher than that of their home country were Peruvians (1.1), Thais (0.6), and Vietnamese, Filipinos, and Brazilians (0.4). All of these are groups for which, in some way or another, there is instability in their home countries.

Next, the gaps between the rating of trust given by foreigners to Japan and to their home countries were 0.7 for companies and economy, 0.3 for the state and politics, and 0.0 for the family. Thus, trust seemed particularly strong in Japan's corporate and economic world, followed by its state and politics. Ethnic groups who gave more than a 0.5 gap in their assessments of companies and economy to Japan over their home countries were Peruvians (1.5), Brazilians and Thais (1.0), Americans (0.8), Filipinos (0.7), and Muslims (0.5). It is notable that all are non-Asian countries, with the exception of the Philippines, which has been heavily influenced by the United States, and Thailand.

Next, looking at assessments of Japanese families, the differences in assessment given by foreign respondents to Japanese families and their own families were, in descending order, tolerance (1.0), individualism (0.7), avoidance of uncertainty (0.6), and power disparities (0.0). In other words, Japanese families were perceived by foreigners as having a high degree of tolerance, to be individualistic, and to have great freedom. In the same way, the gaps between foreigners' assessments of Japanese families and families in their home countries in the four dimensions were: tolerance (1.1), individualism (0.7), power disparities (0.2), and avoidance of uncertainty (-0.1). Thus, they saw Japanese families as more tolerant and individualistic than those in their home countries. On the issue of avoidance of uncertainty, however, they found the tendency to be slightly higher among families in their home countries.

Looking at the differences between ethnic groups in the dimension of tolerance, where the gaps were highest, in terms of the value given to Japanese families compared to their own families, the order was South Koreans (2.0), Filipinos (1.3), Thais (1.2)…and Brazilians (-0.1). Of all the groups, only Brazilians (by a small margin) found Japanese families to be intolerant; the others tended to see them as significantly tolerant. It seems that South Korean families are led to intolerance by Confucianism, Filipino families by Catholicism, and Thai families by Theravada Buddhism. By contrast, the values of Brazilians were by far the most tolerant.

In the same way, looking at the assessments given to Japanese families on the dimension of tolerance compared to families in their home countries, the gaps were, in descending order, South Koreans (2.4), Thais (1.7), Filipinos (1.6)…Brazilians (-0.2), and Americans (-0.6). The tendencies for the South Koreans, Thais, Filipinos and Brazilians were the same as for the families of the respondents themselves, but it is interesting to note that Americans found Japanese families to be extremely intolerant in this regard. From this one can see that there is a notable gap between the intolerance in their own values and the general tolerance of the family system in their own country.

In summary, foreigners generally perceive Japanese society as one with little tolerance but with a great degree of trust. In addition, their assessments of Japanese companies and economy, as well as state and politics, are quite low, whereas those of families are high. This may be one factor behind the recent increase in the number of marriages between Japanese and non-Japanese.

How can Japanese society be opened?

We have looked at the value consciousness of foreigners living in Japan, and now I would like to examine the values of Japanese people themselves and their perceptions of the state of their own society. First, when looking at the values of the Japanese respondents on the different dimensions, they gave themselves the following ratings, in descending order: power disparities (3.8), tolerance (3.6), avoidance of uncertainty (3.1), and individuality (2.7). They showed a medium value on the avoidance of uncertainty, and demonstrated a tendency toward collectivism, but their perceptions of themselves in terms of power disparities and tolerance were close to those of global citizenship. Incidentally, comparing the self-assessments given by the Japanese respondents to those of foreigners cited earlier, those of the foreigners were consistently lower than those of the Japanese respondents, with the gaps being 0.4 for power disparities, 0.4 for individuality, 0.3 for tolerance, and 0.2 for the avoidance of uncertainty. Thus, looking at foreigners as a whole, it seems that the emphasis on relations of superior-inferior and collectivism are stronger than for Japanese.

Whereas the self-assessments given by the Japanese tended toward the values of global citizenship, the assessments they gave to their own country showed the opposite. They were power disparities (3.1), tolerance (2.7), and avoidance of uncertainty and individuality (2.3). Thus, the gaps between the assessments the Japanese respondents gave to themselves and those they gave to Japan were tolerance (0.9), avoidance of uncertainty (0.8), power disparities (0.7), and individuality (0.4). In other words, on all the dimensions, social systems seem to lag behind individual values. From this one can glimpse a part of the suffocation that Japanese suffer from at the end of the 20th century.

The gaps were particularly large with regard to companies and economy, with power disparities (1.5), tolerance (1.5), individualism (1.1), and avoidance of uncertainty (1.0). In other words, individual Japanese feel strong antipathy toward the hierarchical relationships and conformity of workplaces, and feel significant resistance toward coercive collectivism and regulations. The same tendency can be seen at the level of the state and politics, though not as strongly, with the gaps being as follows: tolerance (1.1), individualism (0.4), power disparities (0.3), and avoidance of uncertainty (0.1). Furthermore, the assessment given to Japan by foreigners was only higher than that given by Japanese in the cases of tolerance and avoidance of uncertainty (0.3 each), but in the areas of individualism (0.1) and power disparities (0.0) were at practically the same level.

Since we have examined the views of foreigners as a whole, in the following section I would like to analyze the specific values of different ethnic groups. The nine ethnic groups included in the surveys could generally be divided into five categories. The Chinese respondents and the Americans and South Koreans showed assessments that were closest to the values of global citizenship, followed by Filipinos and Vietnamese, then Latin Americans, with the category of Muslims and Thais being furthest from the global citizenship values.

Looking at the Chinese pattern first, their scores on all categories except for individualism (1.9) were very close to those of global citizenship, with 3.5 for the avoidance of uncertainty, and 3.4 for power disparities and tolerance. It is particularly noteworthy that on the dimension of avoidance of uncertainty, they scored first among all ten ethnic groups, including Japanese.

Next, looking at the category of Americans and South Koreans, for Americans the scores were power disparities (3.7), avoidance of uncertainty (3.1), tolerance (3.0), and individualism (2.6). In the dimension of power disparities they scored higher than all other ethnic groups other than the Japanese, showing a strong tendency toward equality in social relations. For the South Koreans, the scores were power disparities (3.6), tolerance (3.2), avoidance of uncertainty (3.0), and individualism (2.2), showing a similar pattern to the Americans, with the score on power disparities being second, following the Americans. This group can be characterized as leaning toward the values of global citizenship in all dimensions but individualism, with the scores on power discrepancies being particularly high.

Turning to the category of Filipinos and Vietnamese, the Filipinos scored as follows: power disparities (3.3), tolerance and avoidance of uncertainty (3.1), and individualism (2.5), showing a general trend toward global citizenship. Vietnamese showed a very similar pattern, with power disparities (3.3), tolerance (3.2), avoidance of uncertainty (3.0), and individualism (2.5). They represent an average type.

Looking at Brazilians, who constituted one of the Latin American groups, their tolerance was the highest among all ethnic groups, including Japanese, with 3.9, followed by power disparities (3.3), avoidance of uncertainty (2.5), and individualism (2.3). They showed very strong tolerance and a score for power disparities quite close to that of global citizenship, but scored low on the avoidance of uncertainty and individualism. For Peruvians, the scores were tolerance and power disparities (3.5), avoidance of uncertainty (2.6), and individualism (2.1), showing a similar pattern to Brazilians, though the tolerance was not quite as high.

Finally, looking at South Asian Muslims and Thais, the values for the Muslims were tolerance (3.1), power disparities (2.9), avoidance of uncertainty (2.7), and individualism (2.3), with all the values with the exception of tolerance being quite far from those of global citizenship. For Thais, all the values but power disparities were under 3, with power disparities (3.2), tolerance (2.9), avoidance of uncertainty (2.7), and individualism (1.8). In particular, they had the lowest score on individuality among the ten ethnic groups, including Japanese, demonstrating a strong trend toward collectivism.

In this way, among the five categories of ethnic groups, we find that the Chinese had much weaker tendencies to avoid uncertainty than the Japanese, and that the Latin Americans had much higher tolerance than the Japanese. One cannot overlook the category of Americans and South Koreans, also, who had high scores in the dimension of power disparities, though they were lower than the Japanese.

Looking at this and the previous sections, it is clear that foreigners and Japanese alike are victims of Japanese society's companies and economy, and state and politics, which have become inflexible and are showing signs of institutional fatigue. As stated earlier, comparing the values of foreigners and Japanese, one finds in general that those of the Japanese are closer to what I have termed global citizenship. However, I would like to grasp these specific characteristics of the different ethnic groups as potential stimuli for reforming the closed-mindedness of Japanese people and the rigid systems of Japanese society. As I stated in Chapter 6, in the Mogami Region several hundred Filipinas and Korean women came to be the brides of Japanese farmers who could not find Japanese wives, and have loved their husbands, given birth to children, and become rooted in the communities. As a result, the traditional autocratic family system has been shaken, and the region has been transformed into one of the few in Japan with a consciousness that is open to the outside. This precisely typifies the expectations that Japanese society should have of foreign migrants, rather than simply seeing them as workers.

8 A Proposal for a Phasing-in of Civil Rights

Foreign migrants within Japanese society

On the whole, it seems that Japanese society has been successful in accepting foreign migrants with relatively few problems. Marriages between Japanese and non-Japanese have increased regardless of ethnic group, religious facilities have begun to take root in local communities, and there have been very few organized movements aiming to expel foreigners. There are, of course, problems. Irregular foreigners are in a situation where they have practically no rights, incredible human rights violations are perpetrated by immigration authorities, and foreign crime is exaggerated by the police. In addition, it cannot be said that the Japanese have no prejudice or discrimination toward non-Western foreigners. Such attitudes have been strengthened, in recent years, by media reports giving excessive coverage to foreign crime and incidents of smuggling. Discrimination appears in its most typical form in housing; in a situation where many landlords and real estate agents maintain a principle of 'no foreigners allowed,' it is difficult for foreign residents to find places to live. Furthermore, as we saw in Chapter 6, troubles have occurred, albeit a limited scale, between foreign and Japanese residents.

And yet, there are reasons not to be overly optimistic about Japan's future as an immigrant society. As we saw in Chapter 3, we have begun to witness the emergence of a dual labor structure, and it is likely that as this structure further develops, a variety of problems will arise. At the present, most foreign workers are employed in small and tiny enterprises that young Japanese workers tend to avoid, and as a result there is little competition between them and their Japanese counterparts. If the recession deepens and joblessness rises to much higher levels than today, one can reasonably assume that opposition will arise against both Nikkeijin workers and foreign workers in general. It is certain, though, that we have not yet seen any major social tension yet. What were the factors that made this historical development of Japanese society possible?

First, the unfortunate historical experience between Japanese and people from the Korean peninsula, as old-comer foreigners, provided Japanese society with valuable lessons. The opposition by this group against unfair structural discrimination did, though not necessarily adequately, mitigate discrimination against foreigners within Japanese society, and it is clear that this improvement applied to the situation of newcomer foreigners as well.

Second, the number of migrants in Japan is generally low. Foreigners make up just 1.4% or so of the total population, and one third of these people are old-comer foreigners who are already firmly rooted in Japanese society.

Third, the housing pattern in Japan is generally a mixed one, with practically no class-based segregation. This has helped prevent the formation of ghetto districts where certain ethnic groups are concentrated.

Fourth, I would like to emphasize that although the policies of the central government need to be subjected to heavy criticism, the great efforts made at the local government level have had some effects. Among progressive local governments, some hold meetings with foreigners to hear their views, issue signs and public relations bulletins in major foreign languages, offer various administrative services such as acquiring foreign-language books for their libraries, and work to encourage exchanges between foreign and Japanese residents. Since alien registration forms the basis for the provision of administrative services, a considerable number of local governments are now giving registration to irregular foreigners.

Fifth, we cannot overlook the major contribution that NGOs have made. The activities of support groups and Japanese-language instruction volunteers were mentioned in Chapter 6.

It seems clear that respect for this historical heritage will be the key to Japan's future immigration policies.

Thoughts on the new opening policy

In recent years, because of the labor surplus brought about by the collapse of the bubble economy, the controversy over the introduction of foreign workers has virtually disappeared. However, it is clear that because of the low fertility rate, Japan's population will decrease sharply in the future. In response to this, former Economic Planning Agency Director Sakaiya Taichi and the late Chief Cabinet Secretary Kajiyama Seiroku, proposed that consideration be given to bringing in migrants from abroad. In 1999, the Economic Council, an advisory council to the prime minister, added this issue to the agenda of its deliberations.[1] It was not so long ago, in the late 1980s, when in the midst of chronic labor shortages this problem became a major debate, in the form of closed nation versus open nation policies.[2] Thus, it seems valid to call the proposal by Sakaiya and Kajiyama a 'new opening policy.'

In February 2000, the Ministry of Justice formulated its second basic immigration control plan, the first in eight years. In the 1989 revision of the Immigration Control Law, the Ministry of Justice was charged with formulating a framework to ensure the fair implementation of immigration control. The second basic plan meets this requirement. Comparing the new plan with the first, which was formulated in 1992, it can be positively appraised for fundamentally switching to a line of opening the country to foreigners.

The second plan is notable for calling for the following: (1) the smooth acceptance of the foreign labor needed by Japan; (2) the promotion and enhancement of the training and internship programs; (3) smooth settlement for foreigners residing in Japan for long periods of time; (4) realistic and effective policies toward irregular workers; and (5) the appropriate application of the system for refugee recognition.

The stipulation of the first plan was that foreign workers would only be accepted if they had professional skills, and a line was drawn between such individuals and 'so-called unskilled laborers,' to whom very cautious consideration was supposed to be given. At that time, as well, the internship system was still in the planning stage. The first plan also failed to mention the issue of foreigners staying for long periods of time. With regard to overstayers, it merely stated that they should be expelled, and only mentioned the issue of refugee recognition in the context of making sure that 'fake refugees' did not take advantage of the system.

The concrete thinking behind the second plan can be seen in the supplementary explanation given by the Director of the Immigration Bureau.[3]

In this article, he called for setting up residency statuses to smoothen exchanges of international business people and technicians, and particularly for the positive acceptance of professionals and technicians in the IT and other industrial sectors, as well as the setting of statuses to allow the meeting of some needs that could be expected to arise in terms of labor power. Nursing care labor was cited as an area where consensus still must be reached in order to cope with the coming of an aging society with few children. On the issue of internship programs, he called for a quick response to demands for expansion into areas such as agriculture, marine processing, and hoteliery. Incidentally, in March 2000, internships were approved in two types of occupation, each within agriculture and marine product processing.

With regard to irregular workers, who along with Nikkei Latin Americans make up one of the major portions of foreign workers in Japan, the second plan is identical to the first in calling for strengthened activities to apprehend them, but differs with regard to individuals who are considered to have strong links to Japan through, for example, ties with Japanese, permanent foreign residents, or special permanent residents. For these individuals, it calls from a humanitarian viewpoint for special consideration, such as the granting by the Justice Minister of special residency permits.

This change is believed to have been reflected in the fact that nearly all overstayers with Japanese spouses are now granted special residency permits, and that out of a group of 21 overstayers who turned themselves in and applied for special permits in September 1999, 16 who had children in junior high school or above (including children who were scheduled to enter junior high school) were given permits in February 2000.

On the issue of refugees, the plan states that a stable status should be granted to people who really need protection as refugees as soon as possible, and is thus a step forward from the first plan.

In this way, in the second plan the direction has changed to trying to accept into Japanese society the foreign labor that this society needs, regardless of whether this labor is 'unskilled' or not.

We can gain insights on the effect of introducing foreign migrants to deal with population decreases in advanced countries from a report published by the ILO in 1994. The report stated that not only would Canada and Spain need to import 700,000 workers per year to make up for their shortages, but when these original groups began to age it would be necessary to bring in new workers to replace them. Needless to say, such large-scale introductions of foreign labor are unrealistic. Consequently, the ILO concluded that 'The only long-term solution to the problem of decreasing populations in the advanced countries is to promote (domestic) births.'[4]

The influx and settlement of newcomer foreigners into Japanese society, though slightly delayed compared to Europe and the United States, had already begun in the 1970s, and thus has a history of more than two decades. In the following paragraphs, I would like to examine the history of newcomer foreigners, and to consider the policy implications of the new country opening policy as a partial measure to overcome the problem of shrinking populations.

Judging from the historical record, what kinds of socioeconomic effects would arise if a new country opening policy were to be even partially adopted? As we saw in Chapter 1, the number of migrants with high professional expertise or technical skills is relatively low, and it is unlikely that these individuals will have any strong impact on Japanese society. With regard to refugees, an issue on which heated debates have occurred in Europe and the United States following their acceptance, Japan has been taking an ultra-conservative stance, and it is unlikely that this will change in the future. Consequently, it seems that the debate in Japan will focus mainly on so-called 'foreign workers,' meaning people employed in unskilled jobs and in service industries.

The source for this labor will most probably continue to come from neighboring Asian countries, where migrant networks have already been formed, but will also come from Islamic and African countries, where population explosions are taking place, as well as from countries in Latin America. What this means is that the social and cultural differences with Japanese people will grow in comparison to the time when most foreign workers were from neighboring countries or were Nikkeijin Brazilians.

A second, and crucial problem will be how to integrate these foreign workers into Japanese society. Up until today, the labor market for foreign workers has been generally characterized by employment in medium-, small- and tiny-sized firms. The reason for this is that because of the poor working conditions, such firms faced chronic labor shortages in both good and bad economic times. These features will likely endure even if the 'new country opening' policy is adopted, for the simple reason that it is the fundamental structure of Japanese capitalism. Given this, it seems that, as in the present, the foreign workers who are accepted into Japan will be confronted from the start by difficult situations, such as unstable employment and low wages. As a result, it can naturally be expected that social tensions, which have already appeared to some extent, will deepen further.

In response to the debate between those who wanted to close the country to foreign workers and those who espoused an open policy, I have advocated a policy of 'inevitability.' This policy opposes the open country policy, since unskilled workers will invariably be marginalized; however, because movements of people across border are 'inevitable,' it also opposes the closed country policy which attempts to expel foreigners. Instead, it calls instead for respect for the human rights of foreigners who are living within Japanese society.[5] The validity of this policy of 'inevitability' is still clear against the claims of the proponents of the 'new country opening' policy.

The foreign population in Japan will probably continue to increase in the future. However, this increase will not be a fundamental solution to the problem of the low birth rate and the aging of society. Rather, the urgent issue is whether and how to transform our society of few children into one where children can be raised. In this sense, the current population decrease reflects a pathology within Japanese society. What we should aim for is to maintain a stable population level.

A proposal for the phasing-in of civil rights

Previously I have proposed the four following principles for measures toward foreign migrants: (1) respect for their human rights; (2) achieving equality between foreign and Japanese residents; (3) establishing multiculturalism; and (4) taking appropriate international measures.[6] As a concrete way to implement these principles, I would like to propose the idea of a 'phasing-in of civil rights.' This idea is meant to deal with a large-scale influx of 'foreigners coming to settle in Japan,' a group distinct from Japanese nationals as well as from the old-comer Koreans and Chinese.

When considering this 'phasing-in of civil rights,' the first issue to clarify is the separation of nationality and civil rights. In the past, it is fair to say, the only means under the Japanese state's legal system for foreigners to win the same protection of human rights and equality afforded to Japanese nationals was to gain Japanese nationality. However, forcing people to renounce citizenship in their country of origin in order to win Japanese nationality meant that they have to sever both subjective and objective ties with their motherland. This contains unacceptable problems both from the perspective of human rights and of multiculturalism. Needless to say, many old-comer foreigners have deep-seated resistance to the acquisition of Japanese nationality.

The concept of civil rights is based on respect for universal human rights. This means that all individuals who live in a certain community and form part of that community must be assured of a variety of rights, including the right to participate in decision-making. Civil rights in this sense are an extension of the rights of residents guaranteed under the Local Autonomy Law, and represent a questioning of the 'national,' the subject who enjoys self-evident rights. The national is a concept artificially formed based on the fictional concept of race; in a sense it forms the basis for discrimination by the nation-state, which sees its own nationals as absolute, and rejects others.

Looking on an international scale, there is increasing momentum for settled foreigners to be given equal rights to nationals, in terms of civil liberties (freedom of personal liberty, freedoms of expression, thought, and belief, property rights, and right to sue), social rights (the rights to work, receive education, and other social services), and political rights (voting rights and the right to be elected). In the background of this, apart from the fact that the concept of the modern nation-state has a history of only 200 years or so, is the settlement of migrants in various parts of the world that has accompanied the unprecedented movements of people, and the fact that these people have come to make up a significant part of the population of particular countries. Few of these foreigners have acquired nationality in their new homes in spite of the fact that they have moved the basis of their livelihoods to the new place, and are working, paying taxes, and living a family life in these new locations.

These settled foreigners are not temporary visitors but rather members of the societies into which they have moved, and they require a special name. In the place of 'citizens,' the term 'denizens' has increasingly come into use to describe them. The term was originally used to mean 'foreigners who were given special status by the British throne as English subjects,' and was resurrected by T. Hammer, a Swedish scholar specializing on the issue of migration.[7]

Korean residents in Japan, who are rooted in Japanese society, very precisely fit the definition of denizens. Not only were these people suddenly deprived of the Japanese nationality that they once held, but as a result of the lengths of their stays, many are actually descendents of original settlers. Generally speaking, the guarantee of rights to these resident Korean denizens has lagged behind those offered by the advanced nations of Europe.

The British legal system can be of reference on this point. Under the revised Nationality Act of 1951, when subjects of Common-wealth countries, which were once English colonies, moved to the United Kingdom, they were granted a wide range of civil rights as British citizens, including the right to vote and to stand for election, while being allowed to retain their original nationalities. Citizens of Ireland, who are not members of the Commonwealth, are granted similar rights due to their historical position. The Netherlands also accords civil rights to members of its former colonies. Scandinavian countries have granted civil rights to members of other countries in the region, and now have expanded these rights to people with origins in Italy, Asia, and Africa.[8]

However, the clear difference between the concept of 'phased-in civil rights' and that of denizens is that the latter only applies to legal foreigners, and furthermore to those with permanent residence. By contrast, the concept of 'phased-in civil rights' covers even irregular foreigners, and proposes to provide civil rights flexibly in proportion to the degree of settlement. The separation of nationality and citizenship is actually more valid for foreigners who do not wish to settle. The reason for this is that it seems likely that these individuals have a stronger resistance toward the acquisition of Japanese nationality than do settled foreigners.

I would now like to propose phases for granting civil rights, separated from the issue of nationality, in accordance with the degree of settlement in Japan. It should begin with the granting of the right to life, followed by social rights and general civil liberties, and then by political rights at a later stage. Here, the separation between social rights and civil liberties follows the structure of the International Covenant on Human Rights, where social rights, including economic, social, and cultural rights, are contrasted with civil liberties, which include civil and political rights.

The right to life literally means the right to the minimum conditions for a person to live as a human being within Japanese society; it signifies the most basic of social rights. The right to the guarantee of livelihood, medical care, and minimum housing all fit within this concept. In Japan today, irregular foreigners are deprived even of the right to medical protection, and at times the lack of emergency medical care can place them in mortal danger. There is also terrible housing discrimination against foreigners, and many are forced to live in barely livable conditions.

On the issue of social rights, we can use as reference the United Nations' Convention on the Rights of Migrant Workers. It cites a number of rights which, as social rights, should be guaranteed to foreigners on the same basis as nationals. In addition to access to social security and labor protection, it includes the rights of following generations of foreigners and the right to develop one's own culture. The rights for future generations include that of the children of foreign workers to be registered, to choose a nationality, and to receive an education. The right to develop one's own culture includes respect for cultural uniqueness, including ethnic education, and emphasizes the continuation of cultural unity with the home country.

In terms of civil liberties, the International Human Rights Convention (B) includes, in addition to the right of body, movement, housing, emigration, belief, conscience, religion, assembly, and organization, political rights including the right to be appointed to public office. However, in the concept of phased-in civil rights, it seems realistic to separate political rights, where there is significant resistance from domestic residents, and to place it at a higher level than other civil liberties.

Political rights imply the right to participate in public decisions, including those of the state. They include the right to be appointed to civil service, to participate in local politics (both voting rights and the right to stand for office), and national politics (again, voting rights and the right to be elected).

In the following paragraphs, I would like to consider the question of how civil rights could be granted to foreigners depending on their degree of settlement. First, those which involve the right to life should be granted immediately to all foreigners, including those who are only staying for a short period of time to work. They should be granted without condition, regardless of whether they are regular or not. Positive consideration should also be given to the possibility of granting other social rights or civil liberties to all foreigners, regardless of their legal status. With regard to political rights, those at the national level should be granted to settled residents, and at the local level to foreigners with a long period of stay.

By implementing this type of phasing-in of civil rights, it should be possible to take a step forward to satisfying the demand for traditional amnesties or for special residence permits for irregular residents, a movement that is taking place vigorously. The idea behind these schemes is to provide the same treatment as nationals to people who, as a result of a prolonged stay, have moved the base of their livelihood from their home countries to their host countries. Incidentally, past proposals along these lines have limited the choices to either total legalization or none. As a result, great resistance arose in Japanese society based on the concern that this would promote an influx of foreign migrants, and the ideas were never given serious consideration.

In terms of the legislation of 'the phasing-in of civil rights,' it will become necessary to enact what I will tentatively call a 'Law for the Civil Rights of Foreigners.' Its main aim should be to guarantee people without Japanese nationality civil rights in a phased manner, depending on their degree of settlement. It should move from the right to life, to social rights and civil liberties, and finally to political participation. This law would differ by 180 degrees from the current Immigration Control Law, which is based on the spirit of managing and controlling foreigners. In addition, the formulation and granting of the phased-in civil rights will have to take into account the wills of foreigners themselves. It will have to be premised on the acceptance or even encouragement of organizing efforts by foreigners themselves, as a channel for decision-making, and of social movements based on this idea. In this sense, we should take special note of the current movement among old-comer foreigners to demand political rights at the local level, as well as the formation of autonomous organizations involving irregular foreigners that is taking place in various parts of the country.

In Europe, people sometimes say that, 'What we wanted to bring in was labor power, but it was human beings who actually came.' Major social problems arose due to the fact that, because the foreign migrants were human beings, they didn't necessarily return when labor surpluses emerged, but settled instead. In Japan, too, the large-scale settlement of foreign migrants is beginning. We must urgently begin examining the potential contents of 'phased-in civil rights,' on the premise of formulating them into legislation.

Notes

Introduction

1 Minc, Alain, *La vengeance de nations* (The Vengence of Nations), Paris: Editions Grasset & Fasquelle, 1990.

2 This definition is partly based on Barth, Frederic, 'Introduction,' Barth, F., ed., *Ethnic Groups and Boundaries*, Boston: Little Brown and Company, 1969.

3 Sekine Masami, *Esunishiti no seijishakaigaku* (The political sociology of ethnicity), Nagoya: Nagoya Daigaku Shuppan-kai, 1994.

4 Refer to Glazer, Nathan and Moynihan, Daniel P., *Beyond the Melting Pot*, Cambridge, Mass.: Massachusetts Institute of Technology Press, 1963.

5 Anderson, Benedict, *Imagined Communities*, London: Verso Editions, 1983.

6 With regard to the desire of minority groups for recognition, the discourse in Gutmann, Amy, ed., *Multiculturalism*, Princeton: Princeton University Press, 1994 is very interesting.

7 Of course, there is a great volume of literature within ethnic studies on the meaning of identity. For example, see Aoyagi Machiko, tr. and ed., *'Esunikku' to wa nani ka* (What is ethnicity?), Tokyo: Shinsen-sha, 1996.

8 See Castles, Stephen and Miller, Mark J., *The Age of Migration*, London: Macmillan, 1993.

9 Finkielkraut, Alain, *La defaite de la pensee* (The Defeat of the Mind), Paris: Editions Gallimard, 1987.

10 Habermas, Jürgen, *Strukturwandel der Öffentichkeit* (The Structural Transformation of the Public Sphere: An Inquiry into a Category of Bourgeois Society), Luchterhand: Neuwied, 1962; or Habermas, Jürgen, *Theorie des kommunikativen Handelns* (The Theory of Communicative Action), Frankfurt/ Main: Surkamp Verlag, 1981.

11 The Nationality Clause, a ministerial directive issued in 1954, forbids the employment of non-Japanese as civil servants. It was traditionally viewed as applying to local governments as well as the state, but in recent years a series of local governments, beginning with Kawasaki City, have begun to reinterpret it and to allow non-Japanese to work as public employees, albeit under certain conditions.

Chapter 1

1 In general the term 'foreign workers' refers to worker who are working in a country outside of the country where they hold nationality, but in the case of Japan, resident Koreans and Chinese, who hold the status of special permanent residents, are not included. In addition, this term usually refers to manual or so-called unskilled laborers, and even if people working in specialized and managerial or office and highly skilled occupations are included in the broad sense, they are clearly on the borderline.

2 This corresponds to the term 'illegal,' but I have chosen not to use it, for the following reasons. A major portion of any foreign population is generally composed of people who are living or working 'illegally.' These people face deportation, or punishment under migration laws (in the case of Japan, the Immigration Law) of host countries. Some of the crimes listed under Japan's law are 'illegal entry,' 'illegal landing,' 'activities outside of those permitted by status,' 'illegal staying,' and 'assisting illegal labor.'

'Illegal entry' is the act of entering Japan's territory without possessing a valid visa or other document, and 'illegal landing' the act of landing in Japan without receiving a landing permit. 'Activities outside of those permitted by status' means engaging in activities which are not permitted by one's residency status. Concrete examples of this are people who enter Japan using entertainer visas but then work in the sex industry, or people with college or pre-college student visas who concentrate on working but do no study. 'Illegal staying' means remaining in Japan beyond one's permitted period of stay. Thus, the meaning of 'illegality' in

Japan's law can be divided roughly into three main areas: entering Japan in an inappropriate manner, overstaying, and engaging in activities outside of those permitted by one's residency status.

The term 'illegality' has a very strong meaning, as it signifies breaking the law, or in other words violating the principles of social justice. But in the cases of acts expressed as 'illegal entry,' 'illegal staying,' and 'illegal labor,' unlike criminal acts, there is no victim that can be identified. These are merely violations of set formalities, and do not disturb the public order; they are in essence crimes of formality. In addition, the people committing these acts pay income and consumption taxes. This ill-conceived use of the label 'illegal' can lead to the rejection of 'illegal' workers, and to unfair discrimination against them.

All 'illegal' workers face the possibility of being deported at the hand of the state. Deportation procedures mean nothing less than the usurpation of their right of residency, including their livelihoods and places of work. It is unreasonable not to conclude that deportation is generally too strong a measure toward people who have settled in Japan to some extent.

It is also important to note that the human rights of even those 'illegal' workers who manage to avoid deportation are often violated. The question of political rights is out of the question, of course, but social rights and general freedoms, as well as the very basic right of existence, are taken away by the state under the pretext of 'illegality.' In this way, they are deprived of human rights that should be guaranteed universally to all human beings. On top of this, 'illegal' workers are in a weak position because of the fact that discovery could lead to deportation, and as a consequence employers have strong power against them and can easily exploit them. In other words, the use of the label 'illegal' represents the highest level of discrimination against foreigners, and is in fact imposed by the overwhelming power of the state.

This use of the inappropriate and strong label of 'illegal' by the state appears to stem from the line of reasoning that the very existence of such persons threatens the basis of the state and society. More than anything else, under the principle of the nation-state where the state is composed only of its own nationals and excludes others, the questions of distinction between nationals and foreigners, and the permission given to foreigners to stay within the territory, are concepts that necessarily relate to the very sovereignty of the state. One can also state that the recognition throughout the world of the existence of ethnic groups as a major social issue is a condition which has spurred this. In the background of this situation lurks the desire to eliminate the existence of certain specified ethnic groups, and the label 'illegal' serves to provide legitimacy to this exclusion.

3 Refer to Sassen, Saskia, *The Mobility of Labor and Capital*, Cambridge: Cambridge University Press, 1988; Kuwahara Yasuo, *Kokkyo o koeru rodosha* (Workers beyond borders), Tokyo: Iwanami Shoten, 1991; *Honma Hiroshi, Nanmin mondai to wa nani ka?* (What is the refugee issue?), Tokyo: Iwanami Shoten, 1990; and Castles, Stephen and Miller, Mark J., *The Age of Migration*, London: Macmillan, 1993.

4 Nagano Takeshi, *Zainichi Chugokujin* (Resident Chinese in Japan), Tokyo: Akashi Shoten, 1994, pp. 57–.

5 This information is drawn from Kim Chandong, *Ihojin wa kimigayo-maru ni notte* (Aliens on board the vessel Kimigayo), Tokyo: Iwanami Shoten, 1985; Park Kyongshuku, *Chosenjin kyosei renko no kiroku* (Records of Korean forced laborers), Tokyo: Miraisha, 1965; Suh Dengsuku, *Kominka seisaku kara shimon onatsu made* (From the policy of making Koreans into subjects of the Emperor to fingerprinting), Tokyo: Iwanami Shoten, 1989; and Oonuma Yasuaki, *Tan'itsu minzoku shakai no shinwa o koete* (Overcoming the myth of a monoracial society), Tokyo: Toshindo, 1986.

6 Cho Ungtal has proposed the following definition for long-term resident foreigners: 'Non-Japanese nationals (i.e., 'foreigners') whose livelihoods are based in Japanese society, and who are not different from Japanese in terms of social and living conditions.' Concretely, he includes within this definition (1) Koreans, Chinese and Taiwanese who were forced to come to Japan as a result of Japan's imperialist invasion; (2) their descendents, who were born and raised in

Japan; and (3) people who have lived in Japan for at least three years (the minimum period for eligibility for citizenship), whose basis for livelihood is in Japan, and who fulfill their responsibility to pay taxes.

The need for this classification arises from the fact that many of the people in the first two categories are in fact 'citizens' or residents, who make up a portion of Japanese society, and yet they do not seek to gain Japanese nationality. The policy which Japan once took of forcing them to choose between naturalization (assimilation) or exclusion (deportation) has essentially become bankrupt. What is important to note here is that the definition of 'long-term resident' is reserved to those who basis of livelihood is in Japan and who share the same social and living characteristics as the Japanese; it does not employ subjective criteria such as identity or will toward naturalization. Generally speaking, considering the fact that many people settle in foreign countries even while hoping to return to their homelands, it seems appropriate not to rely on subjective criteria. Cho's definition clearly demonstrates that newcomers as well as oldcomers can be included in the definition of long-term resident foreigners.

The traditional policy which equated naturalization with assimilation led to the emergence of discrimination against long-term resident foreigners who refused to accept this connection. Occupational discrimination and the refusal of suffrage gained social attention, and their solution has become a major task today. However, when discussing either the abolition of the Nationality Clause for civil servants or the granting of voting rights, the definition of the term 'long-term resident' becomes problematic as long as these measures only apply to them. There may be no issue for resident Koreans, Chinese, and other people who are defined as 'special permanent residents' under the Immigration Law, but there is a need to create objective criteria, such as number of years of residency, for legal newcomers. Incidentally, I would add that I believe these rights should also be guaranteed to irregular foreigners, as long as they are long-term residents. For more on this subject, see Cho Ungtal, *Teiju gaikokujin no chiho sanseiken* (Local voting rights for permanent resident foreigners), Tokyo: Nihon Hyoronsha, 1992, and Tanaka Hiroshi, *Zainichi gaikokujin (kaiteiban)* (Foreigners in Japan {revised edition}), Tokyo: Iwanami Shoten, 1995.

7 Many hints regarding the tendency toward a multinational state and the ideology of a monoracial one can be gleamed from Ooguma Eiji, *Tan'itsu minzoku shinwa no kigen* (Sources of the myth of monoracialism), Tokyo: Shinyosha, 1995, and Ooguma Eiji, '*Nihonjin' no kyokai* (The boundaries of 'Japaneseness'), Tokyo: Shinyosha, 1998.

8 Both arguments focus on the economic gaps between independent economic units.

9 Japan Immigration Association, *Zairyu gaikokujin tokei* (Annual statistics on resident foreigners), various years. General statistics on registered foreigners are issued every six months. There are also statistics for the end of each year separated by prefecture, nationality, and status of residence, as well as sex, age, and occupation.

10 Ministry of Justice, Immigration Bureau, 'Honpo ni okeru fuho zairyusha su' (The number of illegal foreigners in the country).

11 For a more detailed explanation, see Table 18 of Japan Immigration Association, *Heisei 11–nendo zairyu gaikokujin tokei* (Statistics on resident foreigners for FY1999).

12 For more details, see Ballescas, Maria Rosario Piquero, *Filipino Entertainers in Japan*, Quezon City: The Foundation for Nationalist Studies, 1993.

13 See Tables 2 and 6 of *Heisei 11–nendo zairyu gaikokujin tokei*, op. cit. (Statistics on resident foreigners for FY1999).

14 Amano Yoichi, *Dabao-koku no matsuei-tachi* (The descendents of the country of Davao), Tokyo: Fubaisha, 1990.

15 *Nihon Keizai Shimbun*, December 29, 1995.

16 Yamamoto Kaori, 'Zaikan Nihonjin no tsuma no seikatushi' (Life histories of the wives of Japanese residents of Korea), in Tani Tomio, ed., *Raifu hisutori o manabu hito no tame ni* (For those who want to learn about life histories), Kyoto: Sekai Shiso-sha, 1996.

17 *Asahi Shimbun*, May 9, 1996.

18 Kobayashi Izumi, *Mikuroneshia no chiisana kuniguni* (The small countries of Micronesia), Tokyo: Chuo Koron-sha, 1982.

19 *Asahi Shimbun*, May 12, 1994.

Chapter 2

1 See Tokyo Metropolitan Institute for Labor, *Tokyo-to ni okeru gaikokujin rodosha no shuro jittai* (The reality of foreign workers in the Tokyo metropolis), 1991, introduced in Komai Hiroshi, ed., *Gaikokujin rodosha mondai shiryo shusei* (Compilation of resources on the issue of foreign workers), Tokyo: Akashi Shoten, 1994. This study attempted to elucidate the employment situation of foreign workers in Tokyo in a comprehensive manner by surveying employers and Japanese workers, as well as foreign workers and pre-college students (*shugakusei*). It provides good analysis of the labor aspect of the issue, and is also very interesting from the point of view of theoretical considerations. The aim of the survey, according to the designers, was to step away from existing stereotyped images of foreign workers, and to gain demonstrative insights into their real situation. The survey is composed of a main pillar, (1) a questionnaire survey of employers, in addition to (2) an interview survey of employers, (3) an interview survey of foreign workers, (4) a questionnaire survey of foreigners, and (5) a questionnaire survey of Japanese employees.

The questionnaire survey of employers (1) was carried out by mail from July–August 1989. Questionnaires were sent out using random sampling to 5,200 small- and medium-sized firms employing at least 10 employees. There were 2,080 valid responses, which included 223 firms which were employing foreigners. The interview survey of employers (2) involved visit interviews with 51 firms, principally composed of those which had been found to be employing foreigners in the questionnaire survey of employers (1). It was conducted from December 1989 to October 1990. The interview survey of foreign workers (3) was conducted on 75 individuals selected arbitrarily (out of which 53 produced analyzable results) from July to November 1990. The questionnaire survey of foreigners (4) was conducted on a total of 1,844 persons, composed of 1,588 pre-college students (*shugakusei*) and 256 foreign employees, from December 1989 to February 1990.

Questionnaire forms were distributed and recovered, and the number of valid responses was 793. Finally, the questionnaire survey of Japanese employees (5) was carried out between December 1989 and June 1990, primarily on Japanese employees of the companies which had answered questionnaire (1). The number of forms distributed by companies with foreign employees was 923, with 276 valid responses sent back; 1,500 were distributed by firms that had no foreign employees, with 518 valid responses.

The main items on the surveys were as followed. For (1), they were: outline of business, general employment situation of foreigners, reason and route of employment of foreigners, working conditions and welfare programs for foreign workers, evaluation of and problems involving foreign employees, and requests toward the government. For (2), they were: attributes of the firm, job specifications, employment management, working conditions, and personnel management. For (3) they were: attributes, everyday schedule, work experience, current job and evaluation of this job, household budget, housing, health, future life plans, and family composition. For (4) they were: attributes and background, employment history since coming to Japan, working hours and wage income, and adaptation to workplace and living. For (5) they were: attributes, workplace relations with foreigners, opinions on the employment of foreigners at one's own company, evaluation of foreign employees, and future prospects and requests to the government.

The first point of reservation with the survey is that there is little analysis of the employment of foreigners in the construction industry, an area that carries heavy weight. It seems that more emphasis should have been placed on the construction industry in the interview survey with employers. Second, 18 of the 53 people included in the interview survey of foreigners were pre-college or university students. Admittedly, there are great difficulties in approaching and interviewing irregular workers, but it still seems that the weight of students is too high. Third, many of the pre-college students in the questionnaire survey of foreigners, were self-supporting, and hence it is difficult to claim that they are representative of typical foreign workers. In addition, one could legitimize the survey by seeing it as a survey primarily of pre-college students, but the inclusion of regular foreign workers in the cohort would then make the analysis inconsistent.

2 See Tokyo Metropolitan Institute for Labor, *Gaikokujin rodosha no komyunikeshon to ningen kankei* (Foreign workers: communication and interpersonal relations), 1995–96 (introduced in Komai Hiroshi, *Shinrai/teiju gaikokujin shiryo shusei* (Compilation of resources related to newcomer and settled foreigners), Tokyo: Akashi Shoten, 1998. The aim of this survey was: 'Within this deepest recession of the postwar period, to clarify (1) whether there have been changes in the employment itself and working conditions of foreigners; (2) how Japanese employers and employees are thinking of and dealing with these changes; (3) how foreigners themselves are thinking of and dealing with these changes; and (4) how the attitudes of Japanese people have changed.

For the 'Firm (workplace) survey,' 5,146 business establishments with at least 10 but not more than 300 employees were selected by random sampling based on the 'business establishments statistical survey.' A total of 1,731 valid responses were received, of which 286 were from firms that employed foreigners. For the 'Survey of Japanese employees,' cooperation was received from 90 firms with foreign employees and 348 firms without foreign employees, which had answered the above-mentioned 'Firm (workplace) survey.' 1,021 forms were sent out to the firms with foreign employees, and 254 responses were received; for the firms without foreign employees, 1,489 were sent out and 654 responses were sent back. The 'Interview survey of employ-ers' was conducted on 17 firms with foreign employees which had responded to the 'Firm (workplace) survey.' For the 'Interview and questionnaire survey of foreign workers themselves,' 149 persons were selected through the intro-duction of cooperating firms or by other means. Most of them were overstayers performing so-called unskilled labor, and a small number were people working outside of their residence status. Some were individuals who either lived or worked outside of the Tokyo metropolis.

In terms of nationality, the survey indicated that there were 25 South Koreans, 24 Chinese, 20 Thais, 30 Indonesians, and 50 Bangladeshis.

The main items included in the surveys were as follows. For the 'Firm (workplace) survey': Outline of the business establishment, outline of employment situation of foreign workers, motive and future plans for employment of foreign workers, relations between foreigners and Japanese employees, evaluation of foreign employees, and requests toward the government. For the 'Survey of Japanese employees': attributes, relations and communication with foreign employees, opinion and evaluation of foreign employees, and demands toward the administration. For the 'Interview survey of employers': outline of business, personnel management, problems, and requests to the government. For the 'Interview and questionnaire survey of foreign workers themselves': effects of the recession, joblessness, networks with compatriots or people from same region, relations with Japanese, plans to return home or desire to settle in Japan, and future prospects for work in Japan by compatriots.

In terms of reservations regarding this survey, it can be pointed out that both the 'Firm (workplace) survey' and the Survey of Japanese employees' were restricted to firms with at least 10 employees, and hence did not consider small companies with nine or fewer employees. According to the 'Instances of Violation of the Immigration Control Act in 1996,' 84.4% of irregular workers were working at businesses with 10 or fewer Japanese employees. This indicates that this report contains biases, such as placing much too little weight on businesses in sectors such as construction and restaurants.

3 I would like to give an outline of research in the period of expansion. The pioneering study was the Shinagawa Ward Labor Administration Office's *Gaikokujin no koyo ni kansuru ishiki/jittai chosa* (Attitude and situation survey of the employment of foreign workers) of March 1989, but it was a survey of companies, and made no distinction between legal and irregular workers. The same can be said for the extremely large-scale survey by Tezuka Kazuaki, 'Gaikokujin rodosha no shuro jittai: Shutoken to Osaka no jittai' (The working situation

of foreign workers: the situation in the Tokyo metropolis and Osaka), included in Tezuka Kazuaki, Komai Hiroshi, et al., eds., *Gaikokujin rodosha no shuro jittai* (The working situation of foreign workers), Tokyo: Akashi Shoten, 1992. Inagami Takeshi, Kuwabara Yasuo, et al., *Gaikokujin rodosha o senryokuka suru chusho kigyo* (Making foreign workers into weapons for small and medium-sized enterprises), Tokyo: Chusho Kigyo Research Center, 1992, is a survey of managers of small- and medium-sized enterprises, and is rich in content.

For the national situation in the period of stagnation, in 1993 the Ministry of Labor established a 'System for Reporting on the Employment Situation of Foreigners,' with the results published annually. In terms of contents, it includes an outline of businesses employing foreigners, as well as the types of jobs and labor turnover. However, the number of foreigners reported in 1998 was only 189,814, and thus the value of the data is low as it only covers a small portion of all foreign workers.

4   JICA (Japan International Cooperation Agency), *Nikkeijin honpo shuro jittai chosa hokokusho* (Field survey on the employment situation of Nikkeijin in Japan), 1992, introduced in Komai Hiroshi, *Gaikokujin teiju mondai shiryo shusei* (Compilation of resources on the issue of foreign settlement in Japan), Tokyo: Akashi Shoten, 1995. The aim of this survey was to gain an overall grasp of the real state of Nikkeijin, including what type of individuals they were, and how they were working and living.

With regard to methodology, survey forms were distributed and retrieved between April and July 1991, by the Overseas Japanese Association (Kaigai Nikkeijin Kyokai). A total of 3,225 forms were distributed, and 1,027 valid responses were received, meaning a recovery rate of 31.8%. Looking at the countries of origin of the respondents, 62.4% were from Brazil, 22.1% from Peru, 9.2% from Argentina, 2.2% from Bolivia, 3.2% from Paraguay, 0.6% from Dominica, and 0.2% unknown. The form was written in Portuguese, Spanish, and Japanese. The distribution and recovery was done 'in major prefectures where there are high concentrations of Nikkeijin...in accordance with population distributions compiled by the Overseas Japanese Association...with consideration given to the ratios of men and women.' The forms were distributed by hand through coordinators during home visits, as well as through support organizations, and to individual Nikkeijin at meetings, stations, and on the street. The eight major prefectures where the Nikkeijin were living were Kanagawa (24.8%), Aichi (20.0%), Shizuoka (8.7%), Tokyo (8.1%), Gunma (7.7%), Saitama (6.3%), Ibaraki (4.7%), and Tochigi (3.9%) (excluding 10 individuals who failed to answer).

The major contents of the survey were: basic attributes, Japanese language ability, motivation for coming to Japan, dependent family members, employment situation, everyday life, desire to return home and future plans, and requests regarding support and services. A particular focus was placed on basic attributes, employment situation, and everyday life. The items included in basic attributes were sex, age, birthplace, birthplaces of parents, number of visits to Japan, period of stay, residence status, number of generations in household, marital status, educational background, occupation in country of origin, and current place of residence. The items included in employment situation were labor contract, information on work and living, changes of employment, period of employment, type of job, health and safety environment, welfare and insurance, discrimination, working hours and days, wages, degree of satisfaction with job, and possibility of making later use of experience in Japan. The items included in everyday living were adaptation to life in Japan, feelings of incompatibility, identity, friendships, persons to whom they went for advice, social life, relationships with relatives in Japan, housing, and household expenditures.

I can point out the following reservations with this survey. First, problems can be cited regarding the validity of the analysis by country of origin, which is the basic framework of the survey. There were respondents who were not Brazilians and Peruvians – 94 Argentineans, 33 Paraguayans, and 23 Bolivians. Even if cross analysis is applied, the Paraguayans and Bolivians become statistically insignificant; great care is also needed in deriving any meaning for the Argentineans.

However, the emphasis is placed on country of origin without any scrutinization of this point. Another limitation of the survey is that there is little cross analysis of variables other than country of origin. In addition, stating my own wishes, I would like to point out that because Nikkeijin are legal workers, it may have been possible to use a random sampling method. However, considering the immense difficulty of conducting fact-finding surveys on foreign workers, this may be asking for the impossible.

5　JICA (Japan International Cooperation Agency), *Heisei yo-nendo Nikkeijin honpo shuro jittai chosa hokokusho* (Field survey on the employment situation of Nikkeijin in Japan in 1992), 1993, introduced in *Gaikokujin rodosha mondai shiryo shusei* (Compilation of resources on the issue of foreign workers in Japan), *op. cit.* The aim of this survey was to grasp the situation of Nikkeijin in Japan under the economic recession, based on the contents of consultations, and thus to contribute to migration-related projects in the future.

With regard to methodology, the survey was based on work by the Nikkeijin Consultation and Service Center (Nikkeijin Sodan Sabisu Senta), which was established by the Overseas Japanese Association. The center records the contents of consultations through telephone on prepared forms. This survey was based on the information obtained from 3,044 cases of consultation with the center between August 1992 and February 1993. It interpreted this high number of consultations in such a short period of time as an indication that Nikkeijin workers trust the center, and that it acts as a bridge (or liaison) between them and Japanese society. The consultation forms include items such as date of consultation, name, sex, occupation in Japan, time of arrival in Japan, citizenship, whether Nikkeijin or not, educational attainment, contact information, and contents of consultation.

The nationalities of the 3,044 individuals receiving consultations were as follows: 2,040 Brazilians (67.0%), 616 Peruvians (20.2%), 290 Japanese (9.5%), 32 Bolivians (1.1%), 33 other Nikkeijin (1.1%), 10 non-Nikkeijin who were married to Nikkeijin (0.3%), and 23 unknown (0.8%).

This distribution is not dissimilar to the results of the survey introduced in Note 4. In terms of the distribution of current place of residence, the nine top prefectures were: Tokyo (14.0%), Aichi (12.4%), Kanagawa (11.2%), Saitama (9.6%), Shizuoka (6.2%), Chiba (5.8%), Tochigi (4.4%), Gunma (3.8%), and Osaka (3.7%) (excluding 1,138 cases where the address was unclear). Compared to the actual distribution, these results seem to be biased toward Tokyo and its surrounding prefectures.

With regard to reservations about this survey, I would like to point out that because it was based on telephone consultations, there is inadequate data to make in-depth analysis. In particular, the information obtained on occupation in Japan and educational attainment was very inaccurate. Moreover, only people with extreme difficulties tend to call consultation hotlines, and thus these results may well not reflect the usual situation of the majority of Nikkeijin. Also, though this may be asking for too much, I wish there had been more background explanation on the activities and stances of the Overseas Japanese Association and the Nikkeijin Consultation and Service Center.

6 Hamamatsu City International Affairs Office, *Survey on Living Situation and Attitudes of Foreigners in Hamamatsu City* (1993), '1996 Survey on Living Situation and Attitudes of Nikkeijin,' in *Shinrai/teiju gaikokujin shiryo shusei* (Compilation of resources related to newcomer and settled foreigners), *op. cit.* The first survey was conducted between 1992 and 1993, and published in 1993. In terms of purpose, the survey stated that, 'There is an urgent need to grasp the living situation, etc., of the increasing number of foreigners, and in particular Nikkei Brazilians, to consider what roles the administration and local communities should play, and to build a social system for accepting foreigners in an appropriate manner. This survey aims to provide basic data for such administrative measures.' The aim of the follow-up survey, carried out four years after the initial one, was to assist in the further building of a symbiotic society, in view of the fact that coexistence with foreigners had become commonplace. The first report contains, in addition to the results of an interview

survey of Nikkeijin (hereafter the 'core survey'), results from an attitude survey of local residents and a field survey conducted in Brazil.

For the core survey, a questionnaire in Portuguese, Spanish, and Japanese was used. Interviews were carried out in five places within the city, and questionnaires were also left and then collected from three restaurants and three other places which were frequented by Nikkeijin. A total of 429 responses were recovered. The ratio of Brazilians to Peruvians was 4:1. The attitude of local residents was conducted through questionnaires as well as hearings held for members of neighborhood associations. For the questionnaire survey, 1,500 survey forms were distributed in some 30 towns where many foreign worker residents were living, and 870 responses were collected. The hearings were held in 31 towns. For the field survey in Brazil, 110 homes were visited in five Nikkeijin *colonias*, with a heavy emphasis placed on the families of migrant workers or persons who had once worked as migrant workers; interviews were conducted with 122 individuals. The follow-up survey was conducted in the form of interviews in four places within the city, with 210 responses.

The major items in the core survey were as follows: attributes including nationality, Japanese language ability, and type of visa; reason for coming to Japan, including mediation agencies; job in Japan, including working conditions and relations with other employees and employer; life and problems in Japan, including prejudice, discrimination, troubles and worries; identity; communication with Japanese society; contact with the media, future plans including desire to settle in Japan or to return home; preference of housing location; health and medical care; and expectations with regard to government services. The follow-up survey included, in addition to these items, questions on children's education and language used at home. The main items of the questionnaire survey of local residents included attributes, real state of interchanges with foreigners, desire to interact with foreigners, uneasiness, and requests toward the government. The hearing survey focused on troubles. In the field survey conducted in

Brazil, questions were asked concerning the lives of the families left behind, and life after returning home.

In terms of reservations about the main survey, a survey was actually conducted of companies hiring foreign workers, but the results were, for all intents and purposes, not released. In addition, it is regrettable that there was a lack of systemic analysis between the core survey and the other surveys. Additionally, the report from the follow-up survey is presented merely as an explanation of raw statistics, with no analysis.

7   On the issue of Nikkeijin, in addition to the surveys presented in this chapter, see the following: the pioneering survey by the Okinawa International Foundation (Okinawa-ken Kokusai Koryu Zaidan), *Nanbei ijusha shitei no 'dekasegi mondai' ni kansuru jittai chosa hokokusho* (Report on field survey of the 'migrant labor' problem among offspring of people who migrated to South America), 1990; Watanabe Masako, ed., *Dekasegi Nikkei Burajirujin* (Migrant Nikkei Brazilians), Tokyo: Akashi Shoten, 1995; Kajita Takamichi (lead researcher), *Toransunashonaruna kankyoka deno aratana iju purosesu* (The new migration process under a transnational environ-ment), Report financed by Funds for Promoting Science and Technology, 1999.

8   Komai Hiroshi, *Migrant Workers in Japan*, London: Kegan Paul International, 1995, pp. 45–. A report of this survey can also be found in Komai Hiroshi, ed., 'Gaikokujin rodosha no rodo oyobi seikatsu jittai ni kansuru kenkyu: kenshusei no bunseki' (Research on the working and living situation of foreign workers: analysis of trainees), in *Gaikokujin rodosha no shuro jittai, op. cit.*

9   For recent research on trainees, see Asano Shinichi, *Nihon de manabu Ajiakei gaikokujin: kenshusei, ryugakusei, shugakusei no seikatsu to bunka henyo* (Asian foreigners studying in Japan: changes in the living and culture of trainees, college students, and pre-college students), Tokyo: Daigaku Kyosoku Shuppan, 1997; and Kanbayashi Chieko, *Gino jisshu seido no genjo to kadai* (Current state and problems of the intern system), Study result financed by

funds from Grant-in-Aid for Scientific Research (Kaken), 1997.

10 *Asahi Shimbun*, June 27, November 18, November 19, November 22, November 23, and December 8, 1998; January 8 and February 18, 1999.

11 NHK General TV, Tokuho Shutoken '97 (Special Report Metropolitan Area '97), 'Gaikokujin kenshusei: totzusen no kikoku' (Foreign trainees: sudden repatriation), broadcast on June 22, 1997.

12 *Amakudari*, which translates directly as 'descent from heaven,' refers to the practice of retired government officials being offered lucrative jobs in semi-governmental organizations or in private firms hoping to take advantage of their human networks.

13 Ministry of Justice, Immigration Bureau, *Nyukanho ihan jiken* (Incidents of violations of the Immigration Control Law), various years, introduced in *Gaikokujin rodosha mondai shiryo shusei* (Compilation of resources on the issue of foreign workers in Japan), *op. cit.* and *Shinrai/teiju gaikokujin shiryo shusei* (Compilation of resources related to newcomer and settled foreigners), *op. cit.* These materials are concerned with incidents of violations of the Immigration Control Law. They are issued by the Ministry of Justice's Immigration Bureau, and a large number involve irregular employment. Irregular workers are, for all intents and purposes (unless they are smuggled out), unable to leave Japan without going through a deportation procedure by the Immigration Bureau. The data for these reports are collected from these procedures. Although they are limited to those leaving Japan, they are nevertheless extremely valuable as the only nation-wide source of data on irregular workers. Not only can one get an overall picture of irregular workers from the items listed, but starting from 1989, when statistics were first organized, one can compare years in order to grasp movements over time. The majority of cases involve individuals who reported voluntarily to the Immigration Bureau in order to return home, but there are also a few where the individuals were arrested for violations of the Immigration Control Law or the criminal code.

Violations of the Immigration Control Law are classified into illegal entry, illegal landing, activities outside of residence status, illegal staying (hereinafter, I will use the term overstaying), and violations of criminal law, etc.; instances of illegal employment (hereinafter, 'irregular employment') are classified separately. The overwhelming majority of cases of violations of the Immigration Control Law involve overstayers or irregular employment; few involve illegal entry, illegal landing, activities outside of residence status, or violations of criminal law. The numbers of overstayers and irregular workers for whom deportation orders were issued both decreased gradually from between 60,000 and 70,000 in 1993 to just over 40,000 in 1998. To explain this decrease, the Immigration Bureau added the comment that apprehensions have become more difficult as a result of an increased dispersion into local areas and a tendency of foreigners to live and work in smaller groups.

For irregular workers, the data released by the Immigration Bureau include nationality (place of origin), sex, age, status of residence, period of work, place of work (prefecture), contents of work, compensation (daily amount), nationality (place of origin) of employer, management structure of place of work, involvement of criminal organizations, number of employees at place of work, and, for 1993–95, involvement of brokers.

One can cite, as a point of reservation, that the data on irregular workers only include those who were apprehended, and are thus limited in some respects. The majority of apprehensions were carried out against individuals who had surrendered voluntarily to the Immigration Bureau at the time they wished to leave Japan, and hence it cannot be said that the information covers all irregular workers in Japan. For instance, looking at the nationality figures for apprehensions in 1992, Malaysians and Iranians held the number one and two spots, respectively, showing a significant gap from the figures for overstayers, whose top spots were held by Thais and South Koreans. The figure seems to reflect the fact that many individuals from Malaysia and Iran decided to return home voluntarily in 1992.

14 Tokyo Metropolitan Council of Social Welfare, *Zaiju gaikokujin no fukushi/seikatsu kadai ni kansuru jittai chosa hokokusho* (Report from a field survey on issues involving the welfare and living of foreigners in Japan), 1993, included in *Gaikokujin rodosha mondai shiryo shusei* (Compilation of resources on the issue of foreign workers in Japan), *op. cit.* There is no need to emphasize here again the technical difficulties involved in large-scale surveys of irregular workers. Since they are irregular, their existence tends to be hidden, and it is extremely difficult to come into contact with them. In addition, they often refuse to cooperate with questionnaires. This survey is a pioneering work in large-scale surveys, which managed to surmount these difficulties. The aim of the survey was reported to be to reveal the problems of welfare and living faced by foreign workers, and in particular irregular workers. It is worthy of special note that the survey helped to clarify the problems facing irregular workers as members of communities, with a particular focus on medical, working, and living conditions. The survey items included attributes, housing, job, illnesses or injuries caused by work, other illnesses and injuries, ways of spending holidays and free time, ways of dealing with problems, use of public agencies, family and children's education, and future plans to stay in Japan.

The method used by this survey was to approach irregular workers through eight organizations that were either groups formed by foreign workers, or volunteer and labor groups working in support of them. The distribution and collection of questionnaires was done through the cooperating groups between December 1992 and February 1993. A total of 1,530 questionnaires were distributed, and 957 collected, meaning a recovery rate of 62.5%. Analyzing the results, we found that in terms of residence status they were classified into two major groupings: college students and pre-college students (331 persons) and people who could be considered irregular, with 'no residency status,' 'short-term stay,' or 'unknown' (expressed as 'no residency status or unknown' in this report) (509 persons). The emphasis of the analysis was put on the latter group.

Of those with 'no residence status or unknown'), 26.1% were from Iran, 21.4% from Bangladesh, 15.5% from Pakistan, 12.2% from South Korea, 8.3% from Africa, 5.3% from the Philippines, with smaller numbers coming from Malaysia, China, Taiwan, Hong Kong, etc. A full 63.0% came from the Islamic countries of South and Southwest Asia. Questionnaires were prepared in nine languages: Chinese (two types), Hangul, Persian, Urdu, Bengali, Japanese, English, and French. Their places of residence extended from the central Kanto Plain areas of Tokyo, Saitama, Tochigi, Chiba, and Kanagawa Prefectures, to Gunma, Ibaraki, and Yamanashi Prefectures.

The first point of reservation with this survey is that it included very few Thais, who made up the largest group of irregular workers at the time when it was carried out. The numbers of Filipinos, South Koreans and Chinese were also low. As a consequence, the weight of Bangladeshis and Pakistanis was quite high, and it is possible that the methodology, of going through support groups, led to some bias. Second, there were no survey items on religion, which is an extremely important factor in daily living. In particular, religion can be considered a core factor of daily life and culture for people from Muslim and Catholic areas, and it appears to be a theme that cannot be ignored when considering problems such as welfare and daily life.

15   Chiba Prefectural Chiba High School, International Social Studies Group, *Gaikokujin rodosha jittai chosa, 1995-nen–1996-nen* (1995–1996 Field survey of foreign workers), 1997, in *Shinrai/teiju gaikokujin shiryo shusei* (Compilation of resources related to newcomer and settled foreigners), *op. cit.* This is a very notable survey, as to my knowledge it is the first full-fledged attempt to compare working and living conditions using different ethnic groups as its cohorts. It is believed that the only other survey to have used this method is the 'Zainichi gaikokujin shijo chosa/deta shu' (Collection of market surveys and data on foreigners in Japan), which I will discuss later. It is also admirable that such a difficult survey was carried out by high school students. The purpose set in the survey begins from the need felt to understand the

problem of foreign workers not in the single framework of 'foreigners in Japan,' but as separate ethnic groups. For this reason, the students set as their target groups members of seven ethnic groups – Nikkei Brazilians, South Koreans, Chinese, Filipinos, Thais, Bangladeshis, and Iranians – living in Chiba Prefecture, mainly in Chiba City.

The survey was conducted by questionnaires and interviews. For the questionnaire, forms were prepared in Japanese, Persian, Portuguese, Hangul, Chinese, Thai, and English, and were given to foreign residents either directly or indirectly in places such as housing, factories, churches, and ethnic shops. It was carried out from 1994 to 1995. The interview survey was conducted between 1994 and 1996. The following numbers of individuals in each ethnic group were surveyed: (figures in parentheses indicate number surveyed by questionnaire and by interview): Nikkei Brazilians (30 and 4), South Koreans (27 and 3), Chinese (24 and 3), Filipinos (32 and 2), Thais (15 and 1), Bangladeshis (28 and 5), and Iranians (32 and 7), for a total of 188 and 25 persons.

The questionnaire form for the survey was formulated with reference to *Zainichi Iranjin* (Iranians in Japan), which I edited and published (included in *Gaikokujin teiju mondai shiryo shusei, op. cit.*). The main survey items were attributes both in Japan and at home, present occupation, place of work, troubles with employers, changes of jobs/unemployment, income and remittance to home, housing, Japanese language ability, relations with Japanese, experiences of discrimination, purpose of coming to Japan, and planned period of stay. The main items of the interview survey focused on the interviewees' working and living situations in their home countries and in Japan, but extended to include views of life and future plans.

Looking at the results of this survey, one major feature is that a comparison was made with the data I collected from 1990–91 in Kanagawa Prefecture, differentiated by ethnic groups (included in Komai Hiroshi, *Imin shakai Nihon no koso* (Vision for Japan as a country of immigrants), Tokyo: Kokusai Shoin, 1994), thus providing information about changes in a time series.

In terms of points of reservation, I would like to mention that 21 individuals from outside of Chiba Prefecture answered the questionnaire survey. In addition, among Koreans, many women said that they had come to Japan to 'Increase my skills' or 'Broaden my outlook and knowledge,' indicating that in a relatively large number of cases they were working through the introduction of language schools or working while studying. Thus, in this survey it is difficult to place Koreans within the framework of foreign workers as it applies to other ethnic groups.

16 Prime Minister's Office, Prime Minister's Secretariat, Public Relations Office, 'Gaikokujin rodosha mondai ni kansuru seron chosa' (Public opinion survey on the problem of foreign workers), conducted in 1990, introduced in *Gaikokujin rodosha mondai shiryo shusei* (Compilation of resources on the issue of foreign workers), *op. cit.* For a survey which takes as its cohort the entire Japanese population, this data is somewhat old, but it gives basic information on the attitudes of Japanese toward foreign workers. The Prime Minister's Office conducted two surveys with the same theme in July 1980 and February 1988, entitled 'Gaikokujin no nyukoku to zairyu ni kansuru seron chosa' (Public opinion survey on the entry and residence in Japan of foreigners), and this survey is hence the third in a series. In addition to newspaper opinion polls, another nation-wide survey was the Economic Planning Agency's 'Wagakuni ni okeru gaikokujin koyo to kokumin seikatsu ni kansuru anketo chosa kekka ni tsuite (gaiyo)' (On the results of a questionnaire survey on the employment of foreign workers and national life in our country), conducted in March 1988.

The purpose of the Prime Minister's Office's 1990 survey was to investigate the attitudes of the Japanese population on the issue of foreign workers, as reference for future policies. In terms of methodology, the targets were 5,000 people of at least 20 years of age from around the country, selected through stratified two-stage random sampling. The survey was conducted from November to December 1990, by investigators through direct interviews. There were 3,681 valid responses, meaning a recovery rate of 73.6%. The survey items covered a broad range of areas including experiences of contacts with foreigners, interest and knowledge of the problem of foreign workers, approval or disapproval of illegal work and measures for them, the acceptance of unskilled foreign workers, countermeasures to the labor shortage, and responses of the administration toward foreigners. However, the main focus of the questions was on acceptance or rejection, so it is worth mentioning that there was a lack of attention given to the issue of measures toward people already living and working in Japan.

17 Mitsui Knowledge Industry Research Institute, *Monita o katsuyo shita 'aratanaru jidai no sugata to seisaku hoshin' sakutei no tame no chosa hokokusho* (Survey report for formulating a 'state and policy direction for a new age' making use of monitors), 1999, pp. 58–60.

18 *Chunichi Shimbun*, June 8, 1999.

19 Ministry of Justice, Immigration Bureau, 'Nyukanho ihan gaikokujin no shuchu tekihatsuto no jisshi (daihyorei),' (The implementation of mass apprehensions of foreigners violating the Immigration Control Law (representative cases)), *Kokusai Jinryu* (International People's Exchange), September (or thereabouts) issue of each year.

Chapter 3

1 Okada Emiko, 'Nihon de hataraku – aru Iran-jin seinen no kiroku' (Working in Japan: the chronicle of one Iranian youth,' in Komai Hiroshi, ed., *Nihon no esunikku shakai* (Japan's ethnic society), Tokyo: Akashi Shoten, 1996, p. 28. This chronicle was recorded from a conversation with one 25-year-old Iranian youth. Okada stated that, 'I wanted "him" to tell me about his life and experiences in as great detail as possible, so that I would be able to uncover all the things…country, society, culture, which he shoulders "himself."' She succeeded brilliantly in this.

The following interesting points emerged from her interview. First, because the young man had left Iran illegally before finishing his military service, he was afraid that he would not be able to return. Second, as he had great pride, he felt very humiliated by not being called by his name or being subjected to discrimination. Third, not only was he working hard to learn Japanese, but he was also interested in Japanese women. Fourth, he had a strong sense of jealousy. Finally, he mentioned that he knew of other Iranians who had lost their jobs and done bad things. He also made an impressive statement: 'Japanese people hate us, but I really like Japan. Japanese speak brusquely, but they have simple hearts.'

2 Komai Hiroshi, *Imin shakai Nihon no koso* (Vision for Japan as a country of immigrants), Tokyo: Kokusai Shoin, 1994, p. 96.

3 Watanabe Masako, 'Nikkei Burajiru-jin no seikatsu sekai' (The living sphere of Nikkei Brazilians), in *Toshi Mondai* (Urban problems), Vol. 86 No. 3 (March 1995), p. 22.

4 Hamamatsu City International Affairs Office, *Survey on Living Situation and Attitudes of Foreigners in Hamamatsu City* (1993), in Komai Hiroshi, ed., *Shinrai/teiju gaikokujin shiryo shusei* (Compilation of resources related to newcomer and settled foreigners), Tokyo: Akashi Shoten, 1998, Volume 2, p. 359.

5 Wakabayashi Chihiro's research, 'Nihon o hyoryu suru Banguradeshu no wakamono-tachi' (Bangladeshi young people who drift in Japan), in Komai Hiroshi, *Nihon no esunikku shakai, op. cit.*, is a compilation of the results of three surveys covering roughly six years, and of interviews in Bangladesh of people who had returned from Japan.

6 Nezu Kiyoshi, *Nanmin Nintei* (Recognition of refugees), Diamond-sha, 1992, p. 172.

7 Mya Mya Win, 'Gunji dokusai taisei-ka no Biruma to Zainichi Biruma-jin no minshuka undo' (Burma under military dictatorship and the democratization movement by Burmese in Japan), in Yamamoto Takehiko *et. al.*, eds., *Kokusaika to jinken* (Internationalization and human rights), Tokyo: Kokusai Shoin, 1994, p. 169. In addition, regarding the situation of Burmese residents in Japan, Kura Shinichi compiled the results of a survey that can be called the first in this area, 'Kokusai imin no tayosei to esunikku na rentai – Nihon ni okeru Biruma-jin o jirei ni' (The diversity of international migration and ethnic solidarity: the case of Burmese in Japan), *Nenpo Tsuba Shakaigaku*, No. 10, 1998.

8   JICA (Japan International Cooperation Agency, *Nikkeijin honpo shuro jittai chosa hokokusho* (Report of a fact-finding survey on the employment situation of Nikkeijin in Japan), 1992, introduced in Komai Hiroshi, *Gaikokujin teiju mondai shiryo shusei* (Compilation of resources on the issue of foreign settlement in Japan), Tokyo: Akashi Shoten, 1995, p. 182.

9   Hamamatsu City, *op. cit.* p. 359.

10 Fuchigami Eiji, *Nikkeijin shomei* (Proof of Nikkeijin), Tokyo: Shinhyoron, 1995, pp. 174, 215.

11 Komai Hiroshi, ed., *Zainichi Iranjin* (Iranians in Japan), Tsukuba: University of Tsukuba, Institute of Social Sciences, 1994, introduced in Komai Hiroshi, *Gaikokujin teiju mondai shiryo shusei* (Compilation of resources on the issue of foreign settlement in Japan), *op. cit.* Questionnaires prepared in Persian were handed out to Iranians encountered on streets in the Kanto region, and to have them fill in the questionnaire on the spot. The surveyors studied Persian for three months, but in nearly all cases there were Iranians in the area who could speak either Japanese or English, who helped with the surveys. In addition to this, intensive case interviews, lasting an hour or sometimes more, were conducted with 21 individuals.

The survey was conducted in several locations in the Kanto region. The main locations were the entrance to Yoyogi Park at Harajuku Station, Tokyo, and Kashiwa Station in Chiba Prefecture, where many Iranians gathered at the time, but also included other places in the prefectures of Chiba, Saitama and Ibaraki. The survey was held from July 17 to 25, 1993. There were 245 valid responses, of which 93 were gathered at Harajuku Station. One feature of the responses was that, in terms of residence, the interviewees were distributed throughout a wide area of the Kanto region. Specifically, 47 lived in Ibaraki Prefecture, 38 in Saitama, 34 in Metropolitan Tokyo, 33 in Chiba, 10 in Tochigi, 9 in Kanagawa, and 4 each in Shizuoka, Gunma, and Yamanashi, with 70 providing no answer.

The contents of the survey focused on social and economic attributes in Iran, work, housing, and discrimination in Japan, religious beliefs and activities in Iran and in Japan, and relationships with Japanese. In addition, a space was left where they could answer freely, with the purpose of allowing the surveyees to deliver a message to Japanese people. We received 150 answers in this space, some of them pointing out issues that we had never considered. The profile of the typical Iranian that we obtained from the survey was: an average age of 28.4 years, male, with an average period of stay in Japan of two years and one month. In terms of shortcomings of this survey, it was impossible to conduct sampling as the targets were irregular foreigners.

12 Izutsu Toshihiko, *Isuramu bunka* (Islamic culture) (second collection of writings by the author), Tokyo: Chuo Koronsha, 1993, p. 324.

13 Kano Hirokatsu, *Iran shakai wo kaibo suru* (Analyzing Iranian society), Tokyo: Tokyo Shimbun Shuppan-kyoku, 1980, pp. 169, 221.

14 *Ibid.*, pp. 22, 133, 233.

15 Tokyo Metropolitan Government, Bureau of Citizens and Cultural Affairs, *Ryugakusei shugakusei no seikatsu ni kansuru jittai chosa hokokusho* (Report from a fact-finding survey on the situation of foreign students and pre-college students), 1992, introduced in Komai Hiroshi, *Gaikokujin rodosha mondai shiryo shusei* (Compilation of resources on the issue of foreign workers), *op. cit.* This survey was based on an earlier survey of the same name conducted in 1989, also by the Bureau of Citizens and Cultural Affairs. Also, Study Group on Foreign College Student and Pre-College Students (Gaikokujin Shugakusei/Ryugakusei Kenkyukai), 'Shugakusei/Ryugakusei oyobi sono kikokusha ni kansuru jittai chosa' (Fact-finding survey on pre-college students, college students, and students who have returned to their home countries), introduced in Tezuka Kazuaki, Komai Hiroshi *et. al.*, eds., *Gaikokujin rodosha no shuro jittai* (The working situation of foreign workers), Tokyo: Akashi Shoten, 1992, was based mainly around Kanagawa Prefecture, and included interviews with some people who had returned to their home countries.

The Tokyo Metropolitan Government survey was the most comprehensive and had the largest number of samples of any survey to date. Its aim was to grasp the realities and problems of foreign college and pre-college students living in the metropolis, for the purpose of formulating policy measures. In terms of survey method, cooperation was requested from 110 universities (and two-year colleges) and 40 technical and Japanese language schools in Tokyo and its environs. Questionnaires were distributed from the 65 universities and 29 technical/Japanese language schools which agreed to cooperate, with the questionnaires returned either through the schools or by the individuals themselves by mail. A total of 8,141 questionnaires were distributed, 5,206 through universities and 2,935 through other schools, and a total of 3,102 were returned, 1,750 from universities and 1,352 from other schools. Of the answers, 351 were excluded from the analysis because the respondents lived outside the Tokyo region, leaving a total of 2,751. The recovery rate was thus 38.1%. The survey was conducted from October to December 1991. Survey items included attributes, school being attended, financial assistance and tuition, part-time jobs, budget, housing, health and medical care, school life, life in Tokyo, Japanese language ability, and future plans.

The first point of reservation that can be cited is that there is no regional analysis. One wonders if there are not differences in working and living conditions between those living near major areas such as Shinjuku and Ikebukuro, and those living in outlying areas. In addition, the respondents filled in the questionnaires themselves, so it is possible that some may have given inaccurate information on delicate questions such as number of hours spent working, which involves the Immigration Bureau. In addition, the information on the management and operating situations of Japanese language schools and technical schools should have come from a different form than questionnaires filled out by students. Incidentally, the most common country of origin of pre-college students was South Korea (41.2%), followed by China (22.9%), Taiwan (13.5%), and Malaysia (9.3%), with other places of origin taking up less than 5% each. South Koreans thus seem to have been over-represented.

16 Oka Masumi and Fukada Hiromi, *Chugokujin ryugakusei to Nihon* (Japan and Chinese Foreign Students), Tokyo: Hakutei-sha, 1995, p. 32.

17 Mo Fenf Fu, *Shin-kakyo* (The new Overseas Chinese), Tokyo: Kawade Shobo Shin-sha, 1993, p. 11.

18 In terms of objective surveys on such individuals, there are some area unit-based studies, which do not focus specifically on Chinese, and which are based on interviews. They include Okuda Michihiro and Tajima Junko, eds., *Ikebukuro no Ajia-kei gaikokujin* (The Asian foreigners of Ikebukuro), Tokyo: Mekon, 1991; Okuda Michihiro and Tajima Junko, eds., *Shinjuku no Ajia-kei gaikokujin* (The Asian foreigners of Shinjuku), Tokyo: Mekon, 1993; Okuda Michihiro and Tajima Junko, eds., *Shinpan Ikebukuro no Ajia-kei gaikokujin* (The Asian foreigners of Ikebukuro: new edition), Tokyo: Akashi Shoten, 1995; and Tajima Junko, *Sekai toshi Tokyo no Ajia-kei ijusha* (Asian migrants in the international city of Tokyo), Tokyo: Gakubun-sha, 1998.

19 Editorial Division, Ryugakusei Shinbun, 'Zainichi kajin no jittai: *Ryugakusei Shimbun* dokusha anketo hokoku' (The reality of Chinese in Japan: report from a questionnaire survey of readers of *Ryugakusei Shimbun*,' 1994, introduced in Komai Hiroshi, *Gaikokujin rodosha mondai shiryo shusei* (Compilation of resources on the issue of foreign workers), *op. cit.* This newspaper, *Ryugakusei Shimbun* (literally, 'foreign student newspaper), which is edited and published by Chinese residents of Japan, can be seen as the representative example of an 'ethnic paper.' It was inaugurated in April 1990, and is read not only by college and pre-college students, but by a broad range of Chinese residents in Japan, including people from Taiwan. It is written mostly in Chinese, with Japanese playing a subsidiary role. The contents include not only information on Japan, but also on China, as well as on a broad range of issues ranging from living to culture. As of October 1999, the circulation was 63,000 copies.

The survey was conducted by asking readers to return, by mail, a questionnaire insert in the newspaper. A total of 656 responses were received, showing that many Chinese living in Japan wish to express something to Japanese society. The survey was conducted between November and December, 1993. It was the third such survey, with the first having been done in July 1990, and the second in January 1992. The main contents were basic attributes, economic situation, mental life situation, appraisal of the Japanese, planned future place of residence, attitudes on the Taiwan, Hong Kong, and Tibet issues, and thoughts on Mainland China including the Tienanmen Square Incident. The greatest emphasis seems to have been placed on the two political issues at the end.

Basic attributes included age, sex, and educational attainment, as well as status of residence, number of years stayed in Japan, and place of origin. In terms of economic situation, respondents were asked about their monthly income, balance of savings, housing costs, and effects felt from the recession. Questions on mental life situation included love and marriage, favorite pleasures, and greatest sources of anguish. The section on appraisal of the Japanese included adaptation to Japan, good points of the Japanese, and bad points. In terms of the Taiwan problem, readers were asked about relations between the Mainland and Taiwan, their views on the matter, and the likely reaction of the Mainland to Taiwanese independence. With regard to Mainland China, they were asked detailed questions, including their appraisal of the current situation, their reasons behind this appraisal, their views of post-Deng Xiao-ping China, what system they thought should be adopted, what countries should serve as models, human rights, urgent matters confronting the country, and their appraisal of the Tienanmen Square Incident. One interesting feature to note in the analysis of this survey is that much space was given to free answers, thus providing an extremely interesting chance to hear the raw voices of Chinese living in Japan.

In terms of points of reservation, it seems that the main respondents were people with high educational attainment, who had already attained some social status. Especially considering that there were few responses from Chinese who had come to Japan with Japanese people left behind after the war, it seems likely that the survey failed to include people with relatively low educational attainment or social status. In addition, though this may be unavoidable in a newspaper article, the information was presented as nearly raw data, with little deeper examination of attributes or political attitudes, for example.

20 See, for example, Ide Magoroku, *Owari-naki tabi* (Never-ending journey), Tokyo: Iwanami Shoten, 1986; Nakano Kenji, *Chugoku zanryu koji mondai* (The problem of orphans left behind in China), Tokyo: Joho Kikaku Shuppan, 1987; and Ogawa Tsuneko, *Sokoku yo* (Oh, Motherland) (Iwanami Shinsho), Tokyo: Iwanami Shoten, 1995. Statistical surveys include Chugoku Kikokusha no Kai (Association of Returnees from China), 'Anketo chosa' (Questionnaire survey), 1989; and Ministry of Health and Welfare, 'Chugoku kikoku koji seikatsu jittai chosa kekka no gaiyo' (Overview of the results of a survey on the living situation of orphans returned from China), 1994 and 1995. In the former survey, second- and third-generation descendents made up 60% of respondents. The latter survey only targeted war orphans who had returned at state expense.

21 *Nihon Keizai Shimbun*, November 6, 1998.

22 *Asahi Shimbun*, May 23, 1998.

23 Ministry of Health and Welfare, 'Chugoku kikoku koji seikatsu jittai chosa kekka no gaiyo' (Outline of results of a fact-finding survey on the living situation of war orphans from China), August 1994.

24 Iida Toshiro, 'Toshi shakai ni okeru esunishiti: Chugoku kikokusha no jirei bunseki o chushin ni,' (Ethnicity in urban society: based mainly on case analyses of returnees from China), included in *Nihon no esunikku shakai*, *op. cit.*, p. 271. Iida's paper called for an analytic framework which could grasp the invigoration of urban ethnicity as a movement toward the increase of life chances, which link a growth of choices in social resources and the formation of social networks. For this reason, Iida used as data for his paper a survey of 252 returnees from China conducted by the Chugoku Kikokusha no Kai (Association of Returnees from China).

   In terms of social resources, returnees can choose between dependence on public assistance or independence through work, and in terms of social networks, between solidarity with other returnees or isolation. Using these combinations of life chances, Iida came up with four patterns: dependence/solidarity, dependence/isolation, independence/solidarity, and independence/isolation. He recognized independence/ solidarity as having the greatest potential for invigoration.

25   Komai Hiroshi, ed., *Chugoku kikosha nisei, sansei* (Second- and third-generation returnees from China), Tsukuba: University of Tsukuba, Institute of Social Science, 1996, included in *Shinrai/teiju gaikokujin shiryo shusei* (Compilation of resources related to newcomer and settled foreigners), *op. cit.* The survey was based on questionnaire interviews, and conducted in July 1995. The targets were selected by sys-tematic random sampling from the list of war orphans kept by the Chugoku Kikokusha no Kai. After adding a few individuals, mainly among second- and third-generation returnees, who were 15 years of age and older and participating in Japanese language classes, we achieved a total sample of 147 subjects. Therefore, nearly all were living in Tokyo and in particular within its 23 central wards. The main survey items were attributes, place of origin, Japanese language ability, employment situation, income, type of housing, relations with Japanese, contacts in China, public assistance, reason for returning to Japan, discrimination and prejudice, identity, and desire to go back to China.

Chapter 4

1   Ministry of Labor, 'Gaikokujin koyo jokyo hokoku' (Report on the Employment Situation of Foreigners), November of each year.

2   Ko Sonfi, 'Yokohama-shi A-cho no Saishu tojin to Kankokujin rodosha,' in Komai Hiroshi, ed., *Nihon no esunikku shakai* (Japan's ethnic society), Tokyo: Akashi Shoten, 1996. This survey was conducted on 133 respondents, using a question-naire. The contents of the survey were broad, including background for coming to Japan and past visits to Japan, connections with resident Koreans, jobs done since coming to Japan, problems with everyday living, networks for consultations and information, relationships with Japanese, means of getting information on home country, and future plans. The greatest emphasis, however, was on the networks of Korean workers.

3   Zainichi Gaikokujin Johoshi Rengokai (Ethnic Media and Press Coalition), 'Zainichi gaikokujin shijo chosa/deta shu' (Collection of market surveys and data on foreigners in Japan), 1996, in Komai Hiroshi, *Shinrai/teiju gaikokujin shiryo shusei* (Compilation of resources related to newcomer and settled foreigners), Tokyo: Akashi Shoten, 1998. The Ethnic Media and Press Coalition is an organization founded by representative print media from ethnic communities in Japan. This survey was conducted on readers of the member organization of the Coalition. The purpose of the survey was to provide basic data on readers to advertisers in order to increase advertising. However, the data is presented in a way that allows, with some limitations, comparisons between the attributes and attitudes of the major ethnic groups, and thus, like the Chiba Prefectural High School survey presented in Chapter 2, is very noteworthy. Each publication received 100 responses from readers, for a total of 900 responses. The attached table gives the name of each newspaper or magazine that participated in the survey, as well as the ethnic group to which its readers belong, and its publicly stated circulation (as of 1996).

The contents of the survey included attributes, period of stay in Japan, desire to settle permanently, Japanese language ability, positive or negative views of Japan, ease of living in Japan, income, type of housing, consumption, banking and savings, health and medical care, means of getting information,

Reference Table

Name of publication	Frequency of publication	Publicly-stated circulation	Ethnic group
Ryugakusei Shinbun	Twice/month	50,000	Chinese
Kaibigan	Monthly	32,000	Filipino
Aliran	Monthly	25,000	Korean
Tudobem	Weekly	40,000	Brazilian
Shin-Koryu Jiho	Monthly	39,000	Taiwanese
Sumai	Monthly	30,000	Thai
Malaysia Nippo	Monthly	22,000	Malaysian
Media	Monthly	17,000	Indonesian
Myanmar Times	Monthly	22,000	Myanmarese

newspaper subscriptions, and travel. The compilation and analysis of the data was done on an ethnic group-by-group basis as well as for the aggregate.

As points of reservation on this survey, the results are only presented as raw statistics, with no analysis beyond this. In addition, the purpose was to gain increased advertising, so there is a lot of information on propensity to consume and purchasing power.

4 Ko Sonfi, *op. cit.*, p. 176.

5 Komai Hiroshi, *Imin shakai Nihon no koso* (Vision for Japan as a country of immigrants), Toyo: Kokusai Shoin, 1994, p. 83.

6 See Chapter 3, Note 19.

7 Ballescas, M.R.P., 'Zainichi Firipin rodosha no tayo na jokyo,' (The diverse situation of Filipino workers in Japan), in Komai Hiroshi, ed., *Nihon no esunikku shakai* (Japan's ethnic society), *op. cit.* The survey was conducted on 60 Filipino workers, using a questionnaire. Of the 60, 18 were female entertainers. Practically all of the respondents were irregular workers. The survey data was arranged into current occupation, previous job in the Philippines, place of origin, individual attributes such as educational background, family situation, motivation for coming to Japan, employment situation, and life in Japan. In her paper, Ballescas presented the problematic that the Philippine economy is being incorporated as an informal sector into the formal Japanese economy, which is expanding on a global basis, and that this is triggering the movement of low-waged and unskilled Filipino workers to Japan.

8 See Chapter 3, Note 11.

9 Kura Shinichi, 'Keiki kotai ka ni okeru zainichi Iran-jin' (Iranians in Japan under the economic recession),' in Komai Hiroshi, ed., *Nihon no esunikku shakai* (Japan's ethnic society), *op. cit.* Kura argues that the inclination among Iranians from long-period stays toward settlement is a strategy for gaining life chances, and that this inclination determines their evaluations of Japanese and Japanese society in relation to the society context of their home country.

10 Council for Public Policy (Kokyo Seisaku Chosakai), *Rainichi gaikokujin no shakai futekio jokyo ni kansuru*

chosa (Study on the Situation of Social Non-Adaptation of Foreigners in Japan), 1991, in Komai Hiroshi, *Gaikokujin rodosha mondai shiryo shusei* (Compilation of resources on the issue of foreign workers), Tokyo: Akashi Shoten, 1994, Volume 1, p. 264. This survey is unique in that, while making use of police organizations, it examined the possibility of co-existence between local residents and foreign workers, as well as the potential and contents of frictions which could arise in communities, from both the perspectives of local residents and of foreign workers.

The overall survey was composed of one on the permeation of foreign workers throughout Japan, using data from police stations throughout the country, and another on the consciousness and attitudes of local residents. The latter is the more important of the two. In terms of methodology, six wards and cities were selected from five prefectures – Tokyo, Saitama, Chiba, Kanagawa, and Gunma – where many foreign workers were living and working, either generally or in specific neighborhoods. The survey was then conducted at 10 police boxes in neighborhoods where the police believed many foreign workers lived, and in 6 where they believed there were few. For each police box, 5 to 7 foreign workers were selected (regardless of whether they were irregular or not), for a total of 116 individuals. In addition, 100 Japanese residents over the age of 20 were selected for each police box, for a total of 1,600 individuals. The survey was conducted via questionnaire, with the forms dropped off at homes. The period was February 1 to March 25, 1990 for the foreign workers, and February 1 to March 10 for the Japanese.

Looking at the survey of foreign workers, the contents were organized into three main sections in addition to basic attributes: housing environment and individual living situation in Japan; perceptions of Japanese people and life within Japanese communities; and working and economic life. The questions on basic attributes included age, sex, nationality, marital status, and number of people in the household. The section on housing environment and individual living situation included questions on years lived in the same housing, hopes for future living, and type of housing. For the section on perceptions of Japanese and life within Japanese communities, the questions included impressions of the Japanese, ease of living in Japan, whether they had Japanese friends, desire and satisfaction with relationships with Japanese, and experiences of prejudice, discrimination, and troubles. Finally, the section on working and economic living included questions on work patterns and household expenditures.

The main contents of the survey of Japanese residents included, in addition to basic attributes such as age, sex, and occupation, four sections on foreign workers, including actual contact and the possibility of having relations with them, attitudes and opinions on their coming to Japan, community problems, and individual problems. On the possibility of contact and exchanges with foreign workers, respondents were divided into three categories (those who lived in close proximity, those who lived in the same neighborhood, and those who did not live near foreign workers). They were asked about whether they exchanged 'greetings' or 'had relations' and their degree, and whether they wanted to have relations. If they said they did not want to have relations, they were asked the reasons for this answer. On the issue of attitudes and opinions on foreign workers coming to Japan, they were asked whether they had an interest in the issue, whether they approved of or opposed the acceptance of foreign workers, and the reason for their answer, whether they approved of or opposed foreign workers working in their own town, and their attitudes toward races. Finally, in the category of community problems, they were asked about anxieties they felt and reasons for these feelings, bad experiences they had had, and whether they had ever gone to local authorities or the police for consultations, made phone calls, or negotiated with foreign workers directly to resolve problems.

As points of reservation on this survey, Chinese made up nearly thirty percent of the foreign respondents, with 33 individuals. Many of them were students at the time, and it is thus difficult to see them as typical foreign workers. In addition, the locations of the survey were biased toward the Kanto region. Furthermore, there were no Koreans at all. It should also be noted that, even given the fact that the influx of Latin American Nikkeijin was only beginning at the time, there were no Nikkeijin among the respondents. For the survey of Japanese residents, the main cross analysis was done on the basis of housing situation, between those who lived in close proximity, those who lived in the same neighborhood, and those who did not live near, foreign workers. This is valid in itself, as mentioned above, but considering the fact that there were 169 Japanese who exchanged 'greetings' or had 'relations' with foreign workers, cross compilation analysis with data on the degree to which people exchanged greetings or had relations could have pointed more clearly to a path for Japan becoming a society of multicultural coexistence.

11 Taiwanese were also included in the survey, but they had different attributes from other newcomer foreigners. Their average period of stay in Japan was 15 years, for example.

12 See Chapter 3, Note 19.

13 The most thorough work on this issue remains Shukuya Kyoko, *Ajia kara kita hanayome* (Brides from Asia), Tokyo: Akashi Shoten, 1988.

14 The above data is from Ministry of Health and Welfare, Statistics and Information Department, *Jinko dotai tokei* (Vital statistics), various years.

15 Tokyo Metropolitan Council for Social Welfare, *Zaiju gaikokujin no fukushi/seikatsu kadai ni kansuru jittai chosa hokokusho* (Report from a fact-finding survey on issues involving the welfare and living of foreigners in Japan), 1993, in Komai Hiroshi, *Gaikokujin rodosha mondai shiryo shusei* (Compilation of resources on the issue of foreign workers in Japan), *op. cit.* Volume 2, p. 51.

16 Okada Emiko, 'Nihon de hataraku – aru Iran-jin seinen no kiroku' (Working in Japan: the chronicle of one Iranian youth), *op. cit.*, p. 34.

17 Komai Hiroshi, ed., *Zainichi Iranjin* (Iranians in Japan), *op. cit.*, p. 336.

18 Sugiyama Katsumi *et. al*, 'Seifuzoku sangyo ni juji suru tainichi gaikokujin josei no seikatsu' (The life of foreign women employed in the sex and entertainment industry in Japan), in Rainichi Gaikokujin to no Kyosei Shakai Kenkyukai (Research

Group on Coexistence with Foreigners in Japan), *Rainichi Ajia/ Afurika-kei gaikokujin no seikatsu teikio to Nihonjin to no kyosei ni kansuru kenkyu* (Study on the adjustment to living of Asian and African foreign workers in Japan and their co-existence with Japanese), University of Tokyo, Medical Department, Office of Sociology of Health, 1994.

19 This information is based on visits I made to the Islamic Center Japan, Isezaki Mosque, and Ichinowari Mosque in 1997.

20 Kawasaki City, 'Kawasaki-shi gaikoku-seki shimin ishiki jittai chosa' (Kawasaki City Fact-Finding Survey of Attitudes of Citizens with Foreign Nationality), 1993, in Komai Hiroshi, *Gaikokujin teiju mondai shiryo shusei* (Compilation of resources on the issue of foreign settlement in Japan), *op. cit.*

21 Komai, *op. cit.* (Note 5), p. 81.

22 Chugoku Kikokusha Mondai Kenkyukai (Study Group on the Problems of Chinese Returnees), *Sokoku fukki eno ayumi* (Steps toward return to the motherland), 1990, pp. 46–50, quoted from Imada Katsuji, *Chugoku kikokusha to Nihon shakai* (Returnees from China and Japanese society), University of Tokyo master thesis, undated, pp. 35–36.

23 Kuwayama Norihiko, 'Gaikokujin hanayome no shinri' (The psychology of foreign brides), *Imago*, Seidosha, January 1994, pp. 62–63.

24 Ebata Keisuke, 'Chugoku kikokusha ni mirareta seishin byori,' (Psychopathology seen in returnees from China), *Health Sciences*, Vol. 3, No. 1, 1987, p. 25.

25 Kuwayama, *op. cit.*, pp. 66, 73.

26 See Ito Yasuo, 'Kanto-ken ni okeru shin-kakyo no esunikku bijinesu' (Ethnic businesses by new overseas Chinese in the Kanto region), in Komai Hiroshi, ed., *Nihon no esunikku shakai* (Japan's ethnic society), *op. cit.*, p. 287.

27 Tajima Junko, *Sekai toshi Tokyo no Ajia-kei ijusha* (Asian migrants in the international city of Tokyo), *op. cit.*

28 Ito Yasuo, *op. cit.* The survey was conducted on 18 new Overseas Chinese owners of shops and offices in the Kanto Region, and at 36 firms they ran. He analyzed the businesses they ran with ethnic ties, from the perspective of situational

ethnicity, meaning that subjects selected ethnicity in the way that best served their interests.

29   See Shiramizu Shigehiko, ed., *Esunikku media* (Ethnic media), Tokyo: Akashi Shoten, 1996.

30   The above information is from Shiramizu Shigehiko, *Esunikku bunka shakaigaku* (The sociology of ethnic culture), Tokyo: Nihon Hyoron-sha, 1998, Chapter III.

31   Hamamatsu City International Affairs Office, 'Survey on Living Situation and Attitudes of Foreigners in Hamamatsu City', 1993, in *Shinrai/teiju gaikokujin shiryo shusei* (Compilation of resources related to newcomer and settled foreigners), *op. cit.* Volume 2, p. 389.

32   *Asahi Shimbun*, November 16, 1994.

33   Inaba Yoshiko, *et. al, Gaikokujin kyoju to henbo suru machi* (Foreign residents and changing towns), Tokyo: Gakugei Shuppansha, 1994, pp. 126–127.

34   See Note 19.

35   It is very impressive to see groups of Muslims in white hats walking in broad daylight in Isezaki.

36   Iida Toshiro, 'Toshi shakai ni okeru esunishiti: Chugoku kikokusha no jirei bunseki o chushin ni' (Ethnity in urban society: Centered on the analysis of the case of returnees from China), in Komai Hiroshi, ed., *Nihon no esunikku shakai* (Japan's ethnic society), *op. cit.*, p. 271.

37   Hamatsu City, *op. cit.*, pp. 334–335.

38   Ishii Yuka, *Esunikku kankei to hito no kokusai ido* (Ethnic relations and international movements of people), Tokyo: Kokusai Shoin, 1999, p. 131. In this survey, Ishii attempted to demonstrate the validity of S. Sassen's hypothesis on the links between the globalization of production and movements of people, using Chinese Malaysians, but could not validate it. The survey was conducted by interviews using questionnaires. A total of 96 responses were obtained from the Tokyo metropolitan region, centered around the capital. Looking at the results, the majority of respondents were from urban areas such as Kuala Lumpur and Penang. Many had worked as cooks, in manufacturing, or as construction workers immediately before coming to Japan, and their incomes had been in the middle or higher strata. Half of the respondents had

come to Japan using agents.

39 Komai Hiroshi, *Gaikokujin teiju mondai shiryo shusei* (Compilation of resources on the issue of foreign settlement in Japan), *op. cit.*, p. 565.

40 University of Tokyo, Medical Department, Office of Sociology of Health, 'Ueno no machi to Iran-jin: masatsu to kyosei' (Iranians in Ueno: friction and coexistence), 1992, in Komai Hiroshi, *Gaikokujin rodosha mondai shiryo shusei* (Compilation of resources on the issue of foreign workers), *op. cit.*, Volume 2, p. 199. The purpose of this study was to shed light on the relations between Iranians coming to Ueno and the local town, as well as the attitudes and responses of the local residents to the presence of the Iranians.

The survey, which was conducted in June 1992, was divided into one of Iranians and one of Japanese. The survey of Iranians was done on individuals who gathered at Keisei Ueno Station and the area around Ueno Park. Questionnaires translated into Persian were distributed, and the respondents filled in the answers in either Persian or English. Valid responses were received from 143 individuals. The survey of Japanese was done by random sampling, from among residents of Ueno 2-, 4-, and 6-chome (Japanese towns are divided into sections called '*chomes*'), as well as owners and managers of shops in the Ueno merchants association. I would like to focus exclusively on the survey of Iranians, however. The contents included nationality, age, length of stay in Japan, number of days worked per month, contents of job, place of work, place of living, reason for coming to Ueno, use of shops in Ueno, frequency of contact with Japanese, and impressions of experience in Japan.

The first point of reservation with this survey is that the translation into Persian of the questionnaire was not always accurate. It is a very time-consuming task to translate questionnaires into foreign languages, but it is necessary to be very careful in view of the importance of this task. Second, the report only carried the results of simple computations, without cross compilation. The survey would have been more insightful if it had included analysis by pattern of employment.

41 Iida, *op. cit.*, p. 271.

42 Enari Miyuki, *et. al*, 'Nanbei nikkeijin no shakai kankei' (Social relations of South American Nikkeijin), in Rainichi Gaikokujin tono Kyosei Shakai Kenkyukai, *op. cit.*, pp. 202–203.

43 Hamamatsu City, *op. cit.*, p. 388.

44 Ko, *op. cit.*, pp. 178, 170–171.

45 Ishii, *op. cit.*, p. 145.

46 Wakabayashi Chihiro, 'Tainichi Afurika Kokujin no 'puraido' keisei no tame no nettowaku' (Networks for the building of 'pride' among African blacks living in Japan), in Komai Hiroshi, ed., *Nihon no esunikku shakai* (Japan's ethnic society), *op. cit.* This is the only survey available of Africans in Japan. It is clear that the experience of coexisting with people from Africa has had a considerable impact on the Japanese and Japanese society; the purpose of this survey was to determine the nature of this impact. Some 20 individuals were interviewed, using the roundabout method of finding friends of friends, and allowing them to answer freely to interviews. The survey was divided into three sections: reason for coming to Japan and life in Japan, networks, and Japanese views of blacks.

47 Ballescas, *op. cit.*, p. 106.

48 Tokyo Metropolitan Council of Social Welfare, *op. cit.*, p. 25.

49 Chiba Prefectural Chiba High School, International Social Studies Group, *Gaikokujin rodosha jittai chosa, 1995-nen–1996-nen* (1995–1996 Fact-finding survey of foreign workers), 1997, in *Shinrai/teiju gaikokujin shiryo shusei* (Compilation of resources related to newcomer and settled foreigners), *op. cit*, Volume 2, pp. 48–49.

50 University of Tokyo, Medical Department, Office of Sociology of Health, *op. cit.*, p. 204.

51 Ko, *op. cit.*, p. 185.

Chapter 5

1 Komai, Hiroshi, ed., *Chugoku kikosha nisei, sansei* (Second- and third-generation returnees from China), Tsukuba: University of Tsukuba, Institute of Social Studies, 1996, in *Shinrai/teiju gaikokujin shiryo shusei* (Compilation of resources related to newcomer and settled foreigners), *op. cit.*

2 Higashizawa Yasushi, *Nagai tabi no omoni* (The heavy burden of a long voyage), Tokyo: Kaifu Shobo, 1993, p. 135.
3 University of Tokyo, Medical Department, Office of Sociology of Health, 'Ueno no machi to Iran-jin: masatsu to kyosei' (Iranians in Ueno: friction and coexistence), 1992, in Komai Hiroshi, ed., *Gaikokujin rodosha mondai shiryo shusei* (Compilation of resources on the issue of foreign workers), *op. cit.*
4 Komai Hiroshi, ed., *Zainichi Iranjin* (Iranians in Japan), Tsukuba: University of Tsukuba, Institute of Social Sciences, 1994, in Komai Hiroshi, ed., *Gaikokujin teiju mondai shiryo shusei* (Compilation of resources on the issue of foreign settlement in Japan), *op. cit.*
5 Tokyo Metropolitan Council on Social Welfare, *Zaiju gaikokujin no fukushi/seikatsu kadai ni kansuru jittai chosa hokokusho* (Report from a field survey on issues involving the welfare and living of foreigners in Japan), 1993, in *Gaikokujin rodosha mondai shiryo shusei* (Compilation of resources on the issue of foreign workers in Japan), *op. cit.*, Volume 2, p. 29.
6 Komai Hiroshi, *Imin shakai Nihon no koso* (Vision for Japan as a country of immigrants), Tokyo: Kokusai Shoin, 1994, p. 81.
7 Okada Emiko, 'Nihon de hataraku – aru Iran-jin seinen no kiroku' (Working in Japan: the chronicle of one Iranian youth,' in Komai Hiroshi, ed., *Nihon no esunikku shakai* (Japan's ethnic society), Tokyo: Akashi Shoten, 1996.
8 *Asahi Shimbun*, September 29, 1998.
9 *Nihon Keizai Shimbun*, September 3, 1998.
10 Hashimoto Kohei, 'Zainichi imin rodosha no hanzai to sono suii' (Crime by migrant workers in Japan, and changes), *Kenkyu Ripoto* (Research report), Tokyo: PHP Research Institute, Inc., Research Division, Vol. VIII, June 1994.
11 Management and Coordination Agency, Administrative Inspection Bureau, *Gaikokujin no shuro ni kansuru jittai chosa kekka hokokusho* (Report on field survey on the employment of foreigners), 1992, in Komai Hiroshi, ed., *Gaikokujin rodosha mondai shiryo shusei* (Compilation of resources on the issue of foreign workers), *op. cit.* This report provides very unique, invaluable and interesting material, as its aim was to

cite inadequacies with the various policies and measures of administrative organs toward foreign workers, or problems in coordination between policies, and to offer comprehensive recommendations for resolving these problems. Japan's state administrative organs, such as various ministries and agencies, tend to carefully conceal defects in their own measures, and thus cannot criticize the measures of other organs. On top of this, there is a lack of consideration for overall administrative policies toward foreigners because of turf disputes between different agencies (in Japanese this situation is known as '*tatewari gyosei*'). This report took the stance of overcoming these limitations, which is natural given that it was conducted by the Administration Inspection Bureau of the Management and Coordination Agency. Another merit of this report is that not only does it allow a grasp of the inadequacies of Japanese administrative policies toward foreigners, but also gives an understanding of its overall characteristics.

The report was based on surveys carried out between January and June 1991, toward the National Public Safety Commission, Management and Coordination Agency, Economic Planning Agency, Science and Technology Agency, Ministry of Justice, Ministry of Foreign Affairs, Ministry of Finance, Ministry of Education, Ministry of Health and Welfare, Ministry of Agriculture, Forestry and Fisheries, Ministry of International Trade and Industry, Ministry of Transport, Ministry of Posts and Telecommunications, Ministry of Labor, Ministry of Construction, Ministry of Home Affairs, prefectural governments, local governments, and related administrative bodies. As far as can be gleamed from the contents of the recommendations and the explanations, the methodology was mainly the collection of related documents and interviews, with follow-up surveys conducted through local branches when necessary.

It can be pointed out as a limitation that the report fails to touch upon police-related or judicial policies. Many human rights violations have occurred during raids or investigations concerning violations of the Immigration Control Law carried out jointly by the police and immigration officials. There have also been problems during trials because of the serious lack of interpreters. It would have been desirable to get an overall grasp of this situation. Moreover, local governments have played a large role in compensating for the central government's slowness in implementing policies, but this report failed to adequately address the relationship between the two.

12 Ministry of Justice, Immigration Bureau, 'Joriku kyohisha su' (Number of persons refused entry), various years, Japan Immigration Association, *Shutsunyukoku kanri tokei gaiyo* (Summary of statistics on immigration and emigration), various years. The years 1989–1992 are included in Komai Hiroshi, ed., *Gaikokujin rodosha mondai shiryo shusei* (Compilation of resources on the issue of foreign workers), *op. cit.*. Through these documents, one can get a rough picture of the frequency of cases in which people with valid visas, or from countries that have visa exemption agreements with Japan, are refused entry on the grounds that they may engage in illegal work.

13 With the 1994 revision of the Pension Law, it became possible to make lump sum payments to foreigners leaving Japan.

14 Chiba Prefectural Chiba High School, International Social Studies Group, *Gaikokujin rodosha jittai chosa, 1995-nen–1996-nen*, (1995–1996 field survey of foreign workers), 1997, pp. 85–86. This section was not included in *Shinrai/teiju gaikokujin shiryo shusei* (Compilation of resources related to newcomer and settled foreigners), *op. cit.* Filipinos made up 58% of the respondents, more than 90% were young people in their 20s (58%) and 30s (33%), and 72% were men. Moreover, 61% had been in Japan for at least three years.

15 Kihara Masahiro *et al.*, 'Rainichi gaikokujin no HIV kotai kensa, HIV kotai yoseiritsu oyobi seikansen-sho no doko ni tsuite,' (Trends in the undergoing of HIV tests, rates of HIV positivity, and venereal diseases among foreigners in Japan), *Nippon Koshu Eisei Zasshi* (Japanese Journal of Public Health), Vol. 40, No. 12, 1993.

16 Kihara Masako *et al.*, 'Fuzoku eigyo ni kakawaru rainichi gaikokujin josei no shoku/keireki oyobi kokunai ni okeru seikodo ni tsuite' (The occupations, personal history and sexual behavior in Japan of foreign women involved in the sex industry), *Nippon Koshu Eisei Zasshi* (Japanese Journal of Public Health), Vol. 41, No. 2, 1994.

17 Sugiyama Katsumi *et al.*, 'Seifuzoku sangyo ni juji suru tainichi gaikokujin josei no seikatsu' (The life of foreign women employed in the sex and entertainment industry in Japan), in Rainichi Gaikokujin tono Kyosei Shakai Kenkyukai (Study Group on Coexistence with Foreigners in Japan), *Rainichi Ajia/Afurika-kei gaikokujin no seikatsu tekio to Nihonjin tono kyosei ni kansuru kenkyu* (Study on the adjustment to living of Asian and African foreign workers in Japan and their coexistence with Japanese), 1994, p. 81.

18 Tokyo Metropolitan Council on Social Welfare, *op. cit.*, pp. 41–43.

19 Chiba Prefectural High School, *op. cit.*, p. 88.

20 Nyukan Mondai Chosakai (Immigration Review Task Force), eds., *Misshitsu no jinken shingai* (Human rights violations behind closed doors), Tokyo: Gendai Jinbun-sha, 1996, is full of vivid reports of terrible cases. The group's web site is at *http://www2.odn.ne.jp/nyukan*.

21 Ministry of Education, Science and International Affairs Bureau, '*Nihongo kyoiku ga hitsuyo na gaikokujin jido/seito no ukeire jokyo-nado ni kansuru chosa*' *no kekka* (Results of the 'Survey on the situation of acceptance of foreign children and pupils who require Japanese language instruction'), published every other year, in Komai Hiroshi, ed., *Shinrai/teiju gaikokujin shiryo shusei* (Compilation of resources related to newcomer and settled foreigners), *op. cit.* This document was unique in that it included national data on the situation and policies regarding the acceptance of foreign children and pupils enrolled in Japanese public elementary, junior high, and (since 1993) senior high schools, and who required Japanese language instruction. The first survey was conducted in September 1991, the second in September 1993, the third in September 1995, and the fourth in September 1997. In terms of the situation regarding acceptance, survey items consisted of enrollment by school type, prefecture, school year, sex, period of enrollment, and mother tongue as well as the number of schools and the number of municipalities (since 1995). The survey items on the state of policies and measures were divided by prefectural boards of education and municipality boards of education. For 1991, a

section was included on the degree of understanding of Japanese language and the situation of teaching.

With regard to related documents, since 1996 the Agency for Cultural Affairs has published yearly reports titled 'Nihongo kyoiku no gaiyo' (Outline of Japanese language education) in Japan. They include, in addition to information on educational institutions, numbers of people studying Japanese by country of origin.

22 Nakanishi Akira (chief researcher), 'Gaikokujin jido/seito no ukeire to sono shido/kyoiku ni kansuru jissenteki kenkyu' (Practical studies on the acceptance and instruction/education of foreign children and pupils,' 1994, in Komai Hiroshi, ed., *Gaikokujin teiju mondai shiryo shusei* (Compilation of resources on the issue of foreign settlement in Japan), *op. cit.* With regard to the education of children of newcomer foreigners, it is easy to say, from the perspective of multiculturalism, that multicultural education should be conducted, but in reality there are many obstacles. This report was a pioneering research which approached the issue from the standpoint of pedagogy. The aim of the study was to expose, without ethical or philosophical bias, the problems confronting schools which accept children and pupils from different cultures.

The study was composed of (1) an interview survey of foreign children and pupils; (2) an analysis of the practical instruction given by teachers; (3) analysis including the study journals of schools accepting foreign children; and (4) a questionnaire of regular children and pupils. The methods for the various parts were as follows.

First, (1) was carried out from November 1992 to June 1993, on 29 foreign children. It was a detailed interview, including questions on home life, school life, language, future plans, and impressions of Japan. Of the 29 respondents, a large number, 11, were Brazilians. (2) was carried in January 1994, on 195 teachers who were directly instructing foreign children in schools with many such students, and responses were recovered from 101 individuals. It was done by questionnaire, with questions on the attributes of the children/pupils, early-phase instruction, class instruction, extracurricular instruction, contact with families, communication with parents, and problems and tasks regarding education. For (3), requests were made to designated cooperating schools in the education of foreign children, or schools that put out research journals or records of practical guidance involving education for international understanding, asking them to send copies of their journals. Analyses were done on the journals of 17 elementary schools and three junior high schools from which their concrete experiences could be grasped. An attempt was made to grasp the educational policy and teaching situation using research themes, basic guidelines, and proposed cumulative guidance as material. (4) was conducted from November to December, 1993, on eight public elementary schools (780 pupils) and five junior high schools (734 pupils) in areas where there were many foreign children and pupils, either by dropped off questionnaires or group questionnaire sessions. The contents of the survey were interactions with foreigner classmates, attitudes toward foreigner friends and foreign cultures, relationship between class characteristics and interchanges, and culturo-centric attitudes.

The first point of reservation on this survey is that, unfortunately, there was no introduction to existing literature. Even if work up until that time was fragmentary, it would have been desirable to make reference to it, as this study was pioneering. Second, it appears that the orientation toward theorization was rather weak. There seemed to be few organic links between the chapters, and this may be a manifestation of a lack of effort to build a general model based on the collected data.

23 JICA (Japan International Cooperation Agency), *Nikkeijin honpo shuro jittai chosa* (Field survey on the employment situation of Nikkeijin in Japan), 1992, in Komai Hiroshi, ed., *Gaikokujin teiju mondai shiryo shusei* (Compilation of resources on the issue of foreign settlement in Japan), *op. cit.*, p. 185.

24 Watanabe Masako, 'Nikkei Burajiru-jin jido/seito no zoka ni taisuru kyoiku genba deno mosaku' (Attempts at the educational field level to cope with the increasing number of Nikkei Brazilian children and pupils), *Shakaigaku/shakai fukushigaku kenkyu* (Sociological and social welfare studies), Meiji Gakuin University, Vol. 96, March 1995, pp. 59–60.

25 Regarding this study, see Chapter 6, Note 9.

Chapter 6

1 See Komai Hiroshi, *Imin shakai Nihon no koso* (Vision for Japan as a country of immigrants), Toyo: Kokusai Shoin, 1994, p. 172.

2 Ministry of Home Affairs, 'Jichitai kokusai kyoryoku suishin seisaku taiko no sakutei ni kansuru shishin ni tsuite' (Direction on formulating a policy framework to promote international cooperation by local governments), *Jichikoku* No. 5, April 30, 1995.

3 Looking at the distribution of registered foreigners by prefecture in 1998, by far the greatest concentrations were in Tokyo (17.4%) and Osaka (13.7%), but the number dropped slightly in Osaka compared to the end of the previous year. The rates of increase in Chiba and Saitama prefectures were particularly striking. For Tokyo, the rate was somewhat above the national average. For reference, see Outline Table 5, Japan Immigration Association, *Heisei 11-nendo zairyu gaikokujin tokei* (Statistics on resident foreigners for 1999), 1999.

4 Pioneering literature on the internationalization policies of local governments include Kanagawa Prefecture Self-Government Research Center, *Chikyuka jidai no jichitai* (Local governments in the age of globalization), 1988, and Tokyo Metropolitan Government, Bureau of Citizens and Cultural Affairs, *Tokyo-to ku-shi-cho-son ni okeru kokusai koryu jigyo ni kansuru chosa kekka* (Results of survey on international exchange projects in municipalities in Tokyo), 1989. The 1991 survey by the Administrative Management Research Center (Gyosei Kanri Kenkyu Senta), *Kokusaika jidai to jichitai* (The age of internationalization and local governments), contained examples of activities carried out by advanced local governments throughout the country, but was somewhat fragmentary. The 1991 survey by All Japan Prefectural and Municipal Workers' Union (Jichiro), Research Institute on Local Governance, Central Promotion Committee, *Gaikokujin wa jumin desu* (Foreigners are

residents), proposed measures while making clear the principles they should be based upon. The 1992 survey by the Kanagawa Study Group on the Problems of Foreigners Living in Japan, *Tabunka/taminzoku shakai no shinko to gaikokujin ukeire no genjo* (The development of a multi-cultural/multiracial society and the current state of the acceptance of foreigners) was full of interesting insights, though its scope was limited to Kanagawa Prefecture. Also, Ebashi Takashi, ed., *Gaikokujin wa jumin desu* (Foreigners are residents), Tokyo: Gakuyo Shobo, 1993, while following upon the results of the survey by the All Japan Prefectural and Municipal Workers' Union, was a broad compilation of measures by different local governments throughout the country. In addition, there is, for example, the 1994 survey by the Tokyo Metropolitan Roundtable on International Policies, *Tokyo-to kokusai seisaku kondankai hokokusho* (Report of the Tokyo Metropolitan Roundtable on International Policies).

5   Included in Komai Hiroshi, *Gaikokujin teiju mondai shiryo shusei* (Compilation of resources on the issue of foreign settlement in Japan), Tokyo: Akashi Shoten, 1995. The purpose of this survey was to provide reference materials for the Tokyo Metropolitan Roundtable on International Policies, a private advisory organ to the governor, as well as to provide documents for examining Tokyo's international policies. It was conducted on local governments which were considered to have relatively large numbers of foreigners within their jurisdiction. They included ten prefectural organizations which were the home to ordinance-designated cities, four other prefectural organizations, 12 designated cities, and seven other local governments, for a total of 33 bodies. The survey was composed of two parts, the first on basic philosophy and the second on examples of measures to serve as reference, both in the form of questionnaires with free responses. It was conducted from June to October, 1993, and responses were received from 29 local government bodies.

The major items in the first part included basic philosophy, multilingual services, medical care, education and labor, housing measures, the treatment of so-called illegal workers, support for college and pre-college foreign students, links with volunteer and other groups, the employment of foreigners as government employees, and voting rights for foreigners at the local level. The second part included the provision of information, town signboards, the grasp of foreigners' desires and consultation services for foreigners, natural disaster and crime prevention, medical care, welfare, labor, education, housing, community-based exchange projects, the creation of an environment to nurture the international sensitivity of residents, the employment of foreigners as government employees and the training of civil servants to cope with internationalization, and measures toward so-called illegal workers.

The first point of reservation on this survey is that it did not include the Tokyo Metropolitan Government and the special administrative wards within Tokyo. Even considering that the aim was to examine policies for Tokyo, it should have introduced the existing measures of the Metropolitan Government and the wards. In connection to this, two important designated cities, Osaka and Nagoya, are not included in the survey. The measures of these two cities and Tokyo's special administrative wards would have been helpful for other municipalities around the country. Okinawa Prefecture and Ota City also failed to respond to the questionnaire.

With regard to the methodology, no explanation was given regarding the criteria on which the contents of measures were chosen. Given the fact that internationalization is a new administrative issue, current measures have yet to be solidly systematized. In consideration of this, the survey should have included an explanation of the philosophy upon which it was based. Finally, in terms of the results, merely enumerating responses makes it difficult to grasp the overall situation. At the least, it would have been helpful to have some theoretical analysis.

6 Also included in Komai Hiroshi, *Gaikokujin teiju mondai shiryo shusei* (Compilation of resources on the issue of foreign settlement in Japan), *op. cit.* The proposal was outsourced by Kawasaki City to Prof. Ebashi's laboratory at Hosei University, and written under the responsibility of

the Kawasaki City Study and Research Committee on Measures for Foreign Citizens.

7 Some pioneering literature on administrative demand regarding the international policies of local governments include: Tokyo Minato-ku Cultural and International Exchange Planning Division, *Minato-ku zaiju gaikokujin no ishiki chosa* (Attitude survey of foreigners living in Minato-ku), 1989; and Tokyo-to Toshima-ku Planning Division, *Toshima-ku no kokusaika ni kansuru gyosei juyo chosa* (Survey on administrative demands concerning the internationalization of Toshima-ku), 1989. With regard to old-comer foreigners, there is a significant amount of information, beginning with Kinbara Samon, Ishida Reiko *et. al*, *Nihon no naka no Kankoku/Chosenjin/Chugokujin* (The Koreans and Chinese inside Japan), Tokyo: Akashi Shoten, 1986. Surveys carried out by local governments targeted mainly at Nikkeijin were mentioned in Chapter 3. Recent surveys in similar areas included Part III of Chiba Prefecture Planning Division, Cultural and International Affairs Department, *Chiba-ken kokusaika suishin kiso chosa hokokusho: Heisei roku-nendo jisshi* (Report on a basic survey of the promotion of internationalization in Chiba Prefecture, carried out in 1994), and Tokyo Metropolitan Government, Bureau of Citizens and Cultural Affairs, *Tokyo-to zaiju gaikokujin seikatsu jittai chosa* (Fact-finding survey on the living of foreigners residing in Tokyo-to), 1997.

8 Included in Komai Hiroshi, *Gaikokujin teiju mondai shiryo shusei* (Compilation of resources on the issue of foreign settlement in Japan), *op. cit*. The survey was targeted at 3,000 foreigners of at least 18 years of age, registered in Kawasaki City, selected by random sampling. It was done through mail, and 1,146 valid responses were sent back, meaning a recovery rate of 38.2%. It was conducted from January to March 1993, with questionnaires prepared in Japanese, Hangul, Chinese, English, and Portuguese.

The composition by nationality of the respondents was as follows: 42.1% were South or North Korean, 23.4% from China, Taiwan or Hong Kong, 9.4% Brazilian, 3.1% from

Latin American countries outside Brazil, 6.8% Filipinos, 5.3% from other Asian countries, 8.5% from North America, Europe or Oceania, and 1.4% from other regions. In other words, Koreans made up more than 40% of respondents, and a further nearly one fourth were Chinese, Taiwanese and people from Hong Kong. For the analysis the Koreans were separated into those who had been in Japan for less than ten years and for ten years or more, and the others were analyzed according to their nationalities. The data was also analyzed using three large categories: Asia, Latin America, and Europe/North America/Oceania.

9   Included in Komai Hiroshi, *Shinrai/teiju gaikokujin shiryo shusei* (Compilation of resources related to newcomer and settled foreigners), Tokyo: Akashi Shoten, 1998. In terms of methodology, 3,300 registered foreigners of at least 16 years of age living in the prefecture were selected by random sampling, excluding permanent residents and special permanent residents. Questionnaires were sent by post, and 877 valid responses were recovered, meaning a recovery rate of 26.6%. The significance of the exclusion of the special permanent residents was to limit the analysis to newcomer foreigners. This focus was a special feature of this survey. The survey was carried out from July to August 1996. In addition to Japanese, the questionnaires were produced in English, Chinese, Hangul, Spanish, and Portuguese. Looking at the nationalities of respondents, 35.0% were from China, 13.0% from the Philippines, 8.6% from South Korea, 10.0% from other Asian countries, 16.1% from Brazil, 6.4% from other Latin American countries, 3.9% from Europe/North America, and 1.7% from Oceania/Africa, with 5.4% not answering.

The first point of reservation about this survey is that although a roughly equal number of male and female foreigners were registered in Saitama Prefecture in 1996, 57.8% of the respondents of the survey were women, versus 40.1% men. In addition, whereas 29.3% of registered foreigners in the prefecture were 'spouses or children of Japanese nationals,' they made up a high percentage, or 39.2%, of the respondents. Thus, it is necessary to note that women and spouses of Japanese were over-represented in the survey. In particular, 90% of Filipinos and two thirds of Koreans were women. It is also important to mention that because the subjects were selected from among registered foreigners, it is likely that irregular foreigners, including overstayers, who made up roughly one fourth of all new-comer foreigners at the time the survey was taken, were almost completely excluded.

10 See Komai Hiroshi and Watado Ichiro, eds., *Jichitai no gaikokujin seisaku* (The policies of local governments toward foreigners), Tokyo: Akashi Shoten, 1997.

11 *Nihon Keizai Shimbun*, March 29, 1993.

12 Tokita Tadahiko, *Nihon no iryo keizai* (The economics of medicine in Japan), Tokyo: Toyo Keizai Shimpo Sha, 1995, p. 109.

13 Tokyo Metropolitan Council on Social Welfare, *Zaiju gaikokujin no fukushi/seikatsu kadai ni kansuru jittai chosa hokokusho* (Report from a field survey on issues involving the welfare and living of foreigners in Japan), 1993, in *Gaikokujin rodosha mondai shiryo shusei* (Compilation of resources on the issue of foreign workers in Japan), *op. cit.*, Volume. 2, p. 43.

14 JICA (Japan International Cooperation Agency), *Nikkeijin honpo shuro jittai chosa hokokusho* (Field survey on the employment situation of Nikkeijin in Japan), 1992, in Komai Hiroshi, *Gaikokujin teiju mondai shiryo shusei* (Compilation of resources on the issue of foreign settlement in Japan), *op. cit.*, p. 196.

15 Myrdal, G., *An American Dilemma*, New York: Harper & Row, 1944, Chapter 30.

16 Literature regarding foreigners in communities include: Kawamura Chizuko, 'Shinjuku-ku: kyosei no mainasu men o purasu ni kaeru machizukuri' (Shinjuku Ward: community building in a way that turns the demerits of coexistence into benefits), in Komai Hiroshi and Watado Ichiro, eds., *Jichitai no gaikokujin seisaku* (The policies of local governments toward foreigners), *op. cit.*; and Sakai Kazuko, 'Toshima-ku: kokusaika seisaku no rekishi' (Toshima Ward: the history of policies of internationalization), in the same book. Tomizawa

Hisao, Tamaki Yasuaki, and Inuzuka Kyota made some very interesting discoveries in their survey of foreign workers in *Shizuoka-ken Ogasa-gun Daito-cho zainichi gaikokujin chosa hokokusho* (Report from a survey of foreigners in Daito Town, Ogasa County, Shizuoka Prefecture), Shizuoka: Shizuoka Prefectural University, Division of International Relations, 1993.

17 Council for Public Policy (Kokyo Seisaku Chosakai), *Rainichi gaikokujin no shakai-teki futekio jokyo ni kansuru chosa* (Study on the Situation of Social Non-Adaptation of Foreigners in Japan), 1991, in Komai Hiroshi, *Gaikokujin rodosha mondai shiryo shusei* (Compilation of resources on the issue of foreign workers), *op. cit.*

18 Watado Ichiro, ed., *Ajia toshi 'Tokyo' no komyunitii* (Communities in the Asian city of 'Tokyo'), Tokyo: Meisei University, Division of Humanities, Department of Sociology, 1993, p. 70. The subjects of the study were residents of Shinjuku Ward and Hino City.

19 Sugiyama Katsumi *et al.*, 'Tochigi-ken A-shi ni okeru gaikokujin hanzai no hassei to Nihonjin jumin no hanno' (The occurrence of crimes committed by foreigners in A City, Tochigi Prefecture, and the response of Japanese residents, and Mita Yuko *et al.*, 'Tomo-chiku T-shi ni okeru machi-koba to gaikokujin rodosha' (Local factories and foreign workers in T City, Tomo Region, in Rainichi Gaikokujin to no Kyosei Shakai Kenkyukai (Study Group on Coexistence with Foreigners in Japan), *Rainichi Ajia/Afurika-kei gaikokujin no seikatsu tekio to Nihonjin tono kyosei ni kansuru kenkyu* (Study on the adjustment to living of Asians and Africans in Japan and their coexistence with Japanese), 1994.

20 Tsuzuki Kurumi, 'Nikkei Burajiru-jin ukeire to chiiki no henyo' (The acceptance of Nikkei Brazilians and changes in communities), in Komai Hiroshi, ed., *Nihon no esunikku shakai* (Japan's ethnic society), *op. cit.* Tsuzuki conducted her examinations from the perspective of coexistence. Here, 'coexistence' is defined as 'groups with different characteristics being equal and having communication as they face each other within a society.'

21 Enari Miyuki *et al.*, 'Nanbei Nikkeijin no shakai kankei'

(Social relations of Nikkeijin from South America), in the report in Note 19, pp. 208–209.

22 Agency for Cultural Affairs, Cultural Affairs Department, *Heisei 10-nendo kokunai no Nihongo kyoiku no gaiyo* (Outline of Japanese language education in Japan in 1998), 1999.

23 See Nihongo Borantia Koza Henshu Iinkai, ed., *Ima! Nihongo boranteia: 'Nihongo borantia koza' [Tokyo]* (Now! Japanese language volunteers: 'Japanese language volunteer courses' [Tokyo]), Tokyo: Bonjin-sha, 1996, and Nihongo Borantia Koza Henshu Iinkai, ed., *Ima! Nihongo boranteia: 'Nihongo borantia koza' [Yamagata]* (Now! Japanese language volunteers: 'Japanese language volunteer courses' [Yamagata]), Tokyo: Bonjin-sha, 1996.

Chapter 7

1 Komai Hiroshi (chief researcher), *Zainichi gaikokujin no kachi ishiki* (Value consciousness of foreigners in Japan), Report financed by Grants-in-Aid for Scientific Research, (Kaken), 1998, is a detailed report on this survey.

2 Hofstede used the term 'culture 1' to refer to culture in the narrow meaning of something born from a refined spirit, and 'culture 2' to refer to culture in the broad sense of ways of thinking, feeling, and behavioral patterns. Hofstede, Geert, *Cultures and Organizations*, UK: McGraw-Hill, 1991. My distinction between 'high culture' and 'everyday culture' was inspired by this argument.

3 Parsons, Talcott, *The Social System*, Glencoe, Illinois: Free Press, 1951.

4 Hofstede, *op. cit.*

5 See Habermas, Jürgen, 'Struggles for Recognition in the Democratic Constitutional State,' in Gutmann, Amy, ed., *Multiculturalism*, Princeton: Princeton University Press, 1994.

6 The main areas of survey and numbers of valid responses for the various ethnic groups were as follows. Chinese: Koto Ward, Tokyo, 51; Brazilians: Ooizumi Town, Gunma Prefecture, 67; Koreans: Shinjuku Ward, Tokyo, 94; Filipinos: Chiba Prefecture, 60; Thais: Tsukuba City,

Ibaraki Prefecture, 30; Peruvians: Ooizumi Town, Gunma Prefecture, and Hamamatsu City, Shizuoka Prefecture, 80; Americans: Okinawa Prefecture, 78; Muslims: Isezaki City, Gunma Prefecture, 51; Vietnamese: Nagata Ward, Kobe City, 41; Japanese: Tsukuba City, Ibaraki Prefecture, 59; total respondents: 611.

Chapter 8

1 In the end, because many negative opinions were expressed, it was not included in the *1999 White Paper on the Economy*.

2 The Ministry of Labor 'Study Committee on the Effects of Foreign Workers on the Labor Market, Expert Group,' in the June 1992 report, *Hokokusho* (Report), included a calculation of the long-term costs and benefits of accepting foreign workers, and it concluded that the costs would outweigh the benefits.

3 Machida Yukio, '21–seki no shutsunyukoku kanri gyosei o tenbo shite' (Looking at immigration control administration in the 21st century), *Kokusai Jinryu* (International People's Exchange), March 2000.

4 Stalker, Peter, *The Work of Strangers*, Geneva: International Labour Office, 1994.

5 Komai Hiroshi, *Migrant Workers in Japan*, London: Kegan Paul International, 1995.

6 Komai Hiroshi, *Imin shakai Nihon no koso* (Vision for Japan as a country of immigrants), Toyo: Kokusai Shoin, 1994.

7 Hammer, Tommas, *Democracy and the Nation State*, Aldershot: Avebury, 1990.

8 On the situation in various countries outside of Japan, see Kondo Atsushi, *Gaikokujin no sanseiken* (Political rights for foreigners), Tokyo: Akashi Shoten, 1996, and Kondo Atsushi, *Gaikokujin sanseiken to kokuseki* (Political rights for foreigners and nationality), Tokyo: Akashi Shoten, 1996.

Index